Aberdeenshire Library and Information Service
www.aberdeenshire.gov.uk/libraries
Renewals Hotline 01224 661511

εχc

REES, Jasper

I found my horn

A L I S

I Found My Horn

I Found My Horn

One Man's Struggle with the Orchestra's Most Difficult Instrument

JASPER REES

Weidenfeld & Nicolson
LONDON

First published in Great Britain in 2008
by Weidenfeld & Nicolson

1 3 5 7 9 10 8 6 4 2

A CIP catalogue record for this book
is available from the British Library.

ISBN-13 978 0 297 85225 4

Typeset by Input Data Services Ltd, Frome

Printed and bound at Mackays of Chatham plc,
Chatham, Kent

Weidenfeld & Nicolson

The Orion Publishing Group
Orion House
5 Upper St Martin's Lane
London WC2H 9EA
An Hachette Livre UK Company

The Orion Publishing Group's policy is to use papers that are
natural, renewable and recyclable and made from wood
grown in sustainable forests. The logging and manufacturing
processes are expected to conform to the environmental
regulations of the country of origin.

To Sonia

Contents

I once had a whim and I had to obey it –
To buy a French horn in a second-hand shop.
I polished it up and I started to play it
In spite of the neighbours who begged me to stop.

To sound my horn, I had to develop my embouchure.
I found my horn was a bit of a devil to play . . .

Flanders and Swann,
to the tune of the Rondo of Mozart's Concerto for Horn, K495

Exposition

PERUVIAN PEASANT: *Uh oh.*
LLAMA: *Don't tell me. We're about to go over a huge waterfall.*
PERUVIAN PEASANT: *Yup.*
LLAMA: *Sharp rocks at the bottom?*
PERUVIAN PEASANT: *Most likely.*
    (Pause.)
LLAMA: *Bring it on.*

The Emperor's New Groove (Disney)

One Sunday afternoon I find myself crammed onto a stage with sixty-nine other people. We are from all walks of life. We are male, we are female. We are tall and short, narrow-hipped, broad in the beam. We are young, we are old; we are, in my case, about to be no-further-point-in-denying-it middle-aged. We do have one thing in common, though. Each of us is holding a lengthy piece of coiled brass tubing. One end is pressed to 140 tightly puckered lips. Into the other bell-shaped end, seventy right hands have been inserted. The 210 middle three fingers of seventy left hands each operate a valve. And out of this complex apparatus we all attempting to extract a noise. A harmonious noise.

We are playing the French horn. Or as modernists these days

I

call it, the horn. On the strength of no more than half an hour's rehearsal, an ensemble of seventy massed horns is about to perform the world-famous Hallelujah Chorus from Handel's *Messiah*.

Welcome to the annual festival of the BHS, the British Horn Society. Every year the society musters for a weekend of horn appreciation. It's much like any other single-interest group gathering for a weekend of Byron readings/battle re-enactments/wife-swapping. Perfectly ordinary people: rather arcane pursuit. There are ensembles, talks and concerts, performances by leading professionals; there are masterclasses with a visiting maestro from Dresden. But most of all, at the end of the weekend, there is a massed horn blow. From the thick of it it's hard to say how we sound in rehearsal. Loud, for sure. We are larger than many a professional orchestra. One blast on our horns and we could if necessary bring down the walls of Jericho. Not that this will be necessary. Or indeed desirable.

'No one,' warns our chirpy conductor, whose name is Mike Thompson, 'is going to be impressed if seventy horns can make a big noise. They may just be impressed if we can make a small noise.' Conspiratorially we snigger at the thought of that coiled might: at our disposal we have the biblical version of a nuclear deterrent.

It's a thing to behold, a massed horn ensemble. Horn players don't grow on trees, not like pianists or violinists or choristers. So assembling an ensemble is not like mobilising a small volunteer army to sing *The Messiah*, the way they do each year at the Royal Albert Hall. Anyone can turn up and sing. Not anyone can play the horn. It pretty much says so in *The Guinness Book of Records*. The horn, it says, is the joint hardest instrument to learn. Or it certainly did when I last looked, in 1977. (The other one is the oboe, though who knows how they measure these things?) All we initiates know is that it takes strapping lungs to play the horn, and muscle-bound lips. More than these, it takes nerves of reinforced tungsten, because the horn is treacherous. Cracked notes – clams, as they say in America – are not hard to come by.

If you round up a scratch band of seventy horn players from all over the country, not all of them are going to have all of the above qualities in exactly the same quantities. Some of them are going to be more or less deficient in one or two or, in one or two cases, all of these areas.

Which brings me back to me. Here I am, one of seventy horns attempting the world-famous Hallelujah Chorus. I glance down the two pages of the second horn part and there is not much to slip up on. In skiing parlance it would be classed as an easy blue run: no sheet ice, no beetling moguls you have to get up and over. It is all open landscape, gentle gradients and easy cornering. And yet there is a very big problem. I am a beginner. All right, not quite a beginner. But as near as makes no difference. I am one of those many thousands of people into whose innocent juvenile hands a musical instrument was once upon a time arbitrarily, peremptorily, thrust. In my case it was a French horn, and I was ten. It was not unlike an arranged marriage. Neither party had much say in the matter. We stuck it out for seven years, the horn and me, and then we went our separate ways. Giving it up was more or less the last thing I did before I became an adult. Now, at thirty-nine and three-quarters, I'm about to become a middle-aged adult. My horn has spent the interim gathering dust upstairs in the attic, while I've been downstairs, also gathering a certain amount of dust.

Then something happened. In another hemisphere my own private butterfly flapped its wings. Under a distant ocean a tectonic plate with my name on it shifted. My marriage had come to an end. I was feeling a bit bruised by life. It was in the dead time after Christmas and before New Year – I'd have just turned thirty-nine and the New Person In My Life and I had weight to walk off, lassitude to shake out of our limbs. We got in her car, a ropey old soft-top with holes in the pull-down roof, and drove to Highgate cemetery to look at Karl Marx's grave. Naturally we wanted to listen to some music. The only thing I could find under one of the seats, in a cracked plastic casing, was a Steely Dan compilation. I'm not one of those middle-class males who ever erected a shrine to the chilled white whine of jazz-rock fusion in his bedroom, but no one ever says no to 'Reelin' in the Years'. Except that on this occasion I did say no. It was as if someone had poured quicksilver in my ears. I just couldn't listen to it. It sounded reedy, predictable, thin. It just sounded impoverished.

I ejected the CD and looked for a radio station. This didn't take long: it's a quirk of the New Person's car, along with the holes in the roof, that you can only listen to Five Live and about two-sevenths of the FM band. I landed on Radio Three and heard something that I vaguely recognised. Like a migrating bird return-ing to a vaguely familiar cliff, I roosted. The tune elbowed me in the ribs. What was it? My usual rule of thumb for recognising orchestral music is that I must once have played it in the school orchestra. That narrows it down to three pieces: the first move-ment of a Mozart piano concerto (can't remember which), the first movement of Schubert's Great C major Symphony, and one or other of the two movements of Schubert's Unfinished Symphony. There was no piano coming out of the radio, so that narrowed it down to Schubert.

It's difficult to park in Highgate. Maybe we didn't want to get out anyway, because outside it was one of those days where the bitter cold has departed, leaving behind a muffled, drippy gloom. While we looked for a space I hummed along. From somewhere in my brain I dredged a memory of the French horns entering.

'Horn,' I said out loud, apparently at random.

'What?' In they blast.

'That was the horn bit. Where the French horns come in.'

'What's it to you?'

'I used to be able to play this,' I said. The New Person seemed unsure what to do with this information.

'What, this?' She comes from a family of eminent professional musicians. 'Were you any good?'

'Can't remember. Probably not.'

'When did you . . .'

'Stop? When I left school. Like everyone else, I guess.'

I started to hum along again. As the movement ended, we parked. The announcer said it was the Unfinished.

That afternoon was the catalyst. Suddenly, more or less over-night, I found that the only music I could bear to listen to, was interested in listening to, was orchestral, was choral, was pre-electronic. I didn't want to hear any more pop music, any more rootsy American folk or tragic southern soul or transgressive Seventies power-glam.

I'd heard about this same taste shift happening to other people, but always assumed it was gradual. When very young, I used to go to my mother's hairdresser, from which I retain two memories. One was of lying down on the floor and quite flagrantly levering myself into position, like a mechanic wheeling himself under a car, to look up a hairdresser's skirts and establish whether or not she was wearing any underwear. I must have been four or five. (She was.) The other was a conversation with a gentleman stylist. I asked him who was his favourite pop group and he said no, nowadays he listened to music for grown-ups by Beethoven and Mozart. This would have been around the time the Beatles had split and were going solo. He can't have been more than thirty-five. I remember thinking that this must be the natural order of things. But I couldn't imagine it ever happening to me.

There is no religion in me, nothing to keep my feet off the ground. So looking for a parking space near Highgate cemetery is the closest I have ever come to walking along the road to Damascus. It felt like a conversion, in which in an instant you are suffused with an insight, or a way of feeling things, that was not there before. You go round a corner, and the view is shockingly new.

I took prompt action. Defecting to Radio Three, I began listening. I zipped open my collection of classical CDs, saw how meagre it was and started to shop for symphonies and concertos and chamber music. Gradually I sent feelers out into ever more distant realms of the repertoire. But if there was something I was going to listen to more than anything else, it soon became apparent that it would be music written for the French horn.

Being a male of the species who comes fully pre-loaded with the gender-specific trainspotter chromosome, this rapidly escalated into a top-of-the-range obsession. Within a week I was on one of those travelator walkways you get in airports, with no way off. I had to have classical music on at all times. I was a human hoover. Any minute of the day not soundtracked by classical music in one form or another was to my eyes – to my ears – a wasted minute. I'd want to wake up to the sound of it and go to sleep to the sound of it. I'd want to drive, eat, wash, work, jog to it, go to sleep to it. I'd even want to ablute to it.

Only one thing stopped this from becoming ruinous and all-encompassing, and that was a shortage of funds. Otherwise there would have been nothing to prevent the innumerable recordings of Mozart's four horn concertos currently available on Amazon from finding their collective way into a cardboard package with my address on it. At this point, digital technology intervened. I discovered it was possible to copy CDs onto your laptop. I threw myself into the Sisyphean labour of copying all of mine, then other people's. I accumulated this stuff with the avidity of a miser. Pissing away days when I should have been working, I'd go round to the houses of family, friends, friends' friends, friends' family, and sweep the place for the yellow-and-white spines of Deutsche Grammophon, the tell-tale red of EMI. Within a few weeks I rolled the rock all the way up the hill, and had a library of three or four hundred CDs on my laptop. The obsession was now an addiction; an *affliction*. I had mutated into the music industry's worst nightmare: a ripper.

Then someone told me that you could copy all these files onto a portable device, which you could then wire into your car stereo, your home stereo, your laptop. To someone with my pathology, it was like being directed to a bottomless supply of free drugs. I acquired a Creative Nomad Zen Xtra onto which to copy all this stuff. I decided to think big. These things have variable capacity, measured in gigabytes. Twenty gigs is generally ample. Forty gigs you will never fill. I went and bought myself sixty gigs of storage space. I dumped all the music onto the Nomad. It took up about seven gigs.

Now I was able to plan for something that even five years ago would have been unthinkable: I could fit a significant portion of the entire canon of Western classical music into my top pocket. That is the obvious appeal of the Nomad (and its technological sibling, the i-Pod). For carriers of the trainspotter chromosome, it has an extra benefit. It invites you to categorise, to compartmentalise, to label and shelve, to surrender to your very own anal-retentive inner librarian. As you build your collection file by file, they ask you to identify each new track by title, by artist; most useful of all, they ask you to slot every track into a specific genre.

'What do you think of my genres?' a fellow librarian asked me as he was stacking the shelves of his own music archive. I scrolled down his list. He hadn't gone any further than rock, pop, classical. So I told him, politely but firmly.

'I think your genres are a bit crap.'

'Oh.' He looked hurt. I whipped out the Nomad and directed him to my own bespoke genres, individually tailored to my own needs and specifications. There they all were: aria, ballet, cantata, cello, chanson, clarinet, duet, flute, guitar, harp, harpsichord, lieder, mass, oboe, octet, opera, oratorio, organ, overture, piano, plainsong, quartet, quintet, requiem, symphony, tone poem, trio, trumpet, violin, waltz. There was one I particularly wanted to draw to his attention. It was my French horn genre.

In my horn folder I collected most of the major works for horn – by Mozart, Haydn, Beethoven, Brahms and Strauss – and I also stole a few from other genres – the first Brandenburg Concerto, the *Water Music*, the Nocturne from Mendelssohn's *A Midsummer Night's Dream* – because what seduced me to them wasn't the organic whole, the sound conjured up by the entire musical ensemble. What lured me in, the main thing I wanted to listen to, was the horn part. It was as if I'd walked into the National Gallery with the sole and express purpose of looking at the colour green.

I don't understand where obsessions come from, but I do understand that they are tidal: they rise up and engulf you and then, for some reason, at a certain moment they retrace their way towards the horizon and out of your life, often for ever. This obsession could have gone on until such time as it waned, the way they do. I could have carried on accumulating until my horn collection was something like complete, even in the eyes of a compulsive completist.

But then, with the Niagara of birthdays heaving into view, something big happened. I actually met an actual horn player.

The first I heard of him was when the New Person phoned from her office one day. The New Person is a theatre producer, and after an entire career putting on plays, she was producing the new musical by Andrew Lloyd Webber. It was opening in a few weeks.

'We've got Dave Lee!'

'Is that good?'

'He's the best!'

'Oh. I've not actually heard of him.' At this point I'd not actually heard of any current horn players apart from one called Barry Tuckwell.

'I'm so excited!'

'Is he really the best?'

'Yes!'

'So can I meet him?'

One warm Saturday afternoon in Shaftsbury Avenue, while the Andrew Lloyd Webber musical was in preview, a man of medium height with a cropped beard and dark hair was pointed out to me. I surveyed from a distance. Put him in a pair of braces and he'd look not unlike the missing horn section of Chas and Dave: Chas and Dave and Dave, if you will. I accosted him in the street near the stage door.

'Are you Dave Lee?'

'Yes.'

'I hear you're the best.' Dave laughed, nervously.

'And what's your name?' He had a faded northern accent. I told him who I am, and that I'd been listening to a lot of horn lately.

'Oh yeah?'

'Yes. I used to play. Once upon a time.'

'Oh did you?'

'Yes. Till I gave up. But I've been thinking of taking it up again.'

'Oh good,' he said. 'Well, good luck with it.'

I had not been thinking any such thing, but a silence needed filling and I couldn't think what else to say. As Dave disappeared through the stage door I stood there for a few moments and asked myself whether, when announcing that you are taking up the horn for the first time in twenty-two years, it's necessarily a good idea to blurt it out first to someone who, as I would find out, has been in the horn section, mostly as principal, of the BBC Scottish Symphony Orchestra, the City of Birmingham Symphony Orchestra, the London Philharmonic Orchestra, the Royal Philharmonic Orchestra and the Orchestra of the Royal Opera House. And the Michael Nyman Band.

I became Dave's stalker by self-appointment. This involved various offices and obligations. In the first instance, I was required by myself to talk about Dave a great deal to other people, principally to the New Person. Dave helped me in this department by giving me a copy of his new CD, *Under the Influence*, which as well as luminous pieces for horn by Nyman and Peter Maxwell Davies features ambient renditions of Seventies rock classics like 'Dark Side of the Moon' and 'Life on Mars'. It was the horn as I'd never heard it before: searing and other-worldly and completely hypnotic. It was on the Nomad in a jiffy. Occasionally I would bother him on his mobile. In moments of lucidity I imagined him seeing my number come up and toying with the idea of not answering. But he usually did. We had the odd drink. And I never visited the theatre without looking him up. The conversation was always the same.

'How you doing, mate?'

'Fine thanks, Dave. You?'

'Mustn't grumble. How's the horn playing going?'

'Er . . .'

In the end I had to find a better answer than this, but wasn't quite sure how or where to start.

The Andrew Lloyd Webber musical was about to open. A Prince's Trust gala performance was scheduled with – surreally – a berth reserved in the Royal Box for me. When the Palace asked for some indication of my standing in life, I found myself upgraded on the call sheet from 'journalist' to 'writer'. I had been sanitised. I felt a fraud, but contrived to get through the entire evening without meeting either the royal personage or the royal personage's consort. Then at the end of the night I was standing around near the exit when the heir to the throne, preceded by bodyguards, walked past, caught my eye and ever so discreetly panicked. You could see him thinking – clocked him in the royal box, might be someone important; better say hello just in case.

'And who are you?' he said, fiddling with his cuffs.

'I'm just the producer's boyfriend, sir,' I told him.

'Ah!' he said, tweaking an earlobe. 'You're the boyfriend! I was *wondering* who you were.'

So was I, sir. So was I. (I didn't actually say this.)

Through all this my mind was on other things. Or one other thing. I could think of little else but an instrument I had long since abandoned. *Nothing* else. It began to dawn on me that a die had been cast, that a path was clearing. Whether I really wanted it or no, waters were parting. I had to do what I'd told Dave I was going to do. I had to take up the French horn again. But how?

The answer to everything is online. After a short but intense tour of every horn-related website in the cybergalaxy, I chanced upon the perfect deep end to jump into: the British Horn Society. They meet only once a year for a jamboree of horn playing for all ages and abilities. As luck would have it their annual shindig was two weeks hence. I booked my passage.

The night before taking up the horn again I retrieved my instrument from the attic and brought it into the West End to have my valves oiled by Dave. We met at the stage door and he led me down into the dungeons of the theatre. We found ourselves in a dingy overheated room with a sink. He snapped open his case and out came ointments, unguents, contraptions, little stringy things with bobbly brushes on them.

'What have you got in there then?' he said, pointing at the black case in my hand.

'A horn,' I replied, putting it down.

'No, what type of horn?'

'Eh?'

'The make.'

'Oh.'

I didn't know. I'd never taken the trouble to find out who made my horn, or where they made it. I laid the case flat on the floor, unclipped it and opened the lid. My old horn had a nice gleam to it, even after twenty-two years in the dark.

'Let's have a look,' said Dave. I lifted it from its old velvet-lined case and handed it over. Dave upended the horn and pointed on the underside of the bell to an oval engraving.

'Look,' he said. 'Josef Lídl.' He raised his eyebrows approvingly. 'Any good?'

'Not bad.'

'Oh good.'

'Czech,' he added. 'Czechoslovak.'

He proceeded to administer to my long neglected Josef Lídl horn. Mostly it was a question of running water through the tubes. It took about ten minutes. Dave pulled out slides and greased them, he unscrewed valve caps and oiled them. He drizzled lubricant on rotors. I hung about, feeling useless, stabbing at small talk. Dave was off to play Strauss's first horn concerto in Kraków.

'That's quite hard, isn't it?' Dave didn't even look up.

'Not as hard as Strauss 2,' he chortled.

This is horn humour: black humour. Silently I pondered measurements of difficulty. One man's hard is another man's north face of the Eiger. I was as certain as I was of anything that I would never play Strauss 1 or 2, not in Kraków or anywhere else.

Dave finished and handed me the horn. While he packed away his mobile laboratory, I chose not to blow a note. There was just no knowing what might come out, if anything. Instead I hedged.

'Do any professionals ever play on a Josef Lídl?'

'Lídls?' He shook his head. 'No, they're student horns.'

About forty-eight hours later Mike Thompson, the conductor of the massed horn ensemble, is applauded onto the stage. He and Dave go way back. When they were teenagers they sat next to each other in the National Youth Orchestra. But that was thirty-five years ago. This is now. We all look at our conductor, this random cross-section of society. With an optimistic flourish Mike raises his baton, and we're off. The second horns have a couple of bars' rest and my mind instantly wanders. As I look round the seventy-strong ensemble I privately bet my last brass farthing that I am the only one here who hasn't actually held an instrument in his hands for twenty-two years. A good half of this ensemble weren't even born twenty-two years ago. Some weren't born even eleven years ago. So for one horn player, sharing a music stand in the second horn section with a bloke from West Yorkshire, this is not, as I designated it earlier, the musical equivalent of a blue run. This run is pure, plain, pitch black.

Coincidentally, I think, I did once go skiing after a twenty-year break, on a freebie. You'd have thought that would be enough time for the body to forget all the old errors of technique, but when I pushed off down the hill for the first time, there they all were, imprinted in my very DNA, perfectly preserved like some frozen homunculus trapped in the Arctic ice since 25,000 BC. With the horn, old mistakes are still present and correct: wrong fingering, erratic pitch, inability to hit a top note without requiring three attempts. Amazing what the body can remember, I reflect as I leap into the fray with a split note.

'HALLELUJAH!! Hallelujah! Hallelujah!'

If this second horn ever had any ability, which is in itself open to question, it is a blurred memory; it is a language I used to get by in and now come back to, to discover that I can remember only the words for 'a hot chocolate, please', 'can you tell me the way to the central station?' and 'four'. Twenty-two years. Time enough to fit in another childhood, another adolescence, another induction into the *terra incognita* we know as the opposite sex. Time enough for half this ensemble to be born, grow up and, if they're quick about it, have their own children. Time enough for up to six Olympiads, God knows how many general elections. There were twenty-two years between the Armistice of 1918 and the Battle of Britain. There were twenty-two years between D-Day and Geoff Hurst's hat-trick. In the same month that the Argentine army laid down its weapons in Port Stanley, I laid down my horn. That was in the summer of 1982.

So what am I doing here? I am days shy of forty. The years have been reeled in. Did I mention that there are people in this band a *quarter* my age? What. In. The. Name. Of. Holy. Moses. Am. I. Doing. Here?

These thoughts wander in and out of focus as we announce that the king of kings and lord of lords will reign for ever and ever. In the Albert Hall at this point there would be a single vainglorious trumpet taking on the thousand-strong choir, because Handel had a weakness for the trumpet. It's good for announcing things is the trumpet. It's not good for much else, this side of Louis Armstrong. Suddenly the answer steals up on me. I am here because the horn is not the trumpet. The horn is not the bassoon or the trombone or the flute. The horn is, incomparably, the horn. In the right hands, it is the most beautiful instrument in the orchestra. In the wrong hands, it's still better than the trumpet. You can line up all those instruments in a beauty contest with the horn, and really it's just a question of which other contenders limp onto the podium. Even though I have no religion, I have enough to know the horn is God's representative in the wind section. Or in Schumann's words, 'The horn is the soul of the orchestra.'

Composers were fitful in their appreciation of the horn as a solo instrument. Haydn claimed to have written one of his two surviving horn concertos in his sleep. Beethoven wrote thirty-two piano sonatas, ten violin sonatas, but only one horn sonata. He hadn't finished the piano part by the day of performance, so he improvised it on the night. Richard Strauss, the son of Wagner's principal horn player, wrote his first concerto as a teenager in a burst of filial enthusiasm that didn't last. He left it for sixty years before composing his second in the depths of the Second World War. It was Mozart, through his lifelong friendship with a horn player twenty-five years his senior called Joseph Leutgeb, who composed eternally the most popular concertos written for horn. But even he completed only three, and left three others unfinished.

Over the decades of the nineteenth century the horn's orchestral role was enlarged by successive Germanic composers: Beethoven, Schubert, Brahms, Bruckner and Mahler all reserved for the horns a starring role in their symphonies they denied to, say, the trumpets. In chamber pieces, meanwhile, it was the one member of the brass section that suavely blended not only with woodwind instruments, but also with the strings. With its tonal smoothness and four-octave range, it was a good mixer, an instrument for all occasions. When people queued up to see operas by Rossini, it wasn't the singers they clamoured to hear: it was the horn player.

Further down the century, the horn became the totemic instrumental voice of *Der Ring des Nibelungen*.

From Wagner's Bayreuth, the only logical move was into the movies. The horn has had a parallel career in Tinseltown. Of all the instruments in the orchestra, the horn is one that's never been afraid to make a buck in the Wild West and outer space. In the Swinging Sixties it also had solo spots on the Beach Boys' *Pet Sounds* and the Beatles' *Revolver* and *Sgt Pepper's Lonely Hearts Club Band*, all three of them regularly listed in the top five best pop albums ever made.

And yet there is an image problem. By some strange miscarriage of justice, the horn is somehow deemed among all the brass instruments – with the possible exception of the tuba – to be the most irredeemably uncool. Its ungainly shape, a baroque curlicue of pipes with a comically flaring bell, has something to do with it. It doesn't help that the horn has no Miles Davis. There is no Charlie Parker of the horn. The horn doesn't snap like the trumpet, it doesn't slither and slide like the trombone. The horn didn't hang around Parisian nightclubs in the early 1950s smoking dope and glugging bourbon.

The instrument has never quite shaken off its aristocratic roots, never quite lost that trace of the silver spoon. You don't sound so effortlessly superior without a whiff of privilege attaching to you, like a permanent spray of expensive eau de Cologne. Of all the brass section, the horn players are the ones who look to-the-manor-born in white tie and tails. There is a reason why the horn has never muscled its way into the colliery brass bands of the north of England. It's just not brassy enough. A horn hanging out with euphoniums and cornets is a landowner mucking in with his feudal tenants. It makes everyone feel uneasy.

Which is what I feel on stage at the British Horn Society festival.

My story is the story of most people who learn an instrument. They make some progress but fail to practise enough and, without huge regret, give it up when they leave school. But like a memory of an old flame, they often wonder what might have been if after all they'd carried on. So they fantasise about taking up the instrument again, joining an orchestra, rising to new heights, righting the wrongs of youth. But it's always impossible. There is no time. There is family, work, tiredness. Besides, it's harder to learn anything when you're no longer young. Despite the tug of the old instrument, you ruefully conclude that it's impossible. There is no going back. It cannot be done.

Yet here I am, going back. I have given in to a stupid, quixotic whim. Instead of talking about doing something, I seem to be doing it, publicly, in the company of sixty-nine others. As we move on to the second page, I am regretting it bitterly. There is a passage in the world-famous Hallelujah Chorus when the second horns clamber up towards the top of the register. King of Kiiiiiiings. And lord of Looooooords. Suddenly, on those long sustained notes, I can feel my embouchure going. Anyone who has not played the horn will have no idea what this feels like, or even that it's a physical possibility. It's analogous to the last steep gradient up a Scottish mountain. You've done all the hard work, you can see the summit, it's within your grasp, and suddenly your legs buckle under you and you collapse, vanquished, onto the spongy heather. Only it's not my legs; it's my lips. Actually it's my lip, the upper one. Most people don't realise that the upper lip has any muscle in it at all. It turns out that, at this point, mine doesn't. The lip has not done this sort of work for nearly a quarter of a century, and the going up at this altitude is tough. The sound stuttering out of my horn curls up and dies. I stand there shaking my head, hoping no one notices, which of course they won't. The sixty-nine other horns cover the sound of my silence.

Luckily the home straight is easier. On we all surge towards the tape. A beat's rest, a huge breath, and then we hit it in a slow seventy-strong fanfare.

HAAAALLEEEEELUUUUJAAAAAAH!

Suddenly I am swept back in time, like someone tumbling down one of those laundry chutes in the movies, to a feeling I last had when I was not yet an adult. I recall immediately that there is nothing quite like it. I am a small part of a huge elemental force, a torrent of man-made sound. It swirls around and through me. It ferrets under me and seems to raise me. It is almost impossible not to burst out laughing at the sheer exhilaration of it. All that sound, all that unison.

Amazingly, the walls are still standing as the applause peters out from an audience far outnumbered by our ensemble. I find an emotion welling up inside me with which I've had only a nodding acquaintance in recent years, those years when routine traditionally sets in like a stubborn winter fog, when you set yourself the monthly task of amassing enough money to pay for things you need rather than things you want, when horizons close in and clouds lower dully overhead, when pipedreams of a second home in Tuscany – or, failing that, Wales – shrivel and wilt in the face of steady, remorseless blasts from the blowtorch of life. The swell of emotion is unfamiliar. It isn't any of the usual irritants. It isn't lust or envy or a low-grade self-hatred, a thin film of sadness or a personal brand of existential apathy. I think I recognise it as elation.

That felt unbelievably good, I tell myself. It occurs to me, during this surge of adrenalin, that I'm glad I hauled this thing out of the attic: this old friend, this old foe. Maybe this time, I think, we can get to know each other a little better. And there on the spot I make a ridiculous resolution. On the evidence of the previous two-and-a-half minutes, I cannot play the horn to save my life. But this is my chance, as I slide inexorably towards forty, to slow the surge of time, even to reverse it: to go back and have another go. And this time there will be no distractions that come with being a teenager: laziness, fecklessness, girl cellists. There will be different distractions, none of them available last time round – children, yes, work, yes, the New Person. But this time, I'm going to conquer the *Guinness Book of Records'* most difficult instrument. I'm going to learn it properly, practise it properly, play it properly. I'm not just going to take it up. I'm going to take it on.

This is the really stupid part coming up now. I tell myself that it would be good to have a goal. Standing there as the other sixty-nine members of the massed horn ensemble pack their instruments into cases on the side of the stage, I think the thing to do is to play something on my own. To these people. The thing to do is to see if I can come back in a year's time to the annual festival of the British Horn Society and stand on this stage without sixty-nine other horn players. And play something. A solo.

Why? I am a self-employed journalist. I spend my day telling other people's stories. I interview therefore I am. Take a bow, all you actors, divas and ballerinas. Are you reading, you playwrights and poets and novelists? Comedians, commentators, presidents, presenters, singers, songwriters, supermodels – they've all emptied their lives into my tape recorder. Rockers and royalty, explorers and chefs, gardeners and mountaineers, winners and losers of Olympics and Oscars, World Cups and World Wars. Vegetating on the sofa, I can flick through the satellite channels and see my entire career flash before me. 'Done him, done her, done them, done the lot.' Why, I have even interviewed interviewers.

To the bottom of the bird cage these words all go. But hey, there's always the memory to keep them alive. Now and then I come across one of my subjects at a party or an opening and reminisce about that fascinating gladiatorial encounter we had ... 'was it, God, it must be five years ago now,' I'll say to them. ' ... it was for the ...' I'll name whichever outlet it would have been in. 'We met in ...' I'll name the location. 'No of course of course ... no reason why you should ...' They never remember having met me. And I change the subject back to them. 'So what are you working on now?'

But then why should they? I have done nothing to make myself memorable. It was drummed into me in school never to use the word 'I'. My obedience has been chronic. The pram in the hallway, the self unexplored – that's just how things panned out. On top of which I have always worked at home. There have been no awfully big adventures, not without any more than within. What all this observing has made me, this dogged apostolic witnessing of other people's effort, is an absentee from my own life.

On an inchoate level I have known that at some point in my future this stifling must stop. I've just never known when that might be. I yearn to be counted. I want desperately to contend. As I play my little part in the Hallelujah Chorus, it seems to me that I have stumbled on the gateway to my own adventure.

Sharp rocks at the bottom?
Most likely.
Bring it on.

1
In the Beginning Was the Horn

When the horne bloweth: then let them come vp in to the mounten.
Exodus, ch. 19 v. 13, Tyndale Bible

In the year before I took up the French horn again, an important finding was made about the universe. Scientists at the University of Ulm in Germany, analysing patterns of hot and cold blobs observed by NASA's Wilkinson Microwave Anisotropy Probe, were able to confirm that the universe is finite. The same conclusion had recently been posited by scientists at Montana State University, who contended that space is shaped like a ball. The research of their rivals at Ulm proved that it isn't anything so banal as a sphere. According to their model, the universe narrows at one end to an infinitely distant vanishing point, while at the other it curves outwards, though not for ever. If a spaceship were to travel towards the expanded end, it would at some putative point hit a wall and be deflected back in the opposite direction.

Narrow at one end, curving out into a wide flare at the other? Only one answer seems possible. The universe, far from being spherical, is conical. It exists in the shape of a horn.

I grew up, at least at the weekends, beneath the South Downs in West Sussex. The oldest building in what you'd scarcely call a village goes back to 1680. No one really knows for sure, but our home is of roughly the same vintage. So if it was built in the 1680s, it belongs to the same decade as the births of Handel and Bach who, between them, would give the horn its first orchestral employment.

The cottage was more burrow than house. Once you rose to anywhere near six foot, you had to duck in and out of the sitting room to avoid thudding your head on the door frame. You also had to watch out for a low beam slung across the middle of the room. We are mostly male in my family, mostly six foot or thereabouts. (I am five foot eleven and three-quarters.) We all stoop.

The pockmarked bricks of the hearth were the oldest part of the house. Across the fireplace there was a shiny brass smoke screen in which you could pull faces and watch them wobble and distort back at you. Above, mounted on nails banged into the brick, was a collection of old hunting horns. There was a short round one and, on the other side, a short straight one. Then there was a longer straight one, the kind that often have pennants draped from them and are used to announce the arrival of a royal personage. Running across the top of the wall was the eye-catcher, a magnificent straight horn four feet in length. It had, so far as I could tell, no practical application unless you were planning to summon your two brothers to a medieval joust in the garden. But the centrepiece, the instrument that drew the eye, was a slender round horn of perhaps 15 inches in diameter. Were you to unwrap its coils, it would be just as long as the magnificent straight horn. It had a small bell, and no valves or slides. But this, manifestly, was an ancestor of the instrument I took up on 12 March 1975.

I hardly ever went near them. Occasionally there'd be visitors to whom, as part of a range of hosting duties, we would feel obliged to show off. In such an instance the horns came in handy. The ritual was always the same. We'd start with the smallest and work our way up to the magnificent straight horn. This would be the and-now-ladies-and-gentlemen finale. That was the idea anyway, but it was more or less impossible to tease any form of note out of the two small horns, so mostly we just fought over the bigger horns. We were always genuinely surprised at how difficult it was to extract a presentable noise.

But then these horns weren't designed to sound beautiful. In the pre-orchestral phase of its life, the horn's job was to talk to the animals, or the army, or the enemy. Unlike the lyre, the dulcimer or the lute – at home we also had one of those – it wasn't allowed to bring its muddy boots through the front door. There was no music written for it. It just had to sound loud.

On Saturdays in winter we had first-hand evidence of this. My parents were members of that section of the population that likes to chase small quadrupeds while seated on the back of a large one. In due course my older brother became a willing recruit. He donned the jodhpurs, the tweed jacket, the domed peaked hat, and perched pertly on the back of some sedated pony. My younger brother and I were refuseniks. We kept well away from the saddle. There was no keeping our distance altogether. When we were too young to object we were taken to the meet. The setting was always the same. On top of each horse was a person in uniform: black coat with yellow collar, hard riding hat, whip, coarsely woven white gloves, cravat and pin, knee-high leather boots. Two of these people would be our parents. Perhaps because he spent his week in London, my father seemed determined to go as native as possible at the weekend. He took to wearing a top hat, and even a pink coat. (Pink, as in red. One of the peculiarities of hunting folk is a selective form of colour blindness. They also ticked you off if you referred to a white horse as 'white'. They were always 'grey'.) Everyone else was straight out of central casting, even the foot-followers in black wellingtons, brown trousers and sensible windcheaters. The ladies wore silk headscarves. The men's cheeks were rouged by wind and wine. The scene can have changed very little since the 1680s: the red-brick inn, the naked trees, the sodden earth underfoot, loamy rural vowels in harmonious counterpoint to the clipped, peremptory consonants of the mounted well-to-do. There was only one thing that firmly carbon-dated the scene to the early 1970s: the massively flared jeans worn by my little brother and me as we stood, a glass of warm lemonade in our hands, sulking to one side in our own hermetically sealed boredom.

They were all glugging port. By the time the master of the hounds parped out two short thin notes and a long thin one on his stumpy little pocket horn, everyone was drunk in charge of an animal four times their own size. Occasionally the story would come home from the field of a huntsman being severely injured or paralysed. Some even went the whole hog and got themselves killed. But then death and the horn have gone hand in hand from the beginning.

To see the history of the horn laid out, I go to the eastern outskirts of Paris. There, in a concrete park, is the Musée de la Musique. The place is heaving with instruments of every age and description. On the top floor, past room upon room of spinets and virginals and clavichords, past display upon display of *hautbois* and *viole da gamba* and *mandolini*, I arrive at the horn section.

For a freshly minted horn obsessive who turns up on one of those freezing midwinter afternoons when the sun has clocked off at lunchtime, this is a sight to warm the heart. There, in a glass cabinet, are a dozen or so beautiful instruments. They are arranged in two rows, like a football team posing for a photograph before a final. There are horns from the late seventeenth through to the mid-nineteenth century. The makers' names have a rough artisanal flavour. CG Eschenbach of Germany. Wilhelm Haas of Nuremberg. Charles Joseph Sax of Bruxelles and his son Adolphe Sax (who would invent the saxophone). Most of the makers are from Paris. 'Fait à Paris,' says an engraving on the bell rim of an elegant early hunting horn the size of a bicycle wheel, 'par Crétien ordinair à Roy rue de Laferonerie.' There are several examples from the decades of technological experimentation either side of 1800, when manufacturers looked for ways to expand the limited number of notes that could be sounded on the instrument. One made by Raoux in 1797 has half a dozen detachable crooks, for changing key, stored in a wooden chest. An 1818 horn by the Courtois Frères has no valves. One from two years later has two piston valves (the full complement would turn out to be three). Horticultural decoration sprouts leafily inside the bell. There is a so-called omnichromatic horn by JB Dupont from the same period when some manufacturers went down a blind alley or two. It looks like a plate of spaghetti sculpted in brass.

Alongside all this gleaming metal, at the far right of the front row, is a curling, twisting tube of hollow bone, perhaps two feet in length. '*Trompe en corne de bélier*,' it says. Yemen, eighteenth century. It's a ram's horn. It looks, to say the least, decontextualised. Unlike its neighbours – its teammates – it doesn't look as if it's been *made*. It was with something very akin to this, nonetheless, that it all started. All music, all musical instruments.

Picture a small hunched mostly unclad hunter-gatherer going about his business one afternoon in about 9000 BC. It is the late Stone Age. In the land now known as Iraq, the first attempt at sheep husbandry is being mastered. Neolithic Man is heading back to the cave. A wooden-hafted axe dangles from one fist, a fresh kill from the other. On the ground he spots it: a ram's horn. A skull lies nearby. He has seen this a hundred times, but today he notices that the horn is broken at the tip. Thus it has a hole at both ends, a smaller one, and a larger. He is curious. He picks up the ram's horn and turns it over in his hands. In due course he applies the smaller hole to his lips and, tentatively, or maybe just accidentally, exhales into the aperture. We can only guess at his surprise when out of the far end of this useless dead object there emerges, by some form of sonic alchemy, a note. A tone. He blows again, harder this time, and finds the sound emerging more clearly. Perhaps it even ricochets back off a neighbouring hill. The first note in instrumental history has been sounded.

From here we can speculate at leisure. The discovery seems to him a sort of magic, a potential source of power, and he keeps it secret against the day when it may be useful. Or he takes it straight to his chief, and lays it before him as a token of loyalty. Or he tells everyone, and soon they are all at it: hollowing out rams' horns, fashioning an aperture at the sharp end, and blowing and blowing and blowing for pure joy. It will have been the Neolithic version of the Christmas office lunch, where no one will stop tooting on those extendable paper whistles that come in crackers.

Spool forward some thousands of years. The *shofar* makes its first appearance in the Old Testament in the Book of Exodus, Chapter 19, at the very moment when God on Mount Sinai nominates the children of Israel as his chosen people.

> 16 And the thirde daye in the mornynge there was thunder, and lightenynge and a thicke clowde apo the mounte, ad the voyce of the horne waxed exceadynge lowed, and all the people that was in the hoste was afrayde.
>
> 17 And Moses brought the people out of the tetes to mete with God, and they stode vnder the hyll.
>
> 18 And mounte Sinai was all togither on a smoke; because the Lorde descended doune vpon it in fyre. And the smoke therof asceded vp, as it had bene the smoke of a kylle, and all the mounte was exceadinge fearfull.
>
> 19 And the voyce of the horne blewe and waxed lowder, ad lowder. Moses spake, ad God answered hi ad that with a voyce.

Thus the Tyndale Bible. It's a matter for regret that the scholars elaborating on William Tyndale's translation from Greek and Hebrew sources to produce the 1611 King James version chose to render '*shofar*' as 'trumpet'. But the impact of the ram's horn's first entrance is incontrovertible. In its first recorded note, emerging loud and bodiless from plumes of smoke at the summit of Sinai, the horn provides the musical prelude to the Ten Commandments. It is nothing less than the voice of God.

In due course, a tubular implement that amplifies sound became a proto-nuclear device and accessory to terror. In the Book of Joshua, Chapter 6, at the foot of the walls of Jericho, slightly to the north of the Dead Sea, with no more than fifteen centuries to go till the birth of Christ, God appears to Joshua in a dream and issues his instructions:

> 4 And seven priests shall bear before the ark seven trumpets of rams' horns: and the seventh day ye shall compass the city seven times, and the priests shall blow with the trumpets.
>
> 5 And it shall come to pass, that when they make a long blast with the ram's horn, and when ye hear the sound of the trumpet,

all the people shall shout with a great shout; and the wall of the city shall fall down flat, and the people shall ascend up every man straight before him.

Thus did it come to pass that history's first-ever horn section was formed. They will have needed strong lips, those priests, and big lungs, though less in the way of musical talent. A beginner could have brought down the walls of Jericho.

'I wanted to play the clarinet.' I ask Dave Lee, my new friend, why he took up the horn. 'They said, "Here's a horn." It was at the end of the summer term. I had to teach myself for six weeks in the holidays because I didn't have a teacher. I couldn't get a note out of it. I drove my parents mad.'

As soon as I take up the instrument again, I start to seek out horn players. After we have established to their satisfaction that I'm probably not a slasher, this is the thing I always ask them first. Why the horn?

'As a boy when I went to symphony concerts I had two favourite instruments,' says Peter Damm, a short round jovial man who for thirty-three years was principal horn of the Dresden Staatskapelle. 'Oboe and horn. But at eleven I took up the violin and was in the school orchestra by thirteen. Then suddenly there was a horn available. At fourteen in 1951 I left home to study the horn in Weimar.'

'I was going to take up trombone,' says Phil Myers, principal horn of the New York Philharmonic for the last twenty-six years. 'I grew up in Elkhart, Indiana, where they make a lot of band instruments. My father was a band director so all the instruments were around. He had a sheet of paper where you were supposed to circle what you wanted to play and I was just looking down that list for trombone and I saw a French horn and I thought, well actually I changed my mind. "French horn." That sounds classy, you know.'

'By the age of eleven it was too late for the piano and the violin,' says Andrei Gloukhov, a man of munificent figure and gloomy physiognomy who has played with the St Petersburg (formerly

Leningrad) Philharmonic for thirty-six years. 'I used to be a viola player before,' says Stefan Dohr, principal horn of the Berlin Philharmonic. 'Hermann Baumann lived in the same little village near Essen and I went to his Christmas concert that he gave every year. I heard that and said, "Mm, sounds better than what I do on the viola." I was eleven.' (We will be hearing more from Hermann Baumann.)

Thus an Englishman, a Russian, an American and two Germans, one from each side of the old Iron Curtain, nearly fetched up elsewhere. It is a common experience among horn players to have laboured at something else before seeing the light. Several, I discover, converted from some lesser instrument as late as seventeen, the age at which I gave up. I can't help noticing that they all have barrel chests. Horn players mostly conform to a basic physical mould. They're not thin, reedy types. Phil Myers, in particular, is a globe of a man. Nestled across his torso a horn looks like a cornet. 'My best weight for playing is somewhere between 260 and 290 pounds,' he confides. 'If I get down to 225 or 210 then I feel as though I'm having to work a lot more. I got up to 500 at one point. I was always out of breath, so that didn't work, so I had that operation where they cut your stomach in half. And I got 150 pounds out of that. So now I'm 350. Half that fucking stomach weighed 150 pounds, Goddammit! At 500 I couldn't even stand up.'

Another man mountain I meet is Lowell Greer, the most dis-tinguished soloist on the early, so-called 'natural' horn in America. He is an extremely tall and, despite the heft of his stooping frame, soft-spoken man with a thick beard and dark pebbly eyes. He talks in neatly trimmed sentences at the measured pace of a sonorous andante.

'How did I begin?' he muses. 'It was an accident, I suppose. I had played violin, rather precociously, commencing at the age of four years, learning by rote, as my ability to read anything was not yet developed. At six years, I had an accident with the left hand. My mother pleaded with the doctors not to amputate. They complied, but the left hand has always been clumsy, or at least that's my excuse. When entering the seventh grade, at twelve years of age, I was required to be in the school band. Picking out an instrument was pure accident. All the girls wished to play flute (how decent!), and all the lads were seeking those high-profile posts in the trumpet section. However, by the time the director came to my name, all the available trumpets had been taken by others. The band director looked at me, and, citing my narrow lips, suggested the horn, since thin lips were good for the horn. Later, I came to suspect some collusion with my mother; she detested the trumpet as a solo instrument, along with the saxophone, accordion, saxophone, cordovox, saxophone, and a few other instruments, such as the saxophone. Her fear of the high brass must have been overwhelming. I became fascinated by the sound of the horn, and the director began giving up his Saturday mornings to teach me privately. One day he used the term "professional horn player", at which point I sat up alert. The idea of subbing out of a "real job" and playing the horn for a living was a no-brainer for me. The rest is almost identical to anyone else's story.'

On 12 March 1975, the bell rang. It was a Wednesday, so we'd have just had swimming at school. On the doorstep stood a rather serious man in his twenties. This being 1975, he had slightly too much hair, semi-tamed as big wiry hair was back then by an unnatural-looking side parting. My new horn teacher had a pasty complexion and elbow patches.

In his right hand was an odd-shaped case. He must have switched to his left hand, or put it down, in order to shake hands with my mother. Maybe he also shook hands with the ten-year-old in prep-school grey. We went upstairs to a first-floor drawing room containing high-backed armchairs and a baby grand piano. We sat at the long piano stool. My mother left the room. The visitor, my new horn teacher, unclipped the case and out came this arrangement of metal. It was silver in colour. At one end was a comically huge bell, as flared as one of my trouser legs. It was strewn with dents.

I had never seen a French horn before in my life. I had definitely never expressed an interest in learning one. My father was the musical one, so it must have been his idea, but he in turn may have come under pressure from his mother. Just after the First World War she took the train up from Dolgellau on the fringes of Snowdonia to study piano at the Royal Academy of Music, though she never went on to play professionally. Her younger son inherited her gift. In the Second World War he was a chorister at St George's Chapel in Windsor, the private place of worship of King George VI and Queen Elizabeth. His voice was so prized that they – the school, not the king and queen – wouldn't let my father leave until his voice broke.

My own knowledge of his musicianship was mostly confined to the Gilbert and Sullivan songs he'd sing of an evening. Accompanying himself on the piano, in which he was entirely self-taught, he lived by the credo that where accuracy is lacking, volume is an appropriate substitute. The more wine he'd drunk, the more he assaulted the keys. When we drove to west Wales every Christmas he was wheeled out to sing in more refined style for his parents' friends in an elegant drawing room with Gothic windows, while his mother accompanied him with delicacy and refinement at her own baby grand. Long after he'd emigrated to England and eagerly shucked off all vestiges of his Welshness, music was the one thing my father and grandmother had in common.

Insofar as any talent percolated down a generation, it settled on me. The talent was severely attenuated, a thinned-out thing that was really no more than a vague aptitude. At some point my grandmother must have said, 'Why isn't Jasper learning an instrument?' But why the horn? My father doesn't remember. It seems likely, though, that if he couldn't get me on to a horse, he could get me on to an instrument with stronger links to horses than, say, the cello, the instrument he had given up the minute he left school.

My first horn teacher asked me if I'd ever played the horn before. I said I'd played the horns above the fireplace. He said which fireplace. I said the fireplace in Sussex. He said what sort of horns. I said all sorts but only the big ones work but they don't work very well. He said so you know it's hard work. I said yes and laughed nervously.

We got down to it. He told me how to hold the horn. The smaller end went to the lips, naturally, the three middle fingers on the piston valves. The hole at the larger end – and here was a surprise – housed the right hand. He tweaked and sculpted mine into a position where it could rest on the inside of the bell. It felt unnatural, like the first time you attempt a correct bridge at the snooker table. But it didn't feel as unnatural as the business of forming the correct mouth position. You had to purse your lips and, on pain of excommunication, keep your cheeks in check. No puffing: that was a golden rule. The idea, I was told, was to produce a buzzing sound. What it actually produced, at least to start with, was saliva. I irrigated the carpet. After a few buzzes, he whipped out a small metal mouthpiece from the case and made me blow through it until my face started to settle into the right shape. Then he attached the mouthpiece to the horn.

The initial task of any horn student is to send out a search party and look for a middle C. It's the note that's easiest to find. So I took that first of many deep breaths, and I blew. I blew and blew. And blew. And as happens with many a gifted player as they make their first foray into the world of musical self-expression on this most beautiful of instruments, a note of eloquent purity and sonorous depth, rich in colour and musicality, a note that reached back on some primordial level through the encrusted millennia of history, back past the biblical horn at the foot of the mighty walls of Jericho to Neolithic man chancing one day upon the mystery of amplified sound in the horn of a dead ram, somehow failed to splutter out of the rear end of the twisted metal in my sweaty grip. I looked at the instrument with its battered bell, as if it might somehow be to blame.

'Shall we try again?'

'OK.'

Another deep breath. Eventually, after unnumbered attempts, a wobbly middle C began to take shape, like a creature emerging from the primeval swamp. It was a thing of mud and fog, a blur, a smudge of sound, with no clear definition, no discernible outline. Still, it was a middle C. My first.

'Good. Right. Now press down the first valve with your fore-finger and blow again.'

More mud, more fog, but of a subtly different quality to the middle C. It was, my horn teacher revealed, a D.

'By pressing down a valve,' he explained, 'you are sending the air through a different length of tubing, which changes the note.' I started to experiment. I'd play a C, then a D. A D, then a C, followed by a C and then a D. And so on. By alternately pressing the first valve, then releasing it, I was now officially making music. It was music you wouldn't inflict on someone who had kidnapped your entire family and boiled them alive, flayed your dog and skinned your cat, and, as a final insult, dismembered your impressive collection of Action Men with all-new real hair and gripping hands. But it was music all the same.

With this advanced base camp established, he suggested I head further up the hill and attempt a third note. Like the C, this would be what he called 'an open note'.

'A what?'

'You don't press down any valves.'

'But then it'll be a C.'

'You alter your embouchure.'

'My what?'

'Your embouchure. The opening of your mouth. It's from the French word for mouth. If you make a smaller hole to blow the air through, the pitch will alter.' This sounded most unlikely. Still, tightening my lips – my embouchure – I gave it a crack. It took a while to settle, but as if by magic, the quality of the noise emitted by the horn now changed.

'What note was that?'

'An E. Now press down the first valve again and play an F.'

None of these notes were getting any crisper. The control required to hit a note and stick to it was beyond me. But with a bit of commuting up and down the register, I hit the F. It wavered horribly, like someone struggling to keep their balance on a tight-rope. Every now and then I fell off and dropped down to the D, the other first-valve note. But I had played four notes. I was a natural.

'Now tighten your embouchure again and see if you can play a G.'

'Which valve?'

'None. Keep it open.' I was starting to think this was easy. He set the bar, and I cleared it. Out came the G. A fifth note. In one lesson. Had there ever been a more promising beginner?

'Good. See if you can play the A.' No problem.

'It's first valve again, isn't it?'

'First and second. Forefinger and middle finger.'

'First and ... you mean you press two at once? Are you sure?'

'Press the first and second.' I squeezed and squished my lips together. A thin, reedy, parsimonious emission emerged, a tiny parp, but toxic in the extreme. Coming from another orifice, this critter would have stunk the house out.

'Good,' said my first horn teacher. 'You need to practise before next week.'

'Pardon?'

'To practise. The only way to improve is to work at it.'

'Oh.'

'Just ten minutes a day. Also read the rudiments.'

'The what?'

He produced a book with a picture of a French horn on the cover. *A Tune a Day*. He opened it. It was dense with text, and where there wasn't text there were notes. Whole armies of them, incomprehensible hieroglyphs, scattered apparently at random up and down the page. 'It will help you to learn how music works.' He flicked through to the back of the book and started to write on the inside back page. '<u>March 12 1975</u>. Learn pages 4–7. Also read pages (ii) RUDIMENTS OF MUSIC onwards. Practice [*sic*] long notes on C, E and G, and the scale of C. Learn the <u>fingering</u>.'

He left the battered horn behind.

Three and a half millennia before the birth of Christ, the craft of smelting copper and tin from naturally occurring outcrops of ore, and compounding them into an alloy, was discovered. The new metal gave its name to the Bronze Age. And one of the things they made with this new-fangled technology, alongside swords, shields, coins, jewels, pots and pans, was horns.

Creeping away from the battlegrounds of the Old Testament, the know-how slowly disseminated along the trade routes until it fetched up on the outer rim of the European continent. Some time in the 1820s, in the heart of Ireland, in County Offaly near a village called Dowris, or Doorosheath, men digging potato trenches on the edge of a bog chanced upon an underground stash of metal implements. An agricultural dig turned into an archaeological one as more and more bronze was excavated. In the end, 218 objects were retrieved. They included 44 spearheads, 43 axes, 44 crotals, a bucket, and a magnificent collection of 22 horns.

A good half of the Dowris Hoard is on display in the National Museum of Ireland in Dublin. I pass through one afternoon. Here, in a room bulging with flint tools, cauldrons, axes and gold jewellery brought up from the yielding Irish turf, you can trace the advance of human know-how from 7,000 years before Christ, as man worked out how to sharpen, carve, plane, grind, saw, flange and finally cast. Over centuries of trial and error, Irish metalsmiths came up with ways of casting increasingly complex objects until eventually, after perhaps a thousand years of working with bronze, a technological genius came up with a clay mould in the shape of a horn.

It was the first musical instrument made in Ireland. There are four of them in one display case, curled like a nest of puff adders behind a pane of glass in a reptile house. 'Side-blown horn (*Corn taobhseinnte*),' says the label, 'from a hoard, Derrynane, Co Kerry, 900–500 BC.' 'End-blown horn (*Corn ceannseinte*), from a hoard, Drumbest, Co Antrim.' Two have ornamental tracing, in straight lines or zigzags, scratched into the bell end. One has a pronounced U-bend and collars of decorative spikes, like something you find round the neck of a bulldog.

In a separate casement in the middle of the floor is the Dowris Hoard. The bronze implements have been unceremoniously packed in and piled high to convey an idea of the heap they were found in. I circle the display, counting the horns as they curl in and out of the mounds of spears and crotals. There are eleven of them. They are perhaps 18 inches long, and slightly curved, like a boomerang.

To this day, no one has come up with any clear explanation for the existence of the Dowris Hoard, and others like it in Kerry and Antrim. Did people simply store their possessions in a safe place, and then just forget to retrieve them? The argument in favour suggests that these were centuries of nervousness and insecurity. Homesteads and settlements were built in locations that cut off an enemy advance – on islands, promontories and at the edge of lakes and bogs. The productivity in weapons increased hugely. Perhaps that's why there were so many horns. They were used for signalling danger. But why would anyone want to bury twenty-two of them? And not just for twenty-two years.

I return from the British Horn Society festival inflamed with enthusiasm. I have articulated, if only to myself, the pipedream of going back in twelve months' time and playing a solo. For the moment, I keep my lofty ambition to myself. I don't tell the New Person In My Life. I don't tell Dave. The chances are that it will never happen. I'll never get up to snuff, or I'll lack the nerve to go cap in hand to the society, or I will dredge up the courage but they will snot themselves laughing at the thought of a rank amateur sharing the stage with seasoned professionals.

But I need to begin again somewhere. In privacy, with no one around to listen in, I start to scoot through *A Tune a Day*. I still have my copy. The cover has long since fallen off but there, at the back of the book, are my first horn teacher's instructions. He has curiously bad handwriting. What strikes me now is the book's hectoring tone. It seemed to be shouting at you. From Physical Preparation: 'Breath should be taken through the corners of the mouth. DO NOT PUFF OUR [*sic*] YOUR CHEEKS. Practise in front of a mirror.' From the Care of the Instrument section: 'FAILURE ON YOUR PART ON FOLLOWING OUT REGULARLY THE ABOVE INSTRUCTIONS IN REGARD TO THE CARE OF YOUR INSTRUMENT WILL RESULT IN EXPENSIVE REPAIR COSTS.' The

Method of Holding the French Horn section features snaps of a malnourished young man in blazer and Brylcreem. He has big ears and glasses. 'Pictures posed by Robert Handy; East Orange, N.J.,' it says. They must have been taken at the end of the 1950s. He looks like a jerk.

However, it's all here: the fingerings, the arpeggios, the folk songs, carols, nursery rhymes and ditties so tuneless they have no title other than 'Melody'. There are gems too: snippets of Haydn, oddments of Dvořák, some Brahms, and the theme of the final movement of Beethoven's Choral Symphony makes an early appearance on page 8. You don't get to 'Mary Had a Little Lamb' till page 9. Occasionally I succumb to hot flushes of shame as, within spitting distance of forty, I have to furrow my brow over the notational sequencing of 'Twinkle, Twinkle, Little Star'. But these are the hard yards, and they must be traversed.

I make treacly progress. Most of these exercises are so moronic I can't bear to play them more than once. But as I doggedly crank out the baby tunes, the sound coming out of the horn starts to settle. Where notes were previously pocked with cracks and breaks, some of them now have a rather lordly sheen to them. They rise, they resonate, awaking memories of sounds which, with a good following wind, were once known to come out of the other end of this Josef Lídl. At the British Horn Society festival, I couldn't play for toffee. But with all the diligent attention duly paid to 'Yankee Doodle' and 'Skip to My Lou', to 'Polly Wally Doodle' and 'My Bonnie', I begin to make a connection. I am stirred by the music. It's the tone. It's as if I'm reaching down into a pool of mud and, with a stick in my hand, stirring up something that has always been there, submerged under layer upon impacted layer of the sludge we call experience.

At this point, I can boast that I have at least one thing in common with all those professional horn players. They may have grown up in the old Soviet Union, or in an America convulsed by fear of the commie menace. They may ply their trade in a European capital still scarred by the memory of a wall sliced right through its own midriff. But horn players of whatever nationality are united by a connective tissue, plugged into a matrix which only they fully understand. That understanding begins as soon as, like Andrei Gloukhov or Phil Myers or Stefan Dohr, like Lowell Greer or Dave Lee, they find themselves hooked. It may be an accident, but once they chance upon the horn, it seems there is no question of a choice, no possibility of turning back. It's as if there is a call of nature, an atavistic summons. The instrument works its magic. And now it is working its spell on me. For the next year, there will be no release.

2
The Ipso Factor

The call to war resounded from the winding horn.
Seneca: *Oedipus*

The last strains of 'MacDonald's Farm' die away, along with its testing sequence of quavers and semiquavers. I reckon I have the basics licked now. It's time to raise the bar, and the means are to hand. In my horn case, alongside the Josef Lídl student horn and *A Tune a Day*, I have for twenty-two years kept my own personal copies, with piano accompaniment and separate solo part, of the four horn concertos of Wolfgang Amadeus Mozart.

From nursery rhymes to the greatest composer who ever lived – this may seem more than a single gear shift. The reality is that I know these tunes. It's the same for anyone who has ever dabbled in the horn, from the soloist trotting around the globe to the student hunched in the trenches. The concertos stand at the absolute epicentre of the literature. They are the daily bread, the hardy perennial, the Checkpoint Charlie of the repertoire. On the horn, no one makes it through to the other side without going past the Mozart concertos. They are the 'Smoke on the Water'. And although I gave up the instrument at sixteen, the concertos never gave up on me. They have been buzzing around my head ever since. Scarcely a day has gone by in which I have not hummed or whistled or sung at least a snatch of one of them.

The concerto I know best, the one I spent the most time with, is the third. One Sunday, a couple of weekends after the British Horn Society festival, I fish it out of the case. 'Mozart,' it says. 'Concerto no. 3 in E flat major for horn and piano. K447.' It's an American edition. Inside, detachable from the bound piano part, is a loose-leaf sheaf of music of four pages. This time the heading is in German: 'Konzert Nr. 3 Es dur für Horn and Orchester. W.A. Mozart K.-V. 447.'

The concerto is in three movements. Obedient to eighteenth-century convention, a quick opening movement is followed by a slower middle one, before the pace picks up again for the finale. In this case the tempi are Allegro, Larghetto, Allegro. Literally, happy, a bit slow, happy. The slow movement is also known as the Romanze, because that was the word Mozart scribbled on the original manuscript. When I was still at school, and coming towards the end of my tether as a student of the French horn, I spent quite a bit of time with the middle movement. We got to know each other pretty well, the Romanze and me. We were a good match: it was a bit slow, and so was I.

I turn to it again. I think it might be the thing to play at the concert in a year's time.

A Celtic horn known as a *karnyx* proliferated across Europe. In 1816 fragments of a *karnyx* were dug up in the Moray Firth. In 2004 five more were found, all but one decorated with boar's heads, in central France. The instrument is documented in a Celtic attack on Delphi in 279 BC. Three *karnyx* players are represented on the Gundestrup Cauldron from the first century BC performing in some sort of ritualistic ceremony. As few whole horns have been dug up, it's assumed that though the bell and mouthpiece were metal, the curlicued middle section was made of wood. The bell was often fashioned in the ferocious shape of an animal's gaping jaws, typically a boar or wolf. Otherwise it was not unlike the plate-belled Scandinavian *lur*, examples of which have been excavated in boggy ground all over the Baltic seaboard. They date as far back as the twelfth century BC. Both instruments – the *karnyx* and the *lur* – were played aloft, and in symmetrical pairs – perhaps in allusion to the pachydermic tusks on which they may have been modelled. They seem to have had a funerary role, but as signalling instruments on the battlefield they would have been formidable.

Up until a couple of hundred years before the birth of Christ, the horn had every right to think of itself as invincible. Then it came up against something that really was invincible: the Roman army. In 224 BC, the Bronze Age had long since made way for the Iron Age, with implications for the mass production of weaponry. The *karnyx* accompanied an army of 20,000 Gauls who had invaded Italy. The army penetrated as far as what would now be southern Tuscany, only to find itself encircled and out-numbered on the coast. 'The Romans,' wrote Polybius, the second-century BC Greek chronicler of the rise of the Roman empire,

> were on the one hand encouraged by having caught the enemy between their two armies, but on the other they were terrified by the fine order of the Celtic host and the dreadful din, for there were innumerable horn-blowers and trumpeters, and, as the whole army were shouting their war-cries at the same time, there was such a tumult of sound that it seemed that not only the trumpets and the soldiers but all the country round had got a voice and caught up the cry. Very terrifying too were the appearance and the gestures of the naked warriors in front, all in the prime of life, and finely built men, and all in the leading companies richly adorned with gold torques and armlets. The sight of them indeed dismayed the Romans, but at the same time the prospect of winning such spoils made them twice as keen for the fight.

The Roman republic was in the early stages of conquering the known world. When the Gauls were routed, the *karnyx* did not escape. A prize captured from the barbarian enemy, it found itself trudging along one of those straight roads that lead to Rome.

When the defeated hordes were paraded through the streets of the city, one of the spoils of victory displayed to the baying *populus* was this vanquished instrument of terror. As the republic became an empire, the instrument tasted further defeat when Julius Caesar subdued Gaul and Claudius subordinated Britain. The *karnyx* was still being depicted as booty on the column erected in Rome in honour of Trajan's victories over the Dacians early in the second century AD, more than 300 years after the events described by Polybius.

My first horn teacher left after two lessons. The evidence is there at the back of *A Tune a Day*. There are no practice instructions between 'March 17th' and '2/6'. There is a break, in short, between my second lesson and my third of two and a half months. At the end of it, I still seem to be on page 7. Either I was a very poor pupil, or in those ten weeks I didn't play the horn once. The new instructions are in a different hand. And the first thing my second horn teacher did was draw a line – horizontally, across the page. The line seems to herald the dawn of a new age. What it also means is that I didn't give up the horn after seven years, at the age of seventeen. I gave it up at the age of ten. After two lessons. In effect, I first gave up the horn after one hour.

The Romanze may be slow, but it turns out that I am slower. The problem is the first bar. I can't actually play it. The concerto is in E flat. But the horn is in the key of F. I remember enough to know this means you have to play a tone away from the note written on the staves. But which way? A tone higher, or a tone lower? On the page the first bar is written C-F-A-A. But when you see a C, do you play a B flat, or a D?

I experiment with both options. Neither really works, because by the time I've got to the third note of the first bar, I can't remember if I'm playing up a tone or down. This was the sort of short-circuiting I had to contend with when I learned the horn the first time round. It must be a synaptic malfunction, I tell myself. It's some sort of notational dyslexia. I ring Dave Lee. Like all horn players, Dave has been playing K447 since he had his stabilisers removed.

'What does the key of E flat actually mean?' This is the first time I've spoken to him since I got back from the British Horn Society festival. I was planning to astonish him with my progress when I next touched base. That plan's out the window now. I am conscious that at the other end of the line a leading British horn player will now be thinking I am a moron. But this whole E flat situation needs sorting out or I'm stuck with 'The Battle Hymn of the Republic' in perpetuity. 'I mean I know what it means, as it were, I just don't know what the notes, er . . . If you see what I . . .' I trail off.

'If the horn is tuned in F, it means for anything in E flat you play a tone down from the written note.'

'That's what I've been . . .' I stop short of a white lie. 'So just down a tone?'

'Yeah.'

'Right. I'll . . .'

'And don't forget there are three flats. E flat, A flat and B flat.'

'Oh.' I probably will forget that. I hang up. So, a tone down. The great thing about wind instruments is you can only ever play one note at a time. You never have to play a chord of two or more notes. So theoretically this ought to be easy. But if you suffer from notational dyslexia, it just isn't. Reading music where the notes are one away from where you're used to them being is a bit like deciphering a code in which letters are replaced by their neighbour in the alphabet. 'Xpmghboh Bnbefvt Npabsu', for example, may to a gifted musician clearly read as 'Wolfgang Amadeus Mozart'. To me it reads as 'Xpmghboh Bnbefvt Npabsu'. How about 'Uijse dpodfsup gps ipso jo F gmbu'? 'Third concerto for horn in E flat'. In the Second World War, when German U-boats patrolling the North Atlantic sent their deadly encryptions back to the whirring hub of the Nazi machine, the messages were intercepted and sent to Bletchley Park where Cambridge mathematicians crammed in huts used huge proto-computers to help them unjumble this sort of gobbledygook. I have to do it all by myself.

(Though I do like the fact that 'horn' encodes as 'ipso'.)

I decide to treat the music like a block of marble. Somewhere inside it is the second movement of K447. My task is to find it. I start to chip away, thinking positive thoughts. It helps that I know the tune. It helps that a faint memory of the fingering is filed away somewhere in my cerebral cortex. It helps ... but I can't think of another positive thought. With grinding slowness, I falter towards an approximation of the movement's opening statement. I play it over and over and over again. The notes stumble out, dozy and disoriented as if waking from a deep coma. After an hour or so you can see a rough outline grudgingly emerge.

In the right hands, with the right horn player, the Romanze is one of the most enchanting moments in the entire repertoire. It paces quietly along somewhere between lyricism and wit. It's as if, while casting a pall of splendid gloom over the melody, Mozart could not quite repress the natural bounce of his personality. It is mournful and jaunty, yearning and effervescent, melancholy and spry.

In the wrong hands it's none of the above. The days pass. I keep at it. Quite where this sudden sprouting of a Protestant work ethic comes from is puzzling. Why is it that you are prepared to hammer away at something when you're thirty-nine but not when you're fifteen? Surely it isn't simply that as a fifteen-year-old you can't be arsed. There are many things I can't be arsed to do at thirty-nine. The appropriate amount of exercise, to take a bog-standard example. Rustle up an interest in gardening. Deal with important letters from banks, lenders, estate agents, local government, utility suppliers, mobile phone companies, the Inland Revenue. Acquire a golf handicap. Get going on that pile of second-hand Penguin classics I keep telling myself that people like me ought to have read by now. Pliny the Elder, Plautus, Pliny the Younger – here I do not come.

Fecklessness is not just a teenage affliction. It can strike at any age. But more or less by accident I have alighted on something that I want to get better at, and I profoundly understand that the only way to get better at it is to put the hours in. Over these early weeks of practice, I come up with a theory. It's not a complicated theory. It actually boils down to one word: sex. Around the time you leave school, the biological urge to have sex comes on in a Vesuvial eruption. And the first thing to be drowned in the gushing tide of molten lava – literally the first thing – is the musical instrument you're not very good at. You give it up, and take up sex instead. Now spool forward a decade. Cooling waters have passed under the bridge. You have worked methodically, industriously, at your biological impulse. You have had some fun. But in due course, you decide it's time to quit dicking around and actually procreate. You do your bit of repopulating and you settle down to the devouring business of herding your offspring towards adulthood. Another decade ghosts by. At the end of it you are, lo and behold, slightly less interested in sex than you were at seventeen. It gives me no pleasure to insist on this dispiriting truth, but there it is. You just are. Which means that, at a primordial level, having replenished the earth, you are ready for something else.

Of course there is a more specific reason why I'm practising like buggery. According to a vow I've still not shared with anyone, I'm playing the whole of Xpmghboh Bnbefvt Npabsu't uijse dpodfsup gps ipso jo F gmbu at the British Horn Society festival in slightly under a year's time.

Before the rise of Rome, the horn was put to agricultural use on the Italian peninsula. Polybius reports with some astonishment that the humble pig could be trained to respond to its own horn call.

> The swineherd does not follow behind the animals as in Greece but goes in front and sounds a horn at intervals, the animals following him and responding to the call. They have learnt so well to answer to their own horn that those who hear of this for the first time are astonished and loath to believe it.

The Etruscans are among those he credits with this improbable craft. They were also skilled workers in bronze who through their trade with northern tribes may well have heard tell of the Scandinavian *lur*. Horns completing almost an entire revolution are depicted on murals in Etruscan tombs from the fifth to the fourth century BC. They are played in funeral processions by men in diaphanous white robes. As they brutally subsumed Etruscan culture into their own, the Romans borrowed the design for the horn until, in the first century AD, the art of folding a length of brass tubing without the use of casts and moulds was invented. At a stroke, an instrument made out of metal could bend to man's will. Horns were now free to grow to unseen, unseemly lengths. The horn found in Roman murals and bas-reliefs, on sarcophagi and mosaics, curled from the mouthpiece down under the player's arm and back over his head. They called it the *cornu.* It was an instrumental tumescence, so big that it had to be supported by a wooden crossbar. But it was also portable, and could be taken on the long march along the avenues of Empire. As it was longer it was, by extension, louder and, most petrifyingly, deeper than anything the fur-clad enemy – the Gauls, the Goths, the Celts – could blow back at them. Its invention was an act of pure creative sadism.

It was played by a *cornicen.* Two of them are depicted on Trajan's column. One has rippling biceps and forearms. Their instruments, brandished casually over their shoulders, look like weapons. One historian suggests that Trajan's horn players look tired, and posits an explanation that in the absence of marching drums in the Roman army, the *cornicines* may have had to blow to keep long columns moving in time.

Eventually the instrument was domesticated and put to civic service. At funerals it was *de rigueur* to have a horn wailing mournfully over an important corpse. It took centre stage at the games. In all those Roman epics – *Ben Hur, Spartacus, Gladiator* – whenever the emperor or praetor or gubernator has to address the rabble, it's the *cornu* that announces his ceremonial entrance. Five civilian specimens, once played at gladiatorial games but buried in the lava at Pompeii after Vetruvius erupted in AD 79, are displayed in the Museo Nazionale in Naples. They are ten feet in length, and curl round in a circle half that in diameter.

Ovid mentions the *cornu* in *Metamorphoses.* So does Seneca the Younger in his tragedy *Oedipus.* Juvenal in his *Satires* refers to the *cornu* and *cornicines.* From the evidence of an engraving and inscription on an altar stone in the Roman catacombs – 'M. Julius victor ex Collegio Liticinum et Cornicinum' – horn players were members of some form of guild. But these are passing references. It was only as the Roman Empire neared the end of its natural life, with the Goths massing bloodthirstily on the border, that the *cornu*'s instrumental role in the defence of civilisation was put in writing. Vegetius, the fourth-century military historian, marked down the precise musical functions of each brass instrument on the field of battle. Trumpets and cornets, he explained, were given particular roles in regulating the movement of soldiers, but a pivotal assignment was reserved for the *cornu* – or *buccina*, as it was also called. 'The *classicum*, which is a particular sound of the *buccina* or horn, is appropriated to the commander-in-chief and is used in the presence of the general, or at the execution of a soldier, as a mark of its being done by his authority.' The horn was already the boss of the brass section.

Vegetius added a cautionary note for anyone involved in musical signalling as part of military manoeuvres. 'These rules,' he warned direly,

> must be punctually observed in all exercises and reviews so that the soldiers may be ready to obey them in action without hesitation according to the general's orders either to charge or halt, to pursue the enemy or to retire. For reason will convince us that what is necessary to be performed in the heat of action should constantly be practised in the leisure of peace.

No one has ever put it better: practise – or die.

'30/6/75. ABIDE WITH ME. Pg 14. Learn – play all on one note then add rhythm to notes – breath [*sic*] well all the time – play softly.' I made my concert debut on Music Open Day. The music classroom was in an annexe of the church round the corner from the school. At the appointed hour I trudged there with the rest of the fourth form. This being the tail-end of the glam-rock era, we all had long hair. Mr Hunt, in his grey three-piece suit, was tall and angular and, by contrast, classically bald. He had glasses with black rims and a line in sarcasm which only just kept the lid on his contempt for his students and, perhaps, himself.

The rest of the class sat in rows on canvas chairs with metal frames while I edged watchfully to the front. There were the predictable sniggers from the usual suspects, the ne'er-do-wells and vagabonds who would no doubt end up in prison for drug-dealing in West End nightclubs or defrauding tenants on their country estates or some such posh felony. Ignoring them, I uncased my horn and brandished it proudly. This, I thought, will shut the bastards up. It flashed in a column of sunlight shafting through from the high windows. For the first time, I felt pride tingling along my spine as I held the instrument: I was a horn player.

'Has anyone seen one of these before?' This from Mr Hunt.

No answer.

'Does anyone know what it is?'

Silence.

'What is it, Rees?'

'It's a French horn, sir.'

'So you're going to play something for us.' A smirk danced across his face.

'Yes, sir. I just need to warm up a bit.' I retrieved *A Tune a Day* from the case, opened it on page 14 and put it on the music stand in front of me. Hurriedly I blew a note. The sniggering resumed.

'Shush!' Mr Hunt barked. I felt a shallowness in my chest and a tremor in my right knee. This was my introduction to performance anxiety. I was scandalised, even revolted, by the fact that nerves could not be controlled.

'Abide With Me' is known the length and breadth of England as a footballing hymn. It has been sung at the FA Cup Final more or less since footballs were made of pig bladders. Being an obsessive football fan, there was nothing I didn't know about football. Absolutely nothing. Apart from the tune to 'Abide With Me'. The problem was that the FA Cup Final was always on a Saturday, and we spent weekends in Sussex, and we didn't have a television there, so despite being an obsessive football fan, I'd never actually seen the Cup Final. So I'd never heard 'Abide With Me'. So I had no template to follow in the privacy of my head. I was at the mercy of my own musicality.

I waded in. It was only sixteen bars long, but it felt like taking part in the Battle of the Somme. Bombs rained down from somewhere or other, spitting geysers of mud into the air and leaving huge craters for me to stumble into. My second horn teacher had pencilled exclamation marks above the F sharp and the F natural. I played the sharp natural and the natural sharp. I took breaths in all the wrong places – in the middle of phrases; in the middle of *notes*. The ne'er-do-wells and vagabonds had plenty to snigger about now, did they but know it. But they were quiet. They were witnessing a fellow human being, a fellow boy with shaggy mid-Seventies hair like theirs, suffer unimaginable depths of torment. It was no longer funny.

I limped home. There was no applause. People knew it was the end only because I lowered the horn.

'A pleasing and almost original contribution to our Music Open Day. DH.' Almost original. Does Mr Hunt's report mean what I think it does? I mangled the tune so badly that, like someone mauled by lions in the Circus Maximus, it was barely recognisable at all? Within a week I had left the school. My younger brother and I were evacuated to a boarding school a mile or two outside a town identified in Ptolemy's *Geographia* as Noviomagus Regnorum.

As I get further acquainted with the Romanze, it takes shape in front of me as a conversation between two lovers. The horn says something, then the orchestra – or if you can't get hold of an orchestra, the piano – replies. It is ardent but at the same time elegant and terribly polite. If Noel Coward wrote it up it would go something like this:

HORN: I'm frightfully keen on you and you're frightfully keen on me. I'm simply sure of it.
ORCHESTRA: Oh I'm *frightfully* keen on you. And you're frightfully keen on me. I'm sure of it too.
HORN: My heart jolly well aches.
ORCHESTRA: Does it? Does it really, darling?
HORN: Yes my heart jolly well aches.
ORCHESTRA: Can you be sure?
HORN: How could you ask such a silly question? How *could* you

ask such a silly question? Ha ho ho ho ho ho ho ho hoooa!

ORCHESTRA: You're frightfully keen on me, and I'm frightfully keen on you. But what can we do?

HORN: Run away! We must run away.

ORCHESTRA: I'm frightfully keen on you. But I'm going to pretend you didn't just say that.

HORN: Do let's run away. It would all be such ripping fun. If we hurry we can catch the next train to Gretna Green. Or the next! Or the next? Or the next . . .

ORCHESTRA: Goodness! You really mean it! You really do.

HORN: Yes it seems I do. No of course I do! Would you mind awfully if I laid my head on your lap?

ORCHESTRA: I'm frightfully keen on you.

HORN: I'm frightfully keen on you. But you know that.

ORCHESTRA: There's always another day. We could always run away together another . . .

HORN: I'm sure we could . . . It's awfully comfortable in your lap. Frightfully keen, I'm sure of it.

ORCHESTRA: Yes *I'm* sure of it.

HORN: I'm sure of it too. Or am I?

There are some technical issues. After the opening eight-bar phrase ('I'm frightfully keen on you'), the horn comes back in on a yearning high F and tumbles lyrically down through a phrase ('My heart jolly well aches'). And then does it again ('Yes my heart jolly well aches'). Each time the horn returns, there's a new high note to hit upon re-entry. An ardent E flat ('Run away!'), then a manly D ('Do let's run away'). This being the horn, hitting the high note is a lottery. Or maybe it's archery. Somewhere away from you is a round target consisting of coloured concentric circles. Your task, with your bow, is to land the arrow slap dab in the middle of the bull's eye. This is very much easier said than done. High notes are physically more demanding to play anyway. The embouchure tightens. It becomes harder to blow air through the remaining aperture. Cheeks ache. Soon you are prey to strain, worry, stress. All of which make the high note all the more unattainable. It's not even archery. It's blind man's buff.

Professional horn players crack jokes about cracking notes. The horn, they all know, is fundamentally high-risk. They are a hundred times likelier than a flautist to play a wrong note in a concert. 'In quantity operations,' one pro tells me, 'there will be some losses.' Other pros I meet refer to something called 'security in the upper register', as if a formal Latin euphemism will somehow rationalise or even reduce the jeopardy.

Next comes a passage of quaking semiquavers. ('How can you ask such a silly question?') Semiquavers are fiddly, and there are thirty-two of them sardined into four overcrowded bars. Like a shepherd watching his flock, you have to keep a careful eye out. Lose track of just one of them and they're all following it out through the escape hatch and before you know it you're staring gormlessly at a mass of black dots staging some kind of riot right there on the page in front of you. But after the last high entry the ride is smoother. There are no more hurdles you haven't already crossed. In the second half of the Romanze, Mozart reformulates the closing phrase of the opening statement three times. It's as if he's so pleased with it he can't quite bear to leave it behind. It's mostly a question of counting.

I practise incessantly. I work from home, which means that opportunity always knocks. The Lídl glints in its open case, beckoning, summoning. There'll be a pressing deadline. Someone somewhere is waiting for me to deliver a piece of work. They need it now. They need it an hour, two hours ago. They need it yesterday. They need it. I'm doing it, I tell them. It's happening. It'll be with you by lunchtime. I'm just fine-tuning it. I need to go over it one last time and then it's yours. My resistance weakens. Collapses.

'I'm frightfully keen on you ...' I get up ... 'My heart jolly well aches ...' Just four minutes ... 'Do let's run away ...' The Romanze is only four minutes long ... 'Would you mind awfully if I laid my head on your lap?' I'm in love.

There are forty forty-year-olds sitting at an L-shaped table. They are assembled in the New Person In My Life's deconsecrated pub. A fug of drink and conversation warms the long main room. It's my fortieth birthday, and I am having one of the best evenings of my entire adulthood. There are also two parents and two daughters. Food has been served, speeches have been made, glasses raised to this and that. To my surprise and delight, Dave has turned up with a horn and a string quartet called Stringendo. In an alcove, they play excerpts from his album *Under the Influence*, and the first movement of a quintet Mozart wrote for horn and strings. Much of it, I fear, is lost on the assembled company. They have been systematically plied with drink, and it shows.

Deep into the evening Dave steps before us all and announces that he and I are going to play a little something together. It gets people's attention, mine included.

We are? I look at Dave and make the traditional eyebrow signals for 'over my dead body'. Dave ignores both eyebrows.

'It'll be fun.'

'No it won't.'

'We're playing a little piece by Mozart's father Leopold. Easy as falling off a log, pissed.'

'I'm crap at sight-reading, Dave.' That is true. I always have been. I hate it. I used to need hours to work out how to play a piece I didn't know. It's notational dyslexia. And now, to celebrate the start of my fifth decade, I'm being asked to read a piece of music I've never seen before *in front of an actual audience*? I quiver in indignation at some injustice I can't quite put my finger on. This, I guess, is what happens when you come over all obsessive about something. Your bluff gets called and suddenly it's time to walk the walk.

'It'll be fine,' says Dave. 'Just follow me.'

A music stand materialises in the middle of the room, with music by Leopold Mozart on it. I cast my eye down the page. It's bad news. There is a swarm of notes. I try to stall for time.

'Can I warm up?'

'Bollocks to that. You don't need to warm up. It's in two-four, so one two one two. I'll count you in.'

In the background, the string quartet kicks into a bouncy intro. And Dave starts counting. Counting down. There is no going back.

49

Conditions for a successful performance could not be more favourable. It's only a short piece, maybe a minute. It sits bang in the middle of the range. I played most of these notes in my first-ever lesson three decades earlier. There can't be more than sixty notes to play in all, a lot of them the same. But I nail no more than a quarter of them. The rest? Well Dave is kindly playing loud. The applause is long and loud and 100 per cent ironic. I am profoundly embarrassed.

And then the devil gets into me. I met almost everyone here after leaving school. They never knew I once played the horn, let alone ever heard me. But they all know I've been tooling around on the instrument for a few weeks and, so far as they can tell from the available evidence, I have the competence of a ten-year-old beginner. I feel the need for some sort of redress. No no, I want to say, you've got the wrong idea. I am actually better than that. But there is only one way to prove it. I have to play the Romanze. Out loud. Now.

There is no point in equivocating about nerves. If I don't get up and play, I will lose an astonishing amount of face. It's an emergency. I have no alternative. To hand is the New Person's mother, who is a pianist. I've got the accompaniment in my case. We have played through it a couple of times, round at her place. She takes her place at the piano.

'And here's something I prepared earlier,' I announce over the hubbub.

A new sort of hush descends. There are a few giggles, but mostly there is a quiet murmur of collective trepidation as forty forty-year-olds all think the same thought. This could be genuinely excruciating. Much of my audience never got past first base with music. There's my father the chorister, a former member of the little-known early Eighties two-man group The Cleaners from Venus, a world-class countertenor, a bloke who used to bash skins in his lost youth, an amateur oboist, a chick singer or two, and an opera critic. And then there's Dave and Stringendo. But apart from them, the convocation of forty-year-olds is awash with ignorance. It's the oboist who pipes up helpfully amid the back-chat.

'What are you going to play for us, Jas?'

'I'm going to play the slow second movement of Mozart's third horn concerto.' You can see the lot of them thinking, blimey, there's posh.

Without further ado, I raise the Lidl to my lips and plunge into the opening statement. I am acutely conscious that it's important to play this one for laughs, just to ensure they know for sure that I don't actually think I'm good. Lower expectations, that's the ticket. So at the end of the first phrase ('I'm frightfully keen on you'), which provokes an undiscerning round of applause, I use my eight-bar rest to abandon my post, pace over to the long table in front of me, pick up a glass of red wine, and take a calming draught. As intended, it raises a laugh. This is not one for the purists.

After that, it's plain sailing. The actual music borders on the toe-curling. In one phrase ('Would you mind awfully if I laid my head on your lap?'), which soars up to a yearning E flat then rolls slowly down the other side, I go dramatically awry and feel obliged to apologise. It gets another laugh. This is the softest audience I'm ever going to encounter.

It's possible to enjoy yourself too much. I'm standing there thinking how well it's all going when I lose track somewhere towards the back end of a four-bar rest. 'We could always run away together another . . .' I panic and suddenly think I've missed it.

'Is that me?' I say. Counting was never one of my fortes.

'Now!' barks the New Person's mother unflappably from the piano.

The ending is infinitely delicate, with the horn raising its eyebrows knowingly through a series of three short quavers, echoed by the accompaniment, then briefly stated again, to another echo, before the horn exits on a wry little query. Back at home I've played and played these quavers and very rarely got all of them right. They call for more subtlety than I can reliably count on. I trample through to the final bar in hobnailed boots, squashing notes. A B flat quaver, rest, then down an octave with two more brief bouncy B flats. It's over.

People really are very drunk. They give a hearty ovation to a late-night back-street mugging of a Mozartian standard. One of them even stands, though she is ill the next morning. Dave, who has scarcely had a drop, comes and gives me a bear hug. I haven't earned this acclaim. Most of it is the type you reserve for the also-ran who is never going to win anything and gets a consoling slap on the back anyway for limping over the line.

But I feel fortified. I pull Dave to one side and blurt out that I want to play the whole concerto at the British Horn Society festival. Rome may not have been built in a day, after all, but it could conceivably be knocked up in a year. Couldn't it?

3
Who Is This Bethover?

The Count Rollanz, with sorrow and with pangs,
And with great pain sounded his olifant:
Out of his mouth the clear blood leaped and ran,
About his brain the very temples cracked.

La Chanson de Roland

'Oh.'

Dave Lee's response is non-committal.

'What do you think they'll say?' I ask him. 'Any chance they might say yes?'

The thing about Dave is that he has two stock reactions to almost any situation. Like almost all horn players, he finds life funny. But as a pureblood Yorkshireman he can always find something to grumble about. The grumbling is mostly to do with working conditions, violations of Musicians Union rules and regs etc. Occasionally it's provoked by the underhand politicking of his less than favourite colleagues. Talk to Dave and you'd come away with the impression that the horn world is heaving with plotters, backstabbers, agitators, insurrectionaries, Machiavellians, Masonic intriguers, Decembrists, insurgents, heretics, arsonists, sans-culottes, frame-breakers, defenestrators and, of course, egomaniacs. And other such. Show Dave a horn quartet and he'll show you a Gang of Four. (Although some of his best friends are horn players too. Through him I meet a sizeable number of like-minded horn players, mostly in pubs, of whom he thinks the world.)

So this idea of mine seems to confuse him. It doesn't fall within the compass of his two default settings. It's not hilarious, and it's not a scandal. Or maybe it's both. I watch him computing rapidly. This bloke, he's thinking, wants to stand up in front of an entire audience of horn players, who will have come along expecting to listen to the top professionals, and invite the ultimate humiliation. The French horn takes no prisoners, he's thinking. It is uniquely treacherous. Mistakes on it are so much easier to perpetrate than on other instruments, and so much more audible. When you play the horn in public, especially on your own, you either fly, or you plummet into an all-consuming vortex of flames. You can see all these thoughts, and more, right there on Dave's bearded face.

Over his shoulder there are scenes of riot and mayhem. My fortieth birthday party is still in session. Hooligans have taken over the piano. The night is already old, but we have several circles of musical hell through which to descend till we reach a rock bottom of unadulterated din. But all I can hear is the sound of Dave not saying anything. Until he does say something. He tries to sound casual, but there's no mistaking the urgency of the subtext.

'We'd better get together and have a blow.'

I decide to tell everyone. The best way to ensure something goes ahead is to turn it into a self-fulfilling prophecy. So I tell the New Person In My Life. I tell my parents. I tell my friends, who that night disperse to the four winds. Nobody I meet misses out on this news headline. RETURNING ROOKIE TO PLAY MOZART AT BRIT HORN SOC BASH.

The only people I don't tell are the British Horn Society. But the more I think about it, the more I reckon they'll be fine. Won't they? Why wouldn't they be fine about it? They seemed a pleasant bunch when I met them at their last festival in Southampton. Just in case a direct approach is met with a flat no, I decide to have at them from the flanks. I'll let the news *infiltrate* the British Horn Society, like a virus, or a slow-acting poison, or dry rot.

Which is why, a couple of days later, I'm on the phone to a major London orchestra.

'Hi, I was wondering if I could arrange to meet a member of the orchestra's horn section after the concert? ... Why? ... Yes, well, the thing is I've taken up the French horn again, which I gave up when I left school, and I'm giving a concert at the end of a year ... Yes ... Yes I ... Yes people have said that ...' Someone at the other end of the line has just told me I must be a couple of desks short of the full section. 'The British Horn Society thing is in nine months ... No I haven't asked them. Not yet ...' I try to guide the conversation back on to the asphalt. 'I'm aiming to meet horn players. For advice. So you'll ask him? ... Thank you very much ... OK. Bye for now. Thanks again. Thanks.'

The first professional horn player I tell is Martin Hobbs. Martin plays with the London Philharmonic Orchestra. I book a ticket to see the LPO performing Beethoven's Eight and Ninth symphonies at the Royal Festival Hall in London. As everyone knows, the Ninth shattered the mould, being the first-ever symphony to make extensive use of the human voice. Hence its sobriquet: the Choral Symphony. It was also about three times as long as most symphonies which had come before. According to urban myth, it is no coincidence that when Sony and Philips were developing the technology that gave us the compact disc, the new format was able to accommodate seventy-four minutes of music, which just happens to be the length of Beethoven's Ninth. Not a lot of people know about the symphony's other distinction. In the infinitely gentle third movement, which ambles and undulates through sixteen mellifluous minutes, there is an exquisite solo for none other than the fourth horn.

Fourth horns get to play solos the way moons get to be blue for a whole month of Sundays. For a fourth horn, whose role is traditionally confined to supplying the bass line of the section, the third movement of Beethoven's Ninth is as good as it gets. This is the fourth horn's moment in the sun. It's show time. Halfway through the movement the entire orchestra grinds to a halt and, for a brief interval, one lone musician has the attention of the entire concert hall. But if any fourth horn player in 1824, when the symphony was premiered, thought that this was the way things would be from now on – glory, limelight, attention – then he was mistaken. The next solo for fourth horn didn't turn up for another 113 years, in Shostakovich's Fifth Symphony.

Beethoven's last completed symphony was laid before an expectant public in the Kärntnertortheater in Vienna on 7 May. After those convulsive seventy-four minutes, the profoundly deaf composer had to be turned on the podium, as he was unaware of the tumult going on behind him in the audience. They flapped their handkerchiefs to semaphore their frantic appreciation. Nowadays, a tradition has evolved that once the conductor has taken his bow, and the orchestra theirs, and the chorus, and the maestro has gone off and come on again to further rapturous cheering, he points his baton at the fourth horn and directs him to stand and take the applause alone. Attend the performance of almost any nineteenth-century symphony and sooner or later the conductor is going to ask the principal horn, or all the horns, to stand and take a bow. But this is the only time it happens to the fourth horn. Movingly, it has just happened to Martin Hobbs. When he stands, the whole of the Festival Hall cheers to the rafters. It must be a bloody good feeling.

I meet him afterwards at the pass door on the side of the stage through which the orchestra makes its exits and entrances. He is a smallish man in his early thirties, with a round face and dark hair. His girlfriend is there too. She has been shopping and has some sort of coffee-maker in a plastic bag. Martin has his horn. They need to catch a train to Tunbridge Wells, and there isn't much time to talk. As other musicians pass they pat him on the shoulder, the back, raise a hand in salute. 'Great playing, Martin ... Lovely solo ... Good stuff.' And so on. He looks unfazed, as if this sort of acclaim is a daily event. Perhaps it doesn't do to glow too much.

'You wanted to see me?'

I feel self-conscious. Why would a fourth horn player who has just scaled the ultimate peak want to come down from the mountain to talk to me? I am an absolute nobody. But I'm here now, so I ask a few questions about Beethoven 9 – how low the solo goes, how high. It's entry-level geek stuff. He answers. He mentions something called a pedal F, which I've never heard of, though I don't admit this. Instead I wade in with my real question.

'I took up the horn again last autumn and I'm planning to play a solo at this year's British Horn Society festival. I haven't told them yet, but hopefully they'll, you know, say yes. And I was wondering if you had any advice for me?'

There is even the hint of a pause.

'Yeah,' says Martin Hobbs. 'My advice to you is don't.' He's quite affirmative about this. 'Playing the horn at the British Horn Society is *really* scary. I played at the festival when I was twenty-two. I was second horn to Radovan Vlatković. It was *really* horrible.'

I detect a tremor in his voice, as a half-suppressed memory jumps out from under a rock. My heart begins to work its way down to my boots. 'Don't?' This isn't quite the advice I was looking for. '*Really* horrible?' Couldn't he be even a bit more encouraging?

'Plus I don't know how good you are but they may also not want you to do it.'

I can't think of anything to say. Martin Hobbs obviously thinks I'm a complete joker. I need to offer some evidence to the contrary.

'I'm having lessons with Dave Lee,' I say, although I haven't actually had one yet. 'Do you know him?'

'Yes I know Dave,' he says. 'I've lost count of the number of orchestras that guy's worked for.'

'I was planning to play Mozart 3.' He brightens a little.

'Well that's quite easy. My advice is if you're nervous, play louder.'

'OK,' I say gratefully. 'I'll remember that.'

It's late. The backslappers have left the building. Tunbridge Wells beckons for Martin Hobbs, his girlfriend and their new coffee-maker. They scurry off before I can ask one last question. Who the hell is Radovan Vlatković?

My new school occupied an old country house parked in the middle of sports fields. I remember almost everything about it from the two-and-a-half years I was there. A first week of excruciating homesickness. Playing inside right in the under elevens. My Welsh grandmother collaring the headmaster and demanding to know why I wasn't in the choir. Joining the choir, wearing a red cassock and singing descants very loudly. Once getting 91 per cent in a Latin common entrance mock. A visit from the world champion racing driver James Hunt. A craze for James Herriot. Slices of leathery lamb and raw white cabbage for lunch on Mondays in summer. A little blond boy talking about how his older sister's breasts changed shape when she raised her arms. Blackberry and apple crumble and custard. My visceral dread of swimming races, double science, and tackling in rugby. *The Guns of Navarone*. Everyone else's father being in the navy. The heat wave in 1976, and suffering probably the worst attack of hay fever in medical history. A craze for sports manufacturer catalogues. Playing one of the brothers in *Joseph and the Amazing Technicolor Dreamcoat* by Tim Rice and Andrew Lloyd Webber. Winning the snooker tournament two years on the trot. Wilbur Smith. A boy who was so unfit he snapped his tendon in the 100-yard dash on sports day so that his kneecap sprang halfway up his thigh. The whole school watching *Goldfinger* in the library while outside the world turned white. Playing inside right in the first eleven. Someone's little brother drowning in the swimming pool at home. Miming to Status Quo on lead tennis racket in a Christmas show. Boys unstringing their pyjama trousers and using torches to cast huge tumescent shadows on the dormitory wall.

I can remember it all, apart from the horn teacher. Or horn teachers. There were two, according to my school reports: an N Robinson and one LJ Warnes. They have fused in my memory as an oldish cove who pootled over from Chichester to teach just about every instrument going apart from the piano. (The piano was the preserve of one of those desiccated spinsters who invariably go by the name of Miss Geraldine Smith.) Lessons were in a tiny music room stocked with tired old trumpets and battered drums dating back to pretty much the Boer War. I have a faint memory of a military title – Captain This, or Major That – and a bustle of enthusiasm which may well have masked the fact that my teacher – whichever one he was – knew next to nothing about the instrument he was paid to teach me. I remember being slightly disgusted that he – they – didn't know the horn was tuned in F. Surely everyone knew this.

'He has been practising well. A little more self-confidence in his playing would be beneficial. N Robinson.' The reports are classics of the genre: encouraging in that hedge-betting, arse-covering way that school reports tend to be. '. . . I think we will see a marked improvement in the coming months. N Robinson.' They convey the impression that the pupil is walking the wrong way on a travelator and therefore both coming along nicely and sliding forever backwards. 'A little more self-confidence in his playing would be beneficial, and perhaps his playing in the school orchestra will bring this on. N Robinson.'

N Robinson had the hapless task of conducting the school band. It contained perhaps twenty instrumentalists of varying ability – varying, that is, across a limited spectrum. Some musicians were so talentless as to be anti-musical. Others were merely beginners. By this stage I could play at least eight notes with some degree of confidence. Even if I could remember the pieces we played, there'd be little point in listing them. We didn't play what was written. We played an approximation, and as each approximation was its own private variation the results were cacophonous. An inordinate amount of time was devoted fruitlessly to tuning.

After a year N Robinson could stand it no more, or was driven out. At any rate, he vanished, and in came LJ Warnes, whose reports issue a veiled rebuke to his predecessor. 'I am sure that he is much happier, now that he knows that he is gaining much needed control of the horn. LJ Warnes.' He the pupil, each report says between the lines, could do so much better. 'A good term. Jasper is really beginning to show a good aptitude on the Horn. LJ Warnes.' Whereas I the teacher could do no better. 'His progress on this difficult instrument is quite good, but working for the

RSM Grade III exam should provide a little extra stimulous [*sic*]. LJ Warnes.'

I never sat an exam on the horn in my life.

'Dave, what's a pedal F when it's at home?'

'A pedal note is a bass note, right down at the bottom of the range.'

'The F down below middle C then. I can just about ...'

'No, the F an octave below that.'

'What, so ... you mean the range goes all the ... Jesus.'

It's my first blow with Dave. I've never had a mentor before, and am not quite sure of the etiquette. Do I look up to him even more than already? Do I sit at his feet, even if only in my head? The unmentionable has not been mentioned: remuneration. Am I meant to be paying for these lessons? Or do I merely buy Dave's drinks? Not having had a lesson in anything since leaving school, I have to remember that I am, to all intents and purposes, seventeen again. The intervening twenty-two years have vanished without trace, wiping out the accretion of knowledge and humility that comes with the tread of time. This leads me into a behavioural minefield that most people never have to cross. The forty-year-old in me knows that I don't know all the answers. The problem is that the teenager doesn't.

It is a Saturday afternoon in the West End. The Andrew Lloyd Webber musical has been running for a few months. Dave is between shows – the matinee done, the evening performance to come. We meet at the stage door and lug our horns up to the fifth floor of a palatial Edwardian theatre, the Edwardian lift being broken. Slightly breathless, we root around for a room, and plump for a disused office with windows looking down on to Shaftesbury Avenue. Someone appears at some stage to have lobbed a small grenade in here. Half the walls are hanging off, there is paper blasted randomly all over the floor, and bits and pieces of old office furniture lie about, some on their side. It's dusty too, and cold. This is to be my private horn school for the next nine months.

At least the acoustic is up to snuff. I scatter a few notes into the room and they boom impressively off those walls that aren't missing. Dave stops me short.

'If you want to learn how to play the horn properly,' he says, 'you're going to need a reliable warm-up.'

He whips a book out of his horn case. Like *A Tune a Day*, it's dog-eared, and has lost its cover.

'Farkas,' he says.

'Eh?'

'Philip Farkas. He was principal horn in Chicago for donkeys' years. It's not easy, but it's what you need.' He flicks through the book. It has rather more text than *A Tune a Day*. And many many more exercises. Neither of us has a music stand, so he balances Farkas on top of a television against its aerial. Occasionally it falls on to the floor. For the next half-hour we work through a punishing series of warm-up routines that go way beyond anything I ever attempted in my youth. Slurred exercises across a three-octave range, staccato exercises across a three-octave range, exercises for small intervals between notes, for large intervals, for surprising intervals. An *interminable* series of long tones, crescendi, diminuendi. It goes on and on, and is monumentally dull.

In between exercises Dave talks about this, about that. He demonstrates the correct way of playing an exercise, and each time I nod and say, 'Hm ... mm ... uh huh.' It's a wordless way of saying, 'Yup, goddit, understand ...' The arrogant, impatient teenage know-all in me is going, 'This is boring. Let's move on. Fast.'

I ask Dave how often I need to do these Farkas exercises, assuming that the answer is in the region of once a week.

'Every time you play. Which should be every day.'

'I have to do this every day?'

'I've had to do it every day for thirty-five years. Buggered if you're going to get out of it.' He does one of his big laughs. It has a slightly sadistic edge. 'There are no short cuts with the horn. And it's a good idea to do some scales too. So you get yourself going with the arpeggios, then work on intervals, work on your breath with the long tones and the scales are good for fingering.

Then give yourself ten minutes' fun at the end. You've got to have fun or else what's the point?'

By fun he means Mozart. So we do a bit of the Romanze. It's not that much fun. We scarcely get past the first bar. Dave wants me to attack the first note, not dribble in like someone trying to sidle into the room unnoticed. It requires confidence. Only I've got rather less of that than I had when I entered this bombsite.

It's a short session. Dave has to eat before the evening show. I pack up and leave. I feel as if a small grenade has been lobbed into my own head. I took up the horn again in order to test myself. But not like this. I wanted to tackle a great piece of classical music, wrestle it to the floor, emerge victorious. But that pleasure is to be deferred, every day for half an hour, while I bore myself rigid with Farkas's exercise regime.

Philip Farkas was born in 1914 in Chicago and took up the tuba until one day a streetcar driver refused to let him board because his instrument was blocking the corridor. The driver, recalled Farkas, 'pointed to a French horn being carried by another bandsman, and told me that I would be allowed to bring "one of them" on board'. By the age of twenty-two Farkas was principal horn of the Chicago Symphony Orchestra. He was a practical man. A story goes around the horn world that in rehearsal a famous guest conductor asked Farkas, when playing a particular solo, to 'imagine you are on one side of a valley and your girlfriend is in a house on the opposite side when you play this'. Farkas's response was withering. 'Do you want me to play it louder or softer?' He is the author of such sober volumes as *The Art of Musicianship: A Treatise on the Skills, Knowledge, and Sensitivity Needed by the Mature Musician to Perform in an Artistic and Professional Manner* and the classic pamphlet, *A Photo Study of 40 Virtuoso Horn Players' Embouchures*. After his death in 1992 a biography appeared entitled *Philip Farkas and His Horn – A Happy, Worthwhile Life*. But the book with which his name is associated by almost every horn player in the world is *The Art of French Horn Playing*. Except they don't call it that. They call it *Farkas*. It's the bible.

The bible turns out to be prodigiously technical and rigidly dogmatic about the sheer range and volume of work required to make a good horn player. The mountain I've elected to climb inevitably starts to look higher and steeper as I read about the Masonic arcana of mouthpiece placement, lip aperture, the mechanics of breathing, endurance, tonguing, muting, lip trills. (Lip trills? I didn't even know they were possible.) The list of potential pitfalls enumerated by Farkas puts me in mind of a crevasse field on an alpine glacier. You know there is peril underfoot whichever way you turn, but you don't know precisely where. He is particularly grim-faced on the issue of mouthpiece pressure. 'Excessive mouthpiece pressure,' he fulminates, 'is definitely one of the most serious faults the horn player can have.' With the horn, when you press the mouthpiece hard against your lips it's usually to encourage a high note to materialise at the top end of your register. The higher you need to go, the harder you press, the more exhausted you get and the worse you sound. I used to do it all the time in the old days, and now I'm doing it again.

Farkas has the answer. 'For a few minutes each day,' he says, 'place the horn on a shelf or table of a height which enables you to blow into the horn without holding it. The smoother the surface the better, as the horn should slide away as soon as the lightest pressure is applied. Try to play some long open notes without touching or moving the horn, progressing higher and higher until the increasing pressure finally moves the instrument away from the lips.' There is a picture of Farkas, a sturdy middle-aged man in a suit and tie, doing just this.

I give it a go. I mount the Lídl on a mantelpiece, which is the closest I can get to a head-high shelf. Stooping down I attempt to blow a note through the horn without applying even the minutest pressure to the mouthpiece. The horn obliges by sliding away. I don't produce a single note, and give up after approximately twenty seconds. I've had more rewarding experiences at traffic lights.

Later in the year I sit down with three disciples of Philip Farkas, top American horn professors who were all taught by the man they regard as the boss, the top dog, the *corno di tutti corni*. They all had their embouchures snapped for *A Photo Study of 40 Virtuoso Horn Players' Embouchures*. One of them is Mike Hatfield. Mike's a thin, wiry man from Indiana. He has a tan, sizeable spectacles, and an extravagant toupee. He must be pushing sixty, but once upon a time he was pretty much Farkas's adopted son, and even took over his old teaching post at the University of Indiana. Mike says that Farkas always regretted not having a chance to do a revised second edition of the bible. There was stuff he would have changed. My ears prick up.

'Oh yeah?' I ask hopefully. 'Such as?' Maybe he'll say Farkas had second thoughts about the whole warm-up routine. That it really wasn't such a big deal. By then I've spent several months on the Farkas warm-up.

'Such as that exercise where you put the horn on a shelf,' says Mike, 'and try and blow without mouthpiece pressure. He always wished he hadn't put that in.'

'Why?'

'He said it didn't work. He said he wished he could have changed it. He said it was a waste of time.'

Count Roland raises the oliphant to his lips. Around him, the corpses of fellow Franks litter the mouth of the mountain pass. Up ahead the bulk of Charlemagne's army proceeds obliviously towards France, but the rearguard has been annihilated. The earth sprawls too with enemy dead but, for all their courage, 20,000 Franks are no match for 100,000. Roland could have summoned reinforcements much earlier with a blast from his horn, but he is a prisoner of his own pride, and disdains to ask for help. Only now that defeat is inevitable, and the dead will need a Christian burial, does he raise to his lips a short curved instrument fashioned from the tusk of an elephant.

Horns crop up all over Europe in the Dark Ages. In Ravenna on the Adriatic coast of Italy, Byzantine mosaics in the church of San Michele in Affrisco, consecrated in AD 545, depict angels blowing on long, narrow, curved horns. In *Beowulf* the hero's uncle Hygelac summons his army with blasts on his 'horn and bieme' (horn and trumpet). Medieval Welsh kings were entitled by law to the possession of three ox horns: one for drinking, one for summoning and a third for hunting. In the early fourteenth century the oliphant has a walk-on role in the Gothic prelude to the Italian Renaissance. Giotto's fresco cycle depicting the life of Christ in the Capella Arena in Padua finds a bystander blowing ostentatiously on an oliphant as Judas betrays Christ to the Romans. A century and a half later, Fra Angelico worked on a life of Christ as the frontispiece for a silver chest for Piero de' Medici. The painter died before he could finish the work, so it was left to lesser hands to complete it, probably working from Fra Angelico's drawings. In one of them, 'The Mocking of Christ', one of the two men deriding him brandishes an oliphant. But aside from the destruction wrought by rams' horns on the walls of Jericho, the desperate wail emitted by Roland's oliphant is the most resonant note sounded by a horn in instrumental history.

La Chanson de Roland is a foundation stone of medieval epic literature. Written in Anglo-Norman French and assembled into a coherent manuscript, according to scholarly consensus, towards the end of the eleventh century, *The Song of Roland* migrated in due course into neighbouring languages. There are versions in Old Norse, Middle High German, Middle English, Middle Dutch, the synthetic literary language of Franco-Venetian, and Welsh. In France its 4,000 mostly decasyllabic lines, divided into verse paragraphs or *laisses* with an assonant rhyming scheme, would have been sung by a *jongleur*, or minstrel, accompanied by a *vielle* (viol). The narrative is based on an actual campaign of Charlemagne's, who entered Spain in 778 at the behest of Suleiman ibn-al-Arabi, the governor of Barcelona. The Frankish reward for military support in the governor's internecine conflict with his fellow Muslim, the caliph of Cordoba, was to be the control of several Spanish cities. But, no sooner had Charlemagne laid siege to Saragossa than he heard news of a Saxon rebellion in the north. As he headed back through the Pyrenees, his rearguard was ambushed by Basques in the pass of Roncesvalles. The leader of the rearguard, according to Einhard's *Life of Charlemagne*, was 'Hruodlandus Brittannici limitis praefectus': Hruodland, prefect of the Breton Marches. Contrary to subsequent legend, he cannot have blown an oliphant to summon help, because the instrument was introduced to western Europe from Byzantium only in the tenth century.

Over the ensuing centuries, Roland's name became a byword for Frankish valour. According to the twelfth-century historian William of Malmesbury, the heroic tale of his doomed resistance was recited to Norman troops before they landed at Hastings in 1066, though not the one which has come down to us. 'Then a song of Roland was begun, so that the man's warlike example would arouse the fighters.' The most complete manuscript of the poem, dating from middle decades of the twelfth century, is in the Bodleian Library in Oxford. It is a literary quilt, with interpolations, corrections and assorted accretions added by a succession of scribes. In this version, copied out around the time of the First Crusade, Roland's legend has mutated into an epic tale of Christian heroism in the face of Saracen treachery. There are no Basques any more. The rearguard is attacked by pagans led by King Marsile of Saragossa, who 'serves Muhammad and calls upon Apollo'.

Thus it is that on the day the Franks enter the mountains, the pagan army approaches from behind, sounding a thousand trumpets. Oliver climbs a hill and sees the armour of a teeming military presence glitter in the sun. 'On the olifant deign now to sound a blast,' he urges Roland, to summon reinforcements. They are hugely outnumbered. Roland refuses.

> 'Never, by God,' then answers him Rollanz,
> 'Shall it be said by any living man,
> That for pagans I took my horn in hand!
> Never by me shall men reproach my clan.'

No sooner has the archbishop blessed the Frankish rearguard than the Saracens attack. Initially the enemy suffers terrible losses, none more than by dint of Roland's sword. With his first blow he slices through a pagan from his helmet, gleaming with carbuncular gems, right through his torso to his groin and saddle of beaten gold and into the body of his horse. Brains spill, blood spurts, guts tumble from gaping wounds. In a scene of hellish slaughter, bodies pile up. The Franks cut and thrust with gruesome efficiency, only for the sound of 7,000 bugles to announce the advance of twenty pagan divisions. Roland and Oliver are towering in their resistance, but after further valiant combat the Franks are reduced to sixty men.

> Then says Rollanz: 'I'll wind this olifant,
> If Charles hear, where in the pass he stands,
> I pledge you now they will return, the Franks.'
> Says Oliver: 'Great shame would come of that
> And a reproach on every one, your clan,
> That shall endure while each lives in the land,
> When I implored, you would not do this act;

Their archbishop rides up and intervenes. 'No help it were to us, the horn to blow,' he reasons but urges Roland to blow it all the same. The king will avenge their deaths and give them a Christian burial; their bones will not be left for wolves and swine to gnaw. Roland is swayed. He raises the oliphant to his lips and, with all his considerable might, blows. His effort is fatal. Blood gushes from his mouth, his temples burst, but the distress signal carries 30 leagues along the Roncesvalles pass towards Charlemagne's vanguard. 'I hear his horn,' says the king.

In due course only three Franks remain. With his vision blurred by blood, Oliver's last blow lands by mistake on Roland, who fights on.

> Great pain he has, and trouble in his head,
> His temples burst when he the horn sounded;
> But he would know if Charles will come to them,
> Takes the olifant, and feebly sounds again.

Charlemagne, drawing nearer, hears the mournful note. 'Right evilly we fare!' he says.

> This day Rollanz, my nephew shall be dead:
> I hear his horn, with scarcely any breath.

He urges 60,000 Franks to blow their bugles, whose terrifying sound only intensifies the assault of 400 pagans on Roland. Once they've killed his mount by hurling spears, they retreat in the knowledge that their nemesis can no longer give chase. With no enemy left to fight, Roland's thoughts turn to the afterlife. One by one, he hauls corpse after corpse across the battlefield to the side of the stricken archbishop for his blessing. The archbishop stretches out an arm, clutches the oliphant and tries to drag himself to a stream to fetch Roland a drink. But he dies. Roland, whose brain dribbles from his ears, knows death nears for him too. He

> Takes the olifant, that no reproach shall hear,
> And Durendal in the other hand he wields.

He points himself in the direction of Spain. According to the feudal code, he must die with his face to the enemy. He faints onto a grass mound, where a pagan feigning death sees him and tries to steal his sword. Roland

> Took the olifant, that he would not let go,
> Struck him on th' helm, that jewelled was with gold,
> And broke its steel, his skull and all his bones,
> Out of his head both the two eyes he drove;
> Dead at his feet he has the pagan thrown:
> After he's said: 'Culvert, thou wert too bold,
> Or right or wrong, of my sword seizing hold!
> They'll dub thee fool, to whom the tale is told.
> But my great one, my olifant I broke;
> Fallen from it the crystal and the gold.'

He has killed a man with a blow from his horn. But he has also killed himself by blowing on his horn. Roland struggles towards a pine and lies down in its shade. Under his suppurating body he tucks his sword and his horn and, weeping, dies.

Allegro. Happy. Up in the bombsite, Dave and I are nibbling our way into the first movement of K447. At this early juncture, happy is a tall order. These things can apparently be faked in the bedroom but not, I fancy, in front of the British Horn Society. As I look through the music, I feel like an athlete on the starting block, staring down the track at an avenue of hurdles which, contrary to the usual laws of perspective, don't grow smaller as they recede into the distance, but bigger.

The first hurdle crops up nice and early. It's not the first note – a common-or-garden F in the very epicentre of the register. I can play that just fine. It's the D that comes after. F to D is an interval of a sixth, and it's surprisingly tricky. Anyone can hear a fifth in their head. The first two notes of 'The Last Post', of Strauss's *Also Sprach Zarathustra* and its reconfiguration as the intro to 'I Lost My Heart to a Starship Trooper' are all a leap of a perfect fifth. But a sixth? It's not a naturally occurring interval. I rack my brains for popular tunes that kick off with a leap of a sixth between the first and second note. I come up with precisely three examples: an old Scottish folk song ('My bonnie lies over the ocean'), a nineteenth-century English hymn ('The lord's my shepherd, I'll not want') and a Sinatra standard ('And now the end is near . . .')

I start asking professional horn players how I should approach the movement.

'Don't be afraid of the second note, please,' says Stefan Dohr, principal horn of the Berlin Philharmonic. 'If you are afraid of the second note, the rest of the piece is gone. We hear it in auditions. Even great players, they come on and go, da deurgh!'

That's just brilliant. The D is a banana skin even for horn players who think they're good enough to join the most prestigious orchestra on the planet.

'It's not an easy note,' says Dave. 'You've really got to dig it out.'

The hours are duly put in. Working hours, weekend hours, childcare hours – all are sacrificed to the task of finding a way along that avenue of hurdles. By the end of a session a bizarre form of physical exhaustion kicks in. It locates itself entirely in the muscles around the lips. They are shredded and I just have to stop. But I start to notice an improvement. I can play for longer, and stop clattering into the hurdles. It doesn't help with a deeper problem I have with the Allegro. I don't know what it's *about*. The Romanze I understand, but with the Allegro I can only guess at what I'm trying to convey. There is an air of sprightly abandon in the opening passages. It's all nudges, winks, skips and slides, until a dark passage intervenes in a mood-altering minor key. In due course the gloom is dispersed as the melody surges spectacularly back into the light, whereupon the main theme is recapitulated. By this time, we're limbering up for fireworks as Mozart's melodic phrases become more frenetic, more insistent, until they trip over themselves in a set of bounding triplets that scurry up and then tumble down into the basement of the register.

But what does it all mean? Until I work it out, I won't get a lot further. Dave lets me play through the mistakes without, for the most part, correcting them. We both know I'm cocking things up. No need to point it out. He confines himself to the basic stuff to do with breathing, fingering and, my favourite, counting.

But he does say one nice thing. After the weeks with Farkas, he's noticed an improvement in the tone coming out of the Lídl.

'It's a much better sound you're making now,' he says.

On the journey home I am exultant.

The bar-restaurant of Salzburg railway station is cavernous, in the magnificent European manner. These days you can fly just about anywhere in Europe for the price of a sandwich. This bar-restaurant, with its air of flagging grandeur, harks back to the days when the trains juddered importantly across frontiers in the Alpine heartlands of the old continent. Even at breakfast time, a faint whiff of Würstel and sauerkraut hangs in the air. What would Mozart not have given for a railway station in Salzburg? He made his long succession of exits and entrances from the city of his birth by slow coach.

'You're a writer. Have you ever thought of writing a film script about Punto?'

Opposite me, in the otherwise empty bar-restaurant, is Radovan Vlatković. It's not the opening gambit I was expecting. I'm here to ask his advice about playing in the BHS festival.

Giovanni Punto is the horn player for whom Beethoven wrote his one horn sonata, improvising the piano accompaniment on the night of the premiere in Vienna in April 1800. 'Though the concert was announced with the Sonata the latter was not yet begun,' noted Ferdinand Ries (who became the composer's pupil the following year). 'Beethoven began his work the day before the performance and it was ready for the concert.' The sonata was so popular with the audience that it was immediately encored. The applause would have been mainly reserved for Punto, the greatest soloist in Europe. 'Who is this Bethover [*sic*]?' wrote the confused critic of the *Ofener und Pester Theatertaschenbuch* when they performed it again in Budapest a month later. 'The history of German music is not acquainted with such a name. Punto of course is very well known, his real name is Wenzel Stich . . .'

Radovan Vlatković grew up in Zagreb, started to learn the horn in Wisconsin, played for years in Berlin, and is now resident in Salzburg. Today, with a suitcase and a horn case hanging from each shoulder, he is on his way to Mainz. He is the leading European soloist. And not only that. Giving all due consideration to the rest of the field, I'd say he wins the Mr Horniverse crown at a canter.

'You could show very exciting moments in history,' says Radovan. 'He escapes because he is sick and tired of being a servant and is chased. That would be an exciting, adventurous moment. And then he is in France at the time of the Revolution and he meets Mozart, he meets Beethoven later on. He tries desperately to be a concert master. He is already the best horn player but he's useless. So that would be good. And then he goes back home and dies quite poor back in Bohemia but with a grand funeral and the Mozart *Requiem* is playing at his funeral.'

Giovanni Punto was the horn's first celebrity. Born in 1746, his original Czech name was Jan Václav Stich, though as he grew up in the village of Tetschen (now Jehusiče) in German-speaking Bohemia, it is also translated as Johann Wenzel Stich. His father was a serf. In due course the boy showed so much talent at the horn that Count Thun, to whom he was bonded, sent him to learn his craft with the greatest tutors of the age in, successively, Prague, Munich and then Dresden. After four years back in service in the count's rural estate, he was showing signs of insubordination. His sword was confiscated as a precaution, and the count threatened to throw him into the army if he didn't manage his temper.

Here was the frustration of the musician in the Age of Enlightenment. His gift was not his own. Mozart would have a similar difficulty with the prince archbishop of Salzburg, which he articulated in his letters home to his father. 'The only thing that bothers me about Salzbourg –' he wrote from Paris in 1778, 'and I'm telling you this straight from the heart, is that … members of the orchestra are held in such low esteem – and that the archbishop doesn't take advice from knowledgeable people who have been out in the world, for I can assure you that without travelling one remains a poor creature; that goes especially for people in the arts and sciences!' His tone was less moderate five years later when, newly married in Vienna and freed from the yoke of the Salzburg court, he aimed a withering fusillade in the direction of his birthplace. 'I hope it's not necessary to tell you that I care little about Salzburg and nothing at all about the archbishop and that I shit on both of them.'

Stich no doubt entertained similar sentiments about Count Thun. Insurrection was the only way out. At the age of twenty Stich and five others escaped from Thun's estate. An infuriated count sent soldiers in pursuit with orders to knock out Stich's front teeth, the explicit intention being to terminate his horn-playing career. Stich evaded them, crossing the border into the Holy Roman Empire, changed his name to Giovanni Punto and embarked on an itinerant career, initially as a court musician. In 1768 he was principal horn with the court band of the prince of Hechingen. He was soon in Mainz, but left when the elector declined to appoint him *Konzertmeister*. Like many musicians, Punto had a facility with more than one instrument, and fancied that his talents were equal to the post (and presumably higher pay) of principal violin. For a while he found employment at the court of the Elector Palatine in Mannheim, from where he obtained leave to set out on his first extensive tour as soloist.

Although there is no record of his visit in English newspapers, he was evidently in London in 1771. 'The Elector has a good band,' noted the English historian of music Charles Burney, when passing through Koblenz in the Palatinate in 1772, 'in which M. Ponta, the celebrated French horn from Bohemia, whose taste and astonishing execution were lately so applauded in London, is a performer.' Punto was not yet thirty, but in these years his reputation spread across Europe as far as Hungary and Spain. In 1777 in Paris he played a concerto in front of Marie Antoinette at the prestigious Concert Spirituel season. That year he was also back in London teaching the court horn players of George III.

> ... the King understanding that several of the persons selected [for his private orchestra] played well on stringed besides wind instruments, and perceiving considerable indications of talent among them, His Majesty placed them under masters of eminence at his own expence, and the result was such as to gratify his expectations. Moller and E Kellner were consigned to the tuition of PONTO, the famous horn blower.

A year later Punto again performed at the Concert Spirituel alongside fellow musicians from the court orchestra of Mannheim. The *Mercure de France* noted that: 'Les virtuoses, les grands talents ont été applaudis, principalement M. Punto pour le cor de chasse, M. Wendling pour la flûte, M. Raam pour le hautbois et M. Ritter pour le basson.' The twenty-two-year-old Mozart singled him out for praise. '*Punto bläst Magnifique*,' he enthused in a letter to his father.

Mozart was newly arrived in Paris. It was his umpteenth stint abroad, but his first without his father, who could not obtain release from his musical duties at court in Salzburg. Humiliatingly, Mozart was obliged by Leopold to take his mother as a chaperone instead. Her presence would turn out to be a disaster. But early on in his stay, Mozart was hopeful. For Punto and his fellow wind soloists collectively touting their wares in Paris, the composer wrote a Sinfonia Concertante 'in the greatest hurry, I really worked very hard, and the 4 soloists were and still are quite involved with the piece'. Legros, the director of the Concert Spirituel who had commissioned it and taken possession of the manuscript to be copied, seems to have either mislaid or even suppressed the composition. Mozart was exasperated, but powerless. 'I went to the Concert on the 2 days it should have been performed. Ramm and Punto came up to me all worked up and asked why my Sinfonie

Concerto was not on the program – I don't know. It's the first I've heard about it. I know nothing about it.' Mozart always intended to retranscribe it from memory, but never got round to it. So for all his harrying Punto never actually played the composition Mozart wrote for him.

Perhaps the disappointment underpinned his determination to cast aside his horn for the more remunerative violin. Punto finally contrived to gain employment as a concert master in Würzburg, but he soon relinquished it to take up a grander position back in Paris under the Comte d'Artois, the youngest brother of Louis XVI who, after the restoration of the monarchy, would become Charles X in 1824. Punto continued to travel. He toured the Rhineland in 1784, and in 1787 returned to London to play at the Pantheon in Oxford Street. There he met Michael Kelly, a young Irish singer who the previous year had sung in the first performance of *The Marriage of Figaro* in Vienna. Years later, in his *Reminiscences*, Kelly recalled a dim and distant conversation between a nervous Punto, as he was about to perform in the cavernous venue, and Madame Mara, the theatre manager.

> He said to Madame Mara in German, 'My dear friend, my lips are so parched with fear, that I am sure I shall not make a sound in the instrument; I would give the world for a little water or beer to moisten my lips.'
>
> Madame Mara replied in German, 'There is nobody here to send; and yet if I knew where to get something for you to drink, I would go myself.'
>
> During their dialogue, I was standing at the fireside; and addressing Madame Mara in German, I said, 'Madame, I should be sorry for you to have that trouble, and I sit lazy by; I will, with great pleasure, go and get Monsieur Ponte some Porter.' I instantly dispatched a messenger for a foaming pot; and as soon as it arrived, I presented it to the thirsty musician, in the nick of time, for he was called on to play his concerto just at this moment . . .

Returning to Paris in 1789, Punto threw his weight opportunistically behind the revolution. In a horn-playing textbook he produced in the 1790s he referred to himself in his dedication as 'le Citoyen Punto'. He admitted on the title page to his *Seule et Vraie Méthode pour apprendre facilement les Eléments des Premier et Second Cors* that the precepts found inside were 'Composée par HAMPL / Et perfectionnée par PUNTO son Elève'. Anton Hampl had been his tutor in Dresden. The post having fallen vacant during the Terror, he took up his violin to become conductor of the Théâtre des Variétés Amusantes in Paris, leaving only in 1798 to tour Germany.

In Vienna, in 1800, he duly met Beethoven and premiered his horn sonata at the Hoftheater. According to the *Allgemeine Musikalische Zeitung* on 2 July, they 'so excelled and pleased that despite the new Theatre Ordinance, which forbids loud applause and encores, the two virtuosi were compelled by loud clapping to start the piece from the beginning and play it through again'. They played it again in Budapest, and would have performed it a third time at the behest of a family of local Hungarian aristocrats. But Punto had fallen out with the composer by then, and went alone.

Early the following year the prodigal son returned to Bohemia after thirty-three years away. His compatriots cheered him from the roadsides and toasted him in taverns. At his homecoming concert on 18 January 1801 at the National Theatre in Prague he performed a quartet and concerto of his own. According to the *Prag Neue Zeitung*:

> The unanimous applause which this artist, whose genuine fame has come to him under the pseudonym of Punto, earned here when playing this concerto, was aroused by the incomparable perfection which he displayed in handling his instrument. Even the most respected connoisseurs were forced to admit that they had never before heard such a performance on the horn. His delivery on this normally difficult instrument was pure song in both high and low registers alike.

In 1802 Punto and a pianist embarked on an extended tour of Bohemia, during which he returned to Tetschen, the village of his childhood. In the autumn he was taken ill with pleurisy when returning to Prague, and he died five months later. More than 4,000 compatriots attended his funeral on 26 February 1803 in the baroque church of St Nicholas, though most presumably mourned outside in the open air. Mozart's *Requiem* was performed at his graveside, where the Latin epitaph on his tombstone punned on the name he adopted on escaping his homeland with front teeth intact:

Omne tulit punctum Punto, cui Musa Bohema
Ut plausit vivo, sic moriente gemit.

'Punto won every vote; just as the Muse of Bohemia applauded him while he lived, so does mourn him now that he is dead.' Punto left behind a huge array of horn music, written entirely to show off his virtuosity. Among them were 16 horn concerti (five of which are lost), one concerto for two horns, a horn sextet, 21 horn quartets, 47 horn trios and 103 horn duos. Almost none of this vast repertoire is played now. 'As a performer on the horn he was unrivalled by any predecessor or contemporary,' adjudged Beethoven's first great biographer, Alexander Thayer. 'But as a composer he was beneath criticism.'

I ask Radovan if he has dipped his toe in the works of Punto. 'I've looked at them,' he says. 'They are very flashy virtuoso pieces obviously written to show off his technique. Musically there are more interesting pieces, to be polite. But it shows how it's a one-man show. He writes his own music, he travels.'

He was evidently a remarkable musician. Punto is the first horn player for whom a detailed account of his technique survives. 'What distinguished Punto in a way that one has never heard in any other artist heretofore,' wrote a minor composer called Franz Joseph Fröhlich, 'was his most magnificent performance, the gentlest portrayals, the thunder of tones and their sweetest indescribable blending of nuances with the most varied tone production, an agile tongue, dexterous in all forms of articulation, single and double tones, and even chords, but most important, a silver-bright and charming cantabile tone.'

The train to Mainz is due soon. It's Radovan who changes the subject.

'How are you going to prepare?' he says. We have reached the business end of the conversation.

'Er, I don't know,' I say. 'Any advice?'

'Try to make it a regular habit of spending a little time every day rather than big patches and playing more and more towards the concert. Start early. So you get a feel of how different your form is every day. I think you should play the piece as often as you can, with a friend on the piano. Play it by heart if you can because it's quite easy, so that you get the feeling and the adrenalin going, because it's a different feeling. It's like playing football. Ifor James, who was a semi-professional football player, used to say, "Don't worry about missing a note on the horn. When you miss a goal from five yards away in front of 20,000 people, then you are in trouble."'

Ifor James was a much-loved British horn player and teacher who sent sixty pupils out into the profession, twenty of them as principals. He must have passed on his tip about missing an open goal to every single one of them. Sadly he died soon after I took up the horn again, so I never met him. But his advice has been handed down anyway.

'I'll bear that in mind,' I say.

Radovan laughs. I am reminded of Dave's irrepressible laugh. As I move around the horn world the stories accumulate of the one or two arrogant, autocratic, vainglorious horn players who make the lives of all around them unpleasant. One infamous tyrant takes the gold here. At his retirement party after more than thirty years as principal horn of a world-famous European orchestra, he actually pulled a knife on his second horn, with whom he had not exchanged a single word for five years. Giovanni Punto, who argued with Beethoven even after receiving the gift of a sonata, could well have been one of those. But the default setting of most horn players seems to be levity. They are always seeing the funny side. Why?

'You've noticed,' says Radovan. 'And you're absolutely right – that we all start joking. There must be something about the horn. You have to develop a sense of humour. Otherwise you will go and kill yourself.'

4
Le Son du Boa

Early the next morning he gets out of bed, goes to a window which looked out towards the stables, and sounds his French horn, as he called it, which was his usual signal to call his men to go out a-hunting.

Daniel Defoe: *Roxana*

The International Horn Society is known in horn-playing circles as the IHS. It should not be confused with the Indian Health Service, the Indiana History Society, the Institute for Humane Studies, or other international societies variously devoted to head-aches, hearing or, lest we forget, herpetology. If you believe the dissidents of the French horn world, the IHS committee has on occasion mistaken itself for Iesus Hominum Salvator. When the society was formed, practically its first act was to try to change the official name of the instrument. The minutes of the inaugural general meeting, on 15 June 1971, record a recommendation 'that "horn" be recognized as the correct name for our instrument in the English language'.

The meeting was held in Tallahassee, Florida. This explains a thing or two. The IHS is a worldwide organisation in the same way that the World Series opens its arms to baseball teams from all over the world. Every year the society convenes somewhere different for performances, workshops, lectures and a massive fire sale of French horns of every known make and mark. Every other year, that somewhere different is in North America. Host campuses in the preceding decade have included Bloomington (Indiana), Athens (Georgia), Kalamazoo (Michigan) and Banff (Canada). The year I take up the French horn again, it's in Tuscaloosa (Alabama). I decide I cannot afford to go. Or rather, I can afford not to go. It's never been held in France.

In 1971 the world had yet to hear of those cheese-eating sur-render monkeys who refused to join George W Bush's 'inter-national' coalition. But the subtext of those minutes from all those years ago is clear enough. The overwhelmingly American horn players of the IHS wanted nothing to do with the old country.

Of course the horn is not French in France. The French horn, as we still officially call it on the English side of the Channel, is known in France as a *cor*. In Italy it's a *corno*. They say *corn* in Welsh, Romanian and, as we have seen, Gaelic. It's *korno* in Turkish and Esperanto and, in Maltese, *kurnu*. One festive night in Gozo, the small island off the north coast of Malta, I watch a wind band wheezing out tinny Mediterranean standards as they march through the so-called capital, Victoria. I try to engage the *kurnu* player in conversation. He is having none of it. In my whole year of stalking the great horn players of Europe and America, the only one who refused to talk was the principal *kurnu* of the Gozo marching wind band.

In northerly climes, we soften that initial consonant. It's a *Horn* in German, a *horn* in Danish and Swedish and a *hoorn* in Dutch. The settlers in southern Africa who transmuted Dutch into Afri-kaans say *horing*. To the east, the Slavic languages have their own word: *roh* in Czech, *rog* in Russian, Polish, Slovene and Serbo-Croat (or Serbian and Croatian as, despite their almost entire overlap, we are now obliged to call them). It's only when the instrument paddles up the narrower tributaries of Indo-European that discrepancies start to occur. Hungarian and Finnish are always said to have nothing etymologically in common with any other language apart from each other. Not with the horn they don't. In Budapest, a horn is a *vadaszkürt*. In Helsinki they say *käyrätorvi*.

It's not just in the instrument's name that there is variety. One day, after another lesson in the bombsite, Dave Lee and I repair to the pub and he talks about the different sounds associated with different horn-playing regions. There's the refined British sound, the butch American sound, the showy Czech sound, the Russian vibrato. In Germany, where the Iron Curtain no longer slices the country in half, there's still a distinction between the stentorian sound of the western half and the thin, piping, trumpety playing from the old East Germany of the Dresden Staatskapelle and the Leipzig Gewandhaus. It's not to Dave's taste, this one.

'It's the sound,' he opines over a pint, 'made by a horn player who inspects his own shit.'

But in the beginning there was the French sound.

There are hounds everywhere. A yelping pack of them chase tails in and out of denimed legs, booted feet. There are horses too, massy and tensile, buckled and braced into leather and stainless steel. On the horses: men, and a woman or two, all dressed in a smart livery of discreet ostentation, dark blue jackets fringed at cuff, collar and pocket in soft matt gold. Some of them also wear a curious appendage – a leather strap slung over the right shoulder. At the other end, under the left elbow, hangs a small horn-shaped goblet. It's purely ornamental, there being no mouthpiece. But others brandish the genuine article: a full-size horn which they carry over the other shoulder, like a cross-chest ammunition belt.

This is the *trompe de chasse*. Before mounting, four chaps stand in a row and, in attitudes of deadly seriousness, each raise an instrument to their lips. They don't look quite right without a horse under them. Legs in knee-high riding boots are irretrievably bowed. Under one pair of nostrils froths an important grey moustache. Another huntsman, lanky-limbed and bespectacled, has the dorsal curvature acquired from a lifespan spent stooping eagerly forward in the saddle. A third is very short, and very old, but still fastidiously erect. A fourth is in his thirties.

They hold their horns proudly, shoulder-high, with the right hand gripping the bottom of the circular wrap of piping. Before they start, they blow a single introductory note, and only then proceed to the tune. If that's the word. The melody, such as it is, vaults up and down the register with a merry lack of intrinsic character. The most striking thing is not the content, but the timbre. At the end of each phrase the players linger on a long tone that wails and wavers in the air. The note has an indistinctness all its own. Its closest sonic equivalent would be the old-fashioned police siren, but with the oscillations sped up. It's not quite a warble. It's more of a sonic wobble.

We are somewhere in the Loire Valley, in the courtyard of a double-fronted farmhouse. The *équipage de Brissac*, the Brissac pack, is about to trot into the woods in search of roebuck. My father has been installed on a borrowed chestnut. He sits, hunched and contented among like-minded types with whom he is equipped to exchange barely a word. Not as many mounted horn players have shown up as I'd pinned my hopes on. It's one of those days when you know global warming is a reality. Though still early spring, with barely a leaf in bud, it's a scorcher. Apparently on warm dry days the scent of the prey is weak, and the hounds never catch anything. Hence the turnout. My parents have been this way before. They've come for muddy February weekends where an octet of horn players have stood in a semicircle over the day's kill and trumpeted their triumph. They've dined in the huge château de Brissac, where guests have been fanfared by a dozen splendidly dressed *trompistes* on the grand staircase, six on either side.

There's not much contact between the *trompe de chasse* and the French horn. In the classical horn world, you will scarcely hear a good word spoken for its feral forebear. Most orchestral horn players view it as a crude elderly relative who suffers from incurable incontinence. But in the hunting fields of France they take the *trompe de chasse* seriously. There are even national competitions, where huntsmen gather without their mounts to blow loudly at one another in front of adjudicators. By the end of the day I will have been invited to one. But I'm here to see the instrument in its natural habitat.

Before the hunt we visit the duc and duchesse in their country house for an early lunch. The Brissacs have been in these hills for almost as long as the hills themselves. The family stuck its head above history's parapet in the Revolution when the eighth duc, Louis Hercule Timoléon, was put in charge of Louis XVI's personal Swiss bodyguards at the height of the Terror. He was killed during the September Massacres, when half of all prisoners in Paris were murdered by the mob. His descendant is a congenial Pickwickian figure called Bobby, who from brief acquaintance seems every inch the textbook country aristocrat. Through a sequence of events I can't quite fathom my parents have somehow managed to befriend him. And here we are.

The house is a modest pile by the standards of the French aristocracy. The Brissacs have recently bequeathed the magnificent château in the town of Brissac – plus its prodigious heating bill – to the care of their oldest son, the marquis, and moved to this merely sizeable retreat. From the look of it, it has no more than three dozen rooms. Whichever of these you're in, you're never very far from some sign or other of the duc's ruling passion. The hunting ledgers in the library, the pictures of hunting scenes. Even the wall-mounted light fittings are on a hunting theme. The bulbs stand in gilt brackets in the shape of upturned *trompes de chasse*.

In the dining room we sit down under an elegant late-eighteenth-century still life. It depicts a scene from the end of the day, with the light fading behind a bank of clouds on the hills. From the branch of a tree hangs a fresh kill which has been tethered by its hind leg with a patterned scarf. A pool of blood gathers on the ground by its mouth. There is a hunting dog behind the tree, and two more in the foreground. One of them tentatively dabs at the buck's nether regions with a tongue. Hanging from the same branch as the deer is a gleaming French hunting horn.

The *trompe de chasse* is where the horn had got to by the middle of the seventeenth century. Melted in the furnace, a brass horn was finally able to complete a revolution. Once it could wrap all the way round once, like a hungry boa constrictor it could wrap twice, three times. The earliest record of a fully circular horn is on a late-seventeenth-century choir-stall carving in Worcester

Cathedral. The horn is wrapped round the body of the player. Increasingly frequent illustrations of and references to small round horns occur in the sixteenth century in Germany and France. In an anthology of 'Battles, Hunts and Bird-Songs' published in 1545 Tylman Susato describes how 'a la chasse le son de la trompe ou cournet [donne courage] aux chiens': in the hunt the sound of the trompe or cornet encourages the hounds. A woodcut of a 'cornet de chasse' appears in *La Venerie*, a treatise on hunting dedicated to Charles IX in 1561. But the earliest known example of an actual horn dates from the early 1570s. This so-called helical horn was displayed in the Dresden Staatliches Historisches Museum until the war. The coils were densely wrapped, like a wound-up hose. 'GOTT IST MEIN HELFER,' it said on the rim of the bell. The French called these *cors à plusieurs tours*, horns with several turns. This was one of four types of horn listed in 1636 by the French musical scholar Marin Mersenne in his *Harmonie Universelle*. The others were *le grand cor*, which ballooned in diameter to something as big as a modern bicycle wheel, *le cor qui n'a qu'un seul tour* (the horn with but one turn), and *le huchet*. The *trompe de chasse* fell into the last category: a horn with which one calls from afar.

Where other instruments – sackbut and lute, recorder and spinet – took up positions indoors, the horn pursued its atavistic work out in the fresh air. Soon a huge array of melodies was part of its repertoire. Each of them pertained to a specific moment in the course of a day's hunting. Setting off, a sighting, going through water, hiding in a cover, going home having made a kill, going home having failed to make a kill – they all have their individual collection of notes. They're not so much tunes as ritualistic signals.

And here is one of them, a brief, optimistic melody sounded by a huntsman of the *équipage de Brissac* who points his horse towards the gate and the woods beyond. The frenzy of the pack of hounds cranks up a notch. As riders nudge their mounts into the gathering heat of the afternoon, the bell-flares of half a dozen *trompes de chasse*, painted matt black on the inside to stop the sun's reflection glinting in the eyes of the horse behind, stare impassively back at the foot followers.

*

The third movement of Mozart's third horn concerto, K447, is known as the Rondo. It begins with a stated theme, strays near, strays far, but comes back around to it again and again. Hence its name. What goes a rondo comes a rondo. That theme is a hunting tune. You can hear the pounding of hoofs as quavers gallop to get past one another.

As I turn my attention to it, I'm pleased to discover that bits of the third movement verge on the playable. The first four bars, for example, are an utter doddle. A chimp could play them. A chihuahua could. It gets harder straight after that. Some tricksy phrases call for more agility than my tongue can currently manage. Others require speedier communication between brain and fingers than is within my compass. So it's back to the coalface. I take Radovan Vlatković's word for it and start warming up in the morning. It turns out to be good advice. By mid-afternoon I am free to spend hours under the bonnet with Mozart.

In my next lesson with Dave, various questions come up. They're mostly pernickety issues to do with tonguing and slurring – where to do one, when to do the other. How to make it sound like you're not wading through sludge. But the big question for me is this: exactly how slow can you go in a hunting rondo? Dip below a certain pace and the quarry is going to get clean away. Is one obliged to gallop? Could I get away with a lazy canter, or even a brisk rising trot?

Dave lifts his horn to his lips and proceeds to play the opening theme at warp speed.

'That sort of tempo?' he offers. I raise the Lídl and crack the whip. Surprisingly, I don't fall off in those first four bars. It's when the phrase rounds off with a leap over a gate, followed by a sudden landing on the other side, that I'm thrown clean out off my mount.

'That might be a bit too fast for you,' says Dave. But I am not listening. I was always taught in my riding days that, after an unseating, the real man gets right back into the saddle. Even if he's only six, which I was at the time. So I give it another go. And another. Another. Every time, it's the same result. I curse under my breath.

'Hold on, hold on,' says Dave. 'You're never going to get anywhere like that.' Dave's advice is to slow down in order to speed up. 'If you can't play a phrase quickly, playing it over and over again won't make any difference. Slow it down. Take it to pieces and put it back together again. Play the first three notes of the phrase, then add the fourth, and play that over and over again till you've got it. Then add the fifth. And the sixth. And so on. It's boring as hell, but it's the only way.'

I go back home and do what Dave says. I take the movement to pieces, and laboriously put it back together again. And as with the other two movements, the Allegro and the Romanze, I eventually start to do almost as much right as I do wrong.

It helps that the K447 Rondo is one of the most hummable snippets of instrumental music in Mozart's entire canon. It's not quite as famous as the third movement of the fourth horn concerto, K495. But it is famous. And they both begin with an identical premise: a quaver's upbeat on F, then up a fourth to B flat for six more galloping quavers. You know instantly where you are in the Rondo. You are on top of a horse, careering across the countryside. Occasionally an obstacle places itself in your path. There's a rise in the ground, a dip. Now and then a tree needs rounding, or a hedge clearing. And after every change of speed or direction or gradient, you return to the flat and thunder over the turf to the rhythm of those B flat quavers.

The weird thing is it's possible to imagine all this even if, like me, you've suffered from a near-lifelong allergy to things equestrian. Whether you like it or not, Mozart's rondos for horn put you in touch with your inner huntsman.

'Is this right room for *Wassermusik*?'

Two nervous-looking horn players stand in the doorway. The noise of four dozen musicians tuning their wooden instruments ebbs away as like a herd of cows in a field they turn to look at two foreign gentlemen brandishing shiny metal contraptions. From somewhere in the throng comes the voice of a violinist.

'And you are?'

The horn made its orchestral debut in England on, of all places, a barge.

Daily Courant, 19 July 1717

On Wednesday Evening at about 8, the King took Water at Whitehall in an open Barge, wherein were also the Dutcheſs of Bolton, the Dutcheſs of Newcastle, the Counteſs of Godolphin, Madam Kilmanſeck, and the Earl of Orkney. And went up the River towards Chelſea. Many other barges with Perſons of Quality attended, and ſo great a Number of Boats, that the whole River in a manner was cover'd; a City Company's Barge was employ'd for the Muſick, wherein were 50 Instruments of all ſorts, who play'd all the Way from Lambeth, (while the Barges drove with the Tide without Rowing, as far as Chelſea) the fineſt Symphonies, compoſ'd expreſs for the Occaſion by Mr Hendel; which his Majeſty liked so well, that he cauſ'd it to be plaid over three times in going and returning. At Eleven his Majeſty went a-ſhoar at Chelſea, where a Supper was prepar'd, and then there was another very fine Conſort of Muſick, which laſted till 2; after which, his Majeſty came again into his Barge, and return'd the ſame Way, the Muſick continuing to play till he landed.

As an eyewitness account to the premiere of the *Water Music*, the *Daily Courant* comes up short in one key area. There's no mention of the famous debut. It took the discerning eye of the Prussian minister Friedrich Bonet to note that the musicians 'played all kinds of instruments, to wit, trumpets, horns, oboes, bassoons, flutes, recorders, violins and basses'.

The horn was not entirely new to musical performance. Cavalli had horn parts in *Le nozze di Teti e di Peleo*, an opera performed in Venice in 1639. Lully used them at Versailles in a divertissement-ballet, *La Princesse d'Elide*, in 1664. But in both cases its task was to sound hunting calls. Two '*cornes de chasse*' were ushered into the orchestra proper in Hamburg in 1705, in an opera by Reinhard Keiser called *Octavia*. Handel knew Keiser. But this induction into the pit is pre-dated by at least five years by a concerto for posthorn, hunting horn, violins and basso continuo. Johann Beer, who died in 1700, wrote it for the court of Duke Christian of Sachsen-Weissenfels, a passionate huntsman and spendthrift whose determination to rival the splendour of Louis XIV's Versailles had an unhappy result: the supervision of his finances was eventually placed under the Emperor's estate management. Bach's earliest surviving secular cantata, known as the 'Hunt Cantata', was composed as part of his birthday celebrations in 1713, and included horn parts not dissimilar to those that would resurface in the first Brandenburg Concerto.

In England the horn was still seen as a beast of the field, even if it had barged its way indoors in Austria. On the first day of 1717, the year of the *Water Music*'s first performance, Lady Mary Wortley Montagu wrote from Vienna of balls and festivities she had attended: '. . . the music good, if they had not that detestable custom of mixing hunting horns with it, that almost deafen the company'. The horns she would have been more used to are mentioned in the accounts for the Royal Buckhounds for the same year: 'to a person to teach several huntsmen to sound the French horn, £7 6s. John Harris for ten brass French horns and mending two other for H.M. huntsmen, £26 10s'.

According to his first biographer, Handel wrote the *Water Music* to win back the favour of the king. History is silent on the nature of his transgression. Handel had been appointed kapellmeister to George in Hanover seven years earlier, in 1710, but left his service to move to England in 1712. George arrived to claim his crown two years after that. Perhaps the king nursed a grievance that Handel had abandoned him. Perhaps the king, who struggled to master English, was jealous of Handel's competence in the new language. Perhaps there was no grievance at all. But Handel's decision to ornament his new composition with the baroque horn suggests an eagerness to dazzle, and no doubt to please.

The two horn players may well have been Bohemian. In 1680, the eighteen-year-old Count Franz Anton von Spörck embarked from Bohemia on a two-year tour of Europe after the death of his father. His devotion to hunting was such that when he reached Paris he was immensely struck by the sound of the hunting horn, and had two of his entourage learn the instrument. The retainers'

names were Wenzel Sweda and Peter Rölig. They took their French
horns home with them, where German trumpet makers soon
began to copy the instruments. They also passed on their new-
found artistry to an entire school of pupils, who took the craft of
horn playing back into the rest of Europe.

It's possible to speculate that it was pupils of Sweda or Rölig
who turn up together for the first rehearsal of the *Water Music*.

'And you are?'

The braver one mutely holds up a horn. His second, who is
much younger, does the same.

'What the devil is that?' One of the recorder players has never
seen a horn before. He's heard about them, rough and ready noise-
makers who ply their trade in the wind and rain of the great
outdoors, often on horseback.

'We are tell to . . .' says the younger horn player.

'Are you absolutely certain,' enquires a haughty oboist, 'that
you have come to the right place?'

'Herr Handel ask us.'

'Can anyone else,' asks a helpful bassoonist, 'smell horse dung?'
Everyone laughs again.

'Ah, *die Hörner!* Gentlemen! *Willkommen!* A youngish man
with a German accent seated at a harpsichord, looking up dis-
tractedly from a pile of music, hails them from the far end of the
room. 'Please take your seats! We must begin.'

The two Bohemian horn players edge nervously into the room.
They have rarely played with other instruments before, certainly
not with such a large ensemble. They have scarcely even played
in a chair before, unless a saddle counts. In this sea of seated
musicians they are unsure where to head. As they stand there,
tongue-tied, a friendly trumpeter catches the eye of one of them
and furtively, unsmilingly, jerks his head in the direction of two
empty places at the back. This is the tacit solidarity of a fellow
outsider. As the only brass player, he has long experience of his
colleagues' supercilious wit. Here are other players to share the
burden. He little realises, any more than the horn players do, that
trumpeters will in due course surrender their position of primacy
in the brass section, that successive composers will grow so devoted

to the rich, honeyed tones of the horn that by the end of the nineteenth century some orchestras will have eight of them, even on occasion twelve or sixteen, a whole bank of horns serried in rows and segregated from the rest of the brass, that they will be called upon to blow and blow while the trumpets will sit there like wallflowers, barely more integral than trombonists, summoned only now and then to punctuate a passage, fill in with a phrase, shrilly augment an outburst of fortissimo. The trumpet will be so marginalised by the horn that in search of its lost mojo it will have to go off and invent a whole new musical form.

But all this is in the future as the trumpeter tacitly shows the two horn players where to sit. They take their places. They are sweating. It is July. They have been hurrying down the corridor, and there is no time to warm up.

'Gentlemen, gentlemen!' The maestro has an announcement to make. 'I would like on behalf of you all to welcome some new friends to the bosom of our ensemble. Please!'

The murmurs peter out.

'I first heard them out in the hunting fields back home, and was greatly struck by them. I thought it would be amusing to give his majesty a surprise and bring them with us on our river trip. But please, I must ask you to be indulgent with our new friends.'

The horn players look at each other hastily.

'No, you must not be too *judgemental.* The truth is that the horn players may on occasion sound slightly *out of tune.*'

Some musicians stifle an involuntary guffaw.

'Please, please! This is not their fault. It is the fault of the instrument, which cannot alas be tuned.'

A crescendo of ill-suppressed cackles.

'And the other thing of which you must be aware is the limited number of notes available on the instrument.'

Several of the musicians look at one another and start to mutter.

'Gentlemen! Gentlemen!' Handel raises his voice over the hubbub. 'Theirs is the sound of nature, gentlemen! I have been talking to our horn players here! Most interesting. They can blow only a certain number of notes, depending on how tightly their lips are pressed together. The range is extraordinary. Three whole octaves!'

A few musicians seem moderately impressed with this and stop sniggering.

'A. bass note, a fifth above that, then the octave; then an arpeggio including the seventh. Thereafter, at the higher end of the register, the horn player can play more or less any note he chooses. You will find that this is why I have written for it very largely in the higher register. However, I'm told by our new friends that mistakes are not only possible in the upper part of the horn's range, but likely. So I would ask you once again to be patient. But we must stop this fascinating chat. It is time for us to begin. Gentlemen!'

With that, Mr Handel raises his right hand.

'Dear Jasper . . .'

A letter arrives from a learned friend of a friend.

When I enquired after you our mutual friend said that you were researching the French horn and my immediate response was to declaim the haunting monosyllabic line that I attribute to Ronsard:

'*Le son du cor est triste au fond du bois.*'

This line not only reminds me that the origin of the French horn was an instrument of prey but also of the column in the *Daily Express* during my adolescence written under the *nom de plume* 'Beachcomber'. His speciality was nonsense – 'Mayors are born free but everywhere are in chains', 'An Irish vagrant was brought into court and Mr Justice Cocklecarrot asked him how he earned his living. "I am a tinker, Your Honour." "Yes, yes, my man, but what do you actually do?" "Your honour, I tink, therefore I am."'

The relevance to the French horn is that in one article 'Beachcomber' fabricated an elaborate story about a player in the brass section of a French orchestra who acquired a young and adventurous snake by way of a pet. The snake got stuck in the French horn and led the player to exclaim,

'*Le son du boa est triste au fond du cor.*'

I hope that all is well.

It soon becomes apparent, out in the baking spring heat of the Loire Valley, that no animal will be killed in the course of my researches. This is music to the ears of the New Person In My Life, who has never been anywhere near a hunt in all her years, and isn't quite sure whether her presence squares with her abolitionist conscience. On the night that the Andrew Lloyd Webber musical opened, my older brother was in the crowd of pro-hunt protesters outside the Palace of Westminster making a last-ditch effort to halt the ban on hunting foxes with hounds in England and Wales, though not one of the five who penetrated the very chamber of the House of Commons. The ban has recently come into force back home. The New Person is quietly chuffed to bits. Very quietly, in these surroundings.

It's a dull old afternoon. We are in my parents' 4 x 4, my mother tentative behind the wheel as we edge along asphalt-free tracks through a young forest in bud. I guess she's trying quite literally not to frighten the horses. An air of profound inertia prevails as the sun-baked topsoil refuses to yield the faintest trace of a scent for the hounds to follow. Pulses stir briefly when a huntsman materialises out of the woods in front of us, crosses the road and clambers imperiously up a bank to plunge back among semi-clad trees.

'I have to admit that that's a magnificent sight,' says the New Person, ever the aesthete. But she can't keep it up for long. Before the half-hour is out, she is supine on the flat wall of a low bridge and sleeping off the rest of the afternoon under the sun's caress. For those of us still awake, there is the occasional fanfare on a *trompe de chasse* from somewhere deep in the woods to remind me why I'm here. But they don't have much to *trompe* about. We bump into my father.

'Is it always this exciting?' I ask him.

With the wind in the right direction my father can have a tendency to sound imperious. Atop of a chestnut steed, even a rental one, the wind is very much in the right direction. *De haut en bas* some observation or other wafts its way down to ground level. It's something to do with foot followers liking it or lumping it. Especially those who've previously shown a violent distaste for country pursuits. I'm reminded why my younger brother and I gave these gatherings a wide berth as soon as we were old enough.

All I wanted to do was hear the *trompe de chasse* in action, the way the Duc de Brissac's forebears would have done in the reign of the Sun King. But the sun really is king today, and it's not going to happen. A cortège of riders in a sweaty state of mild disgruntlement heads back along the path towards the double-fronted farmhouse. For the horses, the stables beckon; for the hounds, the kennels. For the humans, it's the bar. For me, it's a quiet corner of a foreign field. My father has a commission for me. I'm required on the hoof to write a speech for him, a vote of thanks, to be delivered later this evening. He'd do it himself, only he needs it to be in French. When he started school there was a war on, and people learnt Latin. So it has fallen to me to fall back on my expensive education and rustle up something the duc and his wassailing chums will understand. I have no dictionary, and I don't have a single word of hunting vocab.

There is a road that travels for ten miles in a north-westerly direction from the heart of London to the foot of a hill. On top of that hill, at the age of thirteen, I went to a new school. The road is known, self-explanatorily, as the Harrow Road.

There are two main ways of being an Old Harrovian. Some spend the rest of their days apologetically assuring everyone how much they hated the place. (Subtext: I am *not* posh, promise.) Others take the view that these were the best years of their life. (Subtext: I am exceptionally posh, and a bit dim.) I tend to favour the mythical third way. I quite liked it. Plus it's not my fault I went there. It was more of a sort of hereditary thing. My father was sent up there by his self-made parents from south-west Wales in the years immediately after the war. For my brothers and me, Harrow was a three-line whip.

'An encouraging start to the term,' says my first school report. 'He should be very able as a player in due course. Nice to see an old pupil again.'

What? I read it again.

'Nice to see an old pupil again.'

I'm at a loss to know what to make of this. Is he talking about me? I'm no orthographer but the handwriting doesn't tally with that of the four teachers I came across in the previous three years. His initials are illegible. They could be JPL. They could be DPKG. They could be JJ or JHWM or BMS or EDHG or CHS. They could be any permutation of the above or other letters. Just about the only set of initials I'm prepared to rule out is XYZ. He may have remembered me, but I sure as heck don't remember him.

'Higher notes not causing quite so many problems.' The next term he was still there. His initials had crystallised into something that looks very like MAC. By the third term they solidified into MA Carter, and for the record my playing had become a lot clearer too. Improvement was the watchword. 'Pitching the notes has improved very well, and together with an improvement in rhythm and reading the term overall has seen a lot of improvement.'

The next term he was back to being MAC. And always the same bell tolled: progress constantly vouched for, a promised land of eventual competence sitting just out of reach on the horizon, the ladder perpetually extended upwards as each fresh rung is conquered. 'Some quite difficult pieces have been played this term and with continued hard work some standard repertoire pieces can be tackled next term.'

It sounds as if he was even looking forward to it. But he can't have been – not that much. However nice it was to see an old acquaintance, I never saw MA Carter again.

I am now meeting horn players almost every week. The horn section of the London Symphony Orchestra, for example, allows me to sit quietly on the Barbican stage during a rehearsal of Tippett's *The Rose Lake*. Down the row, I can see seven horn players in profile, blowing their socks off. From the conductor's podium, Sir Colin Davis doesn't seem to notice that on the far end of a row an eighth horn player is not blowing his socks off. Or, indeed, holding a horn.

Over lunch we talk French horn. Specifically we talk British Horn Society, and my aim to play K447 to the annual festival. Although I have leaked this news into the ether, the bush telegraph doesn't seem to be working. The horn section of the LSO, whom you'd kind of expect to be plugged into the matrix, don't know anything about it. So much for my plan.

'Got any advice?'

'K447,' pipes up Jonathan Lipton, a naturalised American who plays fourth horn. 'The easy one.' He coughs theatrically as he says 'easy'. The third concerto does have a reputation for being more navigable than the second and fourth concertos, and the unfinished first (which Mozart actually composed last). A brief glance at the music reveals as much. Of the two other completed concertos, the first movements are bigger, bolder, scarier, the slow middle movements call for more stamina and control, and the rondos are both fiddlier than the one I'm grappling with. But that cough says it all.

'Make sure you hit the second note,' says Jonathan Lipton. 'The D.' The same booby trap was flagged up by the Berlin Phil. John Ryan, a skinny young Irishman on third horn, has a bright idea. He suggests that, to simulate as accurately as possible the physical symptoms which are part of performance, I run up and down the stairs a couple of times before playing the entire concerto. 'That way,' he says, 'you'll know what it feels like to have the adrenalin pumping through you and your heart racing.' I begin to regret soliciting the advice of the horn section of the LSO.

'Positive visualisation,' says David Pyatt. David Pyatt is the orchestra's principal horn, and one of the best-known horn players in the world. He won the BBC's Young Musician of the Year at the age of fourteen, and hasn't spent much time looking back.

He's the perfect shape for a horn player, being shortish, squattish, and compactish, and also appears to have the perfect mentality: an absolute lack of self-doubt. About a month before I took up the horn again, he stood up in front of the Albert Hall on the Last Night of the Proms in a white tux and cantered effortlessly through Strauss's first horn concerto. I don't care how good you are, that takes armour-plated bollocks.

'What do you mean, positive visualisation?'

He fixes me with a laser-blue stare.

'I mean that when you stand up in front of an audience you need to visualise what that will be like. You need to imagine a scenario in which it all goes well. Because if you picture it going badly, you can bet it will.'

It sounds like something they use in sports psychology to get 110 per cent out of super-fit athletes. The rest of the horn section nods discreetly. They've clearly heard this before. I hadn't previously associated the vocabulary of psychobabble, the toolbox of the shrink, with playing the horn. The instrument that has practically prehistoric origins somehow seems to pre-date Freud and the unconscious. The priests at the foot of the walls of Jericho, the Roman *cornicines* sounding the battle manoeuvres, Louis XIV's *trompe de chasse* players announcing the sighting of prey – they didn't trouble themselves with positive visualisation.

On the other hand, one of the world's best-known horn players has given me licence to dream the impossible dream. Like all of us, I've been visited in my sleep by the same old shadows of immortality. The bog-standard wet one of scoring the winning goal in an FA Cup Final? Been there. Rushing modestly up onstage in a black tux to accept an Olivier/Grammy/Academy Award? Done that. That moment when I'm sent along to interview a beautiful woman and end up living with her? I am wearing the T-shirt. (Actually that did happen.)

But I'm now being told by the principal horn of the London Symphony Orchestra that this sort of thinking is legitimate. It's OK to dream. In fact it's positively encouraged. He has advised me to go ahead and project, to imagine myself walking out in front of the British Horn Society and jaunting faultlessly through

K447. His considered recommendation is that I trick myself into playing well. If it's good enough for the Last Night of the Proms . . .

But he has another piece of advice.

'You need to practise.' This much I know. 'Practise performing. You can play something perfectly five times in a row at home, but the first time you step in front of an audience it'll be as if you're playing it for the first time ever. When you play K447 at the British Horn Society festival, make sure that it's not your performance debut. Because if it is . . .' I think I spot the trace of a smirk.

Afterwards we pose for a photograph, with me in the middle. We do two versions of the picture: one to attention, blowing our horns, the other at ease. I grin broadly throughout. It's my first time, and I get an instant taste for it. One lunchtime the nine-strong horn section of the Vienna Philharmonic present themselves at the stage door of the Royal Albert Hall after rehearsing Bruckner's mighty Eighth Symphony. Half of them bring out single F Viennese pumpenhorns, half present themselves with Wagner tubas, a richly toned cross-breed instrument invented halfway through the nineteenth century and rapidly adopted by the composer from whom it takes its name. We pose like a football team, half of us crouching in front.

I meet Günter Högner who became the orchestra's principal horn in 1971, the night before. A very proper Austrian gent, rather stern in his white tie and tails, he answers all my questions methodically and politely. I whip out my copy of the K447 and ask if he has any tips. As he looks down the sheet music, bafflement clouds his Bürgermeister features.

'Is there something wrong?' I ask.

'He says you've still got the fingering written in.' My German being rusty, we are communicating through an interpreter.

The fingering. It's what I've written above some of the notes to ease me through the bumpier bits of the road. I should have realised this might not impress a man who has been blowing with the Vienna Phil for thirty-five years. Günter keeps his counsel, but his advice is written on his face. No one who needs help with fingerings should be unleashing a rendition of this concerto on a paying public.

'Those are old,' I tell him, laughing. 'I wrote all those fingerings in when I was a teenager. Haven't quite got round to rubbing them out.' Some of those fingerings are barely a month old. I make a note to rub them out the minute I get home.

It's only when I catch up with the horn section of the Berlin Philharmonic, who are minutes away from going onstage in the Festspielhaus in Salzburg, that I stumble across one of the eternal verities of horn photography: there is no set way to hold the instrument for the camera. Do you hug? Do you dangle? Where do you point the bell? On the cover of his album *Under the Influence*, Dave favours a manly pose, nestling the horn in the crook of his right arm with the bell pointing skywards. Some soloists prefer the enigmatic option of holding the instrument over their face and peering through the gaps between the network of piping. Enigmatic, and also pretentious. And useless for section shots. In the picture we are all holding our horns differently.

I meet the New York Philharmonic horns backstage in the brass room in Avery Fisher Hall, part of the Lincoln Center, the sprawling hub of the arts on the Upper West Side. It's a low-ceilinged, L-shaped room, lined all around by a rim of bright red lockers. Occupying most of a sofa in the centre of the room is the mighty Phil Myers, all 350 pounds of him. He likes the idea of the photograph and rounds up the section in no time.

'OK, guys,' he says. '*Heldenleben*. Two three four.' While I hold a borrowed instrument mutely to my lips, four horns of the New York Phil blast out a heroic gobbet of Richard Strauss. I've never felt smaller. And not just because I'm standing next to Phil.

As the year proceeds, I find myself growing a rhinoceros hide. I reason with myself that a thick skin will be useful when I do finally walk out onstage to perform Mozart's third horn concerto. Occasionally I worry that my behaviour may to the professional horn player bear some of the hallmarks of the stalker fan. I check for symptoms. Have I lost the plot in the personal grooming department? Not especially. Do my pupils point in alarmingly different directions? They're slightly different colours, but no.

How about autographs? Am I an obsessive-compulsive collector? Ah.

In fact this turns out to be useful. The Chicago Symphony Orchestra are at Carnegie Hall. Tickets are hard to come by, but the New Person and I secure $40 seats somewhere just under the ceiling. Before the concert, I hang around at the stage door waiting for the legendary Dale Clevenger to turn up for work. Dale Clevenger has been sitting in the principal's desk, once occupied by Philip Farkas, since I was a one-year-old. He is now a white-bearded Methuselah of the horn. Eventually he breezes in. I explain at some length what I'm up to. He listens thoughtfully, but I sense that I haven't hooked him. So I produce from my bag a notebook, hand it over and direct him to the back. He flicks through the pages and duly finds a message from pretty much every eminent horn player in the world. Apart from his good self.

'After the concert,' he says, 'the section scatters to the four winds. The only way you're going to catch us all together is onstage at the end.'

'Fine,' I say.

'Come down to the front of the stage and I'll meet you there.'

We sit through the concert, which mostly consists of Dale Clevenger blowing the roof off Mahler 6. No one gets a bigger sound out of a horn. At the end he is invited to take a bow by himself, but I don't stay to cheer because the New Person and I are rushing down countless flights of stairs to get to the front of the stage. We needn't have hurried. The applause goes on for a good ten minutes. Eventually the tumult subsides and the audience rises to leave. I catch Dale Clevenger's eye. He beckons me onto the stage. The New Person wants the earth to swallow her up. Or even better, me up. The hallowed platform is still full of musicians in white tie and tails and her boyfriend is clambering onto it in a battered leather jacket. But I am dauntless.

'That was sensational,' I tell Dale Clevenger. Thanks to Mahler, he is sweating like a boxer.

'Hey, nobody on da stage!' A chair-stacker with a thick Brooklyn accent is waving the book at me.

'This won't take a moment,' Dale Clevenger explains.

I realise that I'm going to need a horn. I don't have the Lídl with me. Without a horn in my hands, the picture will be worthless. Mrs Dale Clevenger, who happens to be in the section, agrees to lend me hers, and walks round the back of the section where her hornlessness will not be visible. The New Person is less cooperative. She flatly refuses to hoist herself onstage to take the picture, so I hand the camera to a passing trumpeter. And bang, it's done. I choose not to ask the horn section of the Chicago Symphony Orchestra to play their instruments for the snap. After Mahler 6, even I know that that would crash through the barriers of the most basic etiquette.

My father's theory of public speaking is simple. Never rise from your seat until you and your entire audience are inebriated. Works a treat every time. Even, it turns out, in French. *Especially* in French.

God alone knows why. The speech is littered with the coarsest rabble-rousing, the cheesiest oratorical bullet points. And it's delivered in an uncompromising Harrovian accent. Veeve la Fronce! Veeve l'Ongletaire! Veeve la chasse! I don't know if it's my idea or my father's to round off his vote of thanks with this spectacular triple somersault, but he delivers it with fire and gusto and much demagogic pointing at the rafters, which can scarcely contain the ensuing tumult.

The duc rises to respond in rather more elegant English. We are always welcome, he tells us, fingers locking across his Pickwickian midriff. He gets a laugh when he recalls the sight of the New Person earlier in the afternoon, caught literally napping on a wall, and evidently less than enthralled by the day's non-events.

We are sitting, thirty of us, on benches at long plain tables in a square dining room in the double-fronted farmhouse. Dusk has fallen outside, and the temperature has dropped. On a shelf running all the way round the room's perimeter is a series of flat wooden figures, cut-outs of huntsmen with their horses, their hounds and, of course, their horns. It's hard to vouch for the hounds, but the human figures, all in the livery of the Brissac hunt, are portraits of characters in this very room. Quirks of girth and gait have been subtly caricatured. But they are all there, and all here – the duc, the duchesse, the solicitor, the physician, the notary, the farmer, the seductress.

The seductress is an interesting one. She is that type of woman who looks straight through, past and around other women, in search of the man, the men, on the other side. After several visits to Brissac country, my mother attests that she has never extracted so much as a squeak from her. Her technique is not subtle. The New Person remarks on it when for five slightly alarming minutes the seductress comes and parks herself more or less between us on the bench. In all my year with the French horn, this is the only time I came across a living breathing pun on the instrument's English name.

In an attempt to keep things decent, I bang on with great enthusiasm about the *trompe de chasse*. After about a minute the seductress's smile starts to look a little fixed. We will never know how long she would have been prepared to put up with this, because a couple of huntsmen stand up to entertain us on their *trompes*. I rub my hands with an overt expression of glee and turn pointedly to face them. The seductress loses scent of her prey and before long departs for another bench.

The musical horsemen are still in their hunting get-up, a couple of hours after dismounting. It's the youngish one in his thirties and the tall chap with the stooping shoulders who play for us. The stoop is particularly visible owing to a unique quirk of the *trompe de chasse*. They play with their backs to the audience, with the bell of their *trompe* pointed past their right elbow and out into the room. A number of old standards are duly banged out. The tunes stick close to a formula. A long note that shudders with vibrato, followed by a series of chases up and down the register. Some of them involve a call and response. In others they play in unison. The youngish one is quite musical but the stooper, I notice, isn't very good at all. He addresses his *trompe* with all the verve of someone blowing up a party balloon. I could do that, I think, when they've finished and the hubbub has risen to replace the noise of the *trompes*.

'I could do that,' I say to the New Person. The New Person,

who looks like she needs something to keep her from taking another kip, passes it on.

'He could do that,' she says to my father.

It's my father who actually insists I stand up and do it. But I don't require much prodding. I rise from the bench, like a supersub, and accost the youngish man. He turns out to be called Jérôme.

'*Je voudrais essayer,*' I say. '*Essayer de jouer une trompe de chasse. Est-ce que vous pouvez me donner une petite leçon?*'

Jérôme looks a bit puzzled. Presumably he's not come across an English *trompiste* before.

'*Sonner,*' he says. It's my turn to look thrown.

'*Sonner,*' he repeats. '*On ne dit pas "jouer". On sonne la trompe.*' You don't play a *trompe*. You sound it.

Clearly I'm not going to impress him with my French. I decide to play my trump card. (My *trompe* card, if you will.)

'*Mon père,*' I say. '*Il a une trompe de chasse. Dans la voiture.*'

It's true. In the boot of the 4 x 4 is a *trompe de chasse* my father picked up in France on one of his previous visits. He's brought it down for ... actually I'm not quite sure why he's brought it, if not for me to play. A rumour fans round the room that Jérôme and the non-hunting English bloke with the narcoleptic girlfriend are going to play for the diners. To sound for them. Thirty hunting folk in a large farmhouse in the middle of the Loire valley – I'm not sure David Pyatt had this in mind when he told me to get used to the feel of performance.

My father lopes back in from the car with the family *trompe* in his grip. He hands it over. In order to warm up, and to post my horn-playing credentials before anyone is properly listening, I play a swift arpeggio on it, as far up the range as I can manage, and then down into the basement. Jérôme thrusts out both lips in a traditional French *moue*. Not bad, the face says. As a grudging hush descends, we face our audience. It occurs to me that I'm not remotely nervous.

'*OK,*' he says, '*suivez-moi.*' Jérôme plays a long note. I join in, rather thinly.

'*Fort. Plus fort.*' He clenches his fist.

I gulp in air and, shoulders pumping with the effort, blow as if blowing up a party balloon. A lingering vibrato expands satisfyingly into every corner of the room. There is a cheer from the floor.

'*Alors*,' says Jérôme. He plays a simple phrase, lowers his *trompe* and looks across at me. I repeat the phrase. It's relatively easy to start with. The thing about the *trompe de chasse* is there are only a certain number of notes you can play. It's bound hand and foot to the harmonic series. There are no valves, and so no fingerings to complicate matters. The sole way of varying the notes is to change the size of aperture made by your lips. The tighter you press, the higher the note. And the higher up the scale you go, the more notes there are available. Thankfully we stick to the middle area of the range, where it's all a bit of a cake-walk. Or so it first seems. But as the succession of phrases mount, they get longer, it turns into a memory test and I begin to flounder. I'm reminded of my fortieth birthday, when Dave made me play Leopold Mozart in unison with him. We were meant to be honking the same melody, only I couldn't hold the tune. And this time I don't even have the music.

It doesn't seem to matter. On we go, calling and responding, or playing together. Mistakes creep into the second half, but nobody seems to care. This is not the Albert Hall. There's applause from a roomful of French huntsmen when we get to the end. My mother looks pleased. The New Person claps in her usual style, hands up at head height. The duc and duchesse look, at the very least, unoffended. Even the seductress is applauding daintily. I spot my father banging a palm on the table. I have inadvertently taken his golden rule for successful speech-making, and applied it to playing the horn in public.

Rehearsals are done. The rest of the ensemble has heard what the horns can do. Now they must do it in public. The barge trundles in the water as the pull of an incoming tide sends it gliding gently upstream towards Chelsea. Under their chairs two Bohemian horn players feel the swell of the old river.

The slow majestic overture of the *Water Music* is given entirely over to the strings, before the oboe joins them in a mournful adagio. For seven or so minutes, eyeing the sheet music on the stands in front of them, the horn players wrestle with their nerves. Nerves have never been kind to horn players. Mr Handel is a reassuring presence. He has been their ally, their champion, but he cannot help them now. Somewhere in their midst, in this waterway heaving with ceremonial craft, is royalty, seated under an awning, listening pleasantly. For the king, who arrived in England only three years earlier, this trip up the river in the temperate warmth of a July evening is a form of tourism.

As the moment draws near, during the slow song of an oboe, the two horn players raise their instruments to their lips in anticipation of the full orchestral chord that is their cue. In the rest at the end of the adagio, they swallow a huge breath and, half a beat after the strings, unleash a sudden fusillade of quavers. On the fifth note, they linger on a glorious harmonised trill, the sound of a fluttering songbird, then repeat the same phrase but with a different chord on the trill. And they rise through the octave until they descend again like water gambolling exuberantly downstream over rocks.

This must have been one of those very rare instances in musical history where everyone stops to listen. It can't have been dissimilar to the moment the sinful glamour of the electric guitar first flared in the ears of the world's waiting youth. As the siren song of the horns echoed out across the water towards the crowded shores of the Thames, everyone from the king jolted from his evening slumber to the commoner watching this water-borne parade of Germanic wealth and splendour from the bank must have been thinking the same thing, even if only briefly, even if none of them actually said it. What in God's name is that extraordinary, unearthly sound?

By the time the Bohemian horn players repaired to bed, long after dawn, having serenaded the king's party from Westminster to Chelsea and back again, they will have been spent. Nine hours is a long night's work for an embouchure. But they could congratulate themselves. Thanks to their playing, by the time the sun rose over London on Thursday 18 July 1717, *le son du bois* had become *le son du roi*.

5
Ass, Ox and Fool

to my daughter I wrote a letter about my golden clock the letter is null and nothing my wife should sell it and the money should go to Ernest's three kids they are poor fools ———— my clothes and linen should all go to my son Fridarich Leitgeb, but not all at once only when my wife wishes each year if she wishes or half year. That is my last will and opinions.

Joseph Leutgeb, Mozart's horn player

I used to have a favourite shop window in London, down a narrow street in Covent Garden. I never resisted the temptation to detour past it. It could easily have been some second-hand bookshop lined from floor to ceiling with dog-eared Penguin classics. Or an aromatic deli hawking crusty cheeses and salty haunches of ham. But it wasn't. It was Paxmans, the outlet of the leading British manufacturer of French horns.

Long after I gave it up, Paxmans was my sole contact with the instrument, a bit like the old boys section of the school magazine is the single tenuous thread connecting you with formative friendships, auld enmities. Except that every time I went past, nothing had changed. There would be six or eight of them gleaming behind the glass, unapologetically flashing their curves for all the world like sex workers in Amsterdam. It was the most explicit window display in the entire city. I used to stand outside it and drool. I always told myself that one day I'd go in.

The Lídl didn't come from Paxmans. They sell only the top brands at Paxmans. Josef Lídl of Brno, Czechoslovakia, is not a top brand. We got the horn from Boosey & Hawkes, a rather less specialist musical superstore off Oxford Street. I remember being intensely embarrassed one Friday afternoon in July as my father and I walked to the tube with our new purchase at a pace set by his preternaturally long legs. On the busiest shopping street in the country, everyone else was carrying shopping bags. I had a cumbersome wooden case which, ridiculously, flared out at one end. My right knee kept bumping into it. Also it was too heavy. I whined to my father that I couldn't carry it. Tetchily he took it off my hands and, in retaliation, lengthened his stride. If I could have given up the French horn there and then, even though my father had just shelled out 500 quid on a new instrument, I'd have jumped at the chance.

But I needed a new instrument. The dented old bit of tin I had been playing since my first-ever lesson was holding me back. So said the experts.

'I think it would be advisable,' advised one of my horn teachers, 'to buy a new instrument in the fairly near future, as the lack of modern additions, such as waterkeys [*sic*], is proving a draw-back [*sic*].'

I haven't mentioned the water yet.

The British Horn Society festival is still six months away. But it's time to secure a place on the performance roster. My softly-softly mode of attack, in which I slip news of my ambition to play Mozart's third horn concert, K447, into the bloodstream of the horn fraternity, has been an outright failure. By now I've met a lot of British horn players – orchestral players, soloists, freelances, professors of horn at the major London academies and colleges, mates of Dave Lee. We've chewed the fat, we've talked horn, we've all chortled fondly at the instrument's feminine wiles and caprices. But until I mention it to them, not a single one has any idea of my grand plan to take the festival by storm. Plainly none of them talk to one another. Or to anyone at the British Horn Society. Or if they do, they don't talk about me.

But I have reason to be hopeful. Practice is going swimmingly. I pick up the Lídl every morning like an addict getting a fix. The Farkas warm-ups are a warm bath. K447 is in goodish nick. Thanks to Dave's tutelage, there are times, behind closed doors with no one listening, not even the New Person In My Life and certainly not Dave, when I can play the Romanze and hardly make a mistake. I am now starting to imbue it with feeling. The Rondo is also presentable in patches, and even the treacherous, unfathomable Allegro has its moments. I'm doing what David Pyatt told me to do. I'm positively visualising. It seems the opportune moment to take the bull by the horns.

Dear Hugh Seenan,
I hope you might remember me from last year's British Horn Society festival in Southampton.

In rasping Glaswegian, the president of the BHS cheerily suggested we sit down some time that weekend over a beer.

We met only briefly . . .

That night, in a rainy Southampton, I tried to tail the president's blue Ford Escort to an Indian restaurant where the great and the good of the BHS committee would be dining.

. . . but as a result of that weekend I caught the bug. I started practising, and I haven't stopped.

Through sheets of rain I can still see the Escort duck through an amber light, nip round a corner and quite flagrantly lose us.

I am now firmly in the grip of an obsession.

When we finally located the Indian restaurant, there was no room at the inn.

In order to give myself an incentive to make the real improvement I somehow failed to achieve as a teenager, I have set myself a target. I have decided to perform in public on my own.

A long table was heaving with eminent horn players, including the great Peter Damm.

The piece I want to play is Mozart's third concerto. It dawned on me that the natural place to do the performance would be at this year's festival ...

The next day, the second of the festival weekend, Hugh Seenan wasn't there.

... a year on from the day I stood on the stage with 69 other horns and played the Hallelujah Chorus. So I am seeking your permission and that of the committee to take up a small amount of the festival schedule in October. But I hope you will feel able to look kindly on my request.

He'd had to go to Germany.

Perhaps we could discuss my request over a beer?
    Best wishes,
    Jasper Rees

That should do the trick.

SERENE HIGHNESS AND NOBLE PRINCE OF THE HOLY ROMAN EMPIRE GRACIOUS AND DREAD LORD!

I have wished to inform Your Serene Highness in profound submission that yesterday one of the hunting-horn players named Knobloch died and will be buried today. And since for the completeness of the musique another two hunting-horn players would be necessary, I wished to recommend to Your Serene Highness Anton Reibisch, whose art and deportment I know well and find suitable. He has lately served with His Excellency, Count Frantz Eszterhazy (who has dismissed his musique), and will most submissively wait upon Your Serene

Highness; and, if considered acceptable, he will also find a
suitable partner ...
  I remain

Your Serene Highness'
Most humble, obedient
Joseph Haydn.

Eisenstad [*sic*], 23 January 1765

In the same letter Haydn asked his employer, Prince Nikolaus,
for medicines. 'I have felt badly several times in the past few days,'
he groaned, 'and much worse than before.' Being January, it was
presumably cold, and since his engagement four years earlier as
vice-kapellmeister to the Esterházy court, an exhausting regime
of composition, rehearsal and performance had worked Haydn to
the brink of exhaustion. A year into his employment he confused
the parts for violins and oboes when completing the orchestrations
for a horn concerto. To the copyist who would write out the parts,
he offered an excuse in the margin: '*im Schlaff geschrieben*'. Next
to a guttering candle he must have slumped into sleep as he wrote.
  The horn was one of the richer, deeper colours Haydn could
summon from the palette of sounds available to him as he
composed the buoyant early symphonies in those first years at
Eszterháza. Most of them are scored for a pair of horns. The death
of Johannes Knobloch encouraged Haydn to think opportunistically and replace one horn player with two. Despite his
recommendation, Reibisch was not engaged, but we know the
names of the pair of horn players who were: Franz Stamitz and
Joseph Dietzl. Thus Haydn acquired for the first time a quartet
of horn players, from whom he felt he could ask for more than
coloration. The result was the Hornsignal Symphony, enumerated
as No. 31 in Haydn's 104 symphonies. It begins and ends with a
rousing horn call, and makes particular demands on the high horn
throughout. The quartet must have passed the audition, because
more symphonies with hugely demanding horn parts followed, as
well as concertos and double concertos. Some are now lost, but
from the evidence of the surviving works, all of them were fiendishly difficult.

The other members of the quartet were Carl Franz and Thad-
däus Steinmüller. There is a contemporary account of Franz's
playing: 'As concerns the execution of chromatic scales by means
of [stopping with] the hand, as well as facility in the high and low
ranges ... and purity of intonation, scarcely any artist was found
in those days who would have come close to him.' He was highly
valued. When Franz fell ill for much of 1774, he was sent away to
recuperate at the prince's expense. Steinmüller, meanwhile, sired
a horn-playing dynasty. Three of his sons, to one of whom Haydn
was godfather, spent a month in Hamburg in 1784.

On 24 January the Brothers Johann, Wilhelm and Joseph
Steinmüller from the Esterházy Capelle gave a public concert
here in the Schauspielhaus. One was already prejudiced in these
virtuosi's favour, since they have a Haydn for a Capellmeister,
and one was not disappointed; they turned out to be truly
virtuosi, genuine connoisseurs of the music and its melody and
of their instrument. It is rare, very rare, that one can hear three
such clever men on this instrument at one time, men who
know each other so well and acquired such routine. Their own
father is their master.

The records from the summer palace at Eszterháza make detailed
reference to sixteen horn players employed during Haydn's decades
as kapellmeister. They offer an intriguing glimpse of a horn player's
life as a court musician. Some stayed no more than a year, but
the longest-serving spent most of their professional lives under
Haydn's wing. Dietzl was there for a quarter of a century, and left
only when the old prince died in 1790 and his son disbanded the
Kapelle. Joseph Oliva and Franz Pauer, both engaged on 1 June
1769, also stayed until Nikolaus's death. The prince paid for their
horns, and agreed to be godfather to one of Oliva's many children.
In 1793 they both reapplied to his heir for positions in the Esterházy establishment, Oliva pleading that 'he had served the high
princely house as musician for 22 years, diligently and faithfully,
but now, alas, he has been a full three years without bread and a
position and must live in a most wretched fashion, although he is

still a man in the prime of life who is capable of work.' They were engaged as violinists.

It was standard practice, and sound economic sense, to be competent on more than one instrument. Several musicians nominally contracted as horn players would spend long periods in the string section sawing at a violin, viola or baryton. But at the point of engagement they would always present themselves as horn players for the simple reason that the pay was better. The Esterházy records list salaries for horn players ranging from 240 to 462 gulden. They were given in addition 24 lb of candles, 3 or 6 fathom cords of wood and one uniform each year. Some also received free lodging in the musicians' quarters, or 30 florins' lodging money. But preferential treatment was discretionary. Martin Rupp, though engaged eight years after Oliva and Pauer, asked for his salary of 300 gulden to be brought closer to theirs. The prince's refusal, allied to other 'slights and annoyances', forced him to resign his contract after four years. He went to Vienna and was employed for 400 gulden. In 1774 Oliva, who had received a pay rise of 50 gulden per annum the previous year, had to crave the prince's pardon when he breached his terms of employment to play in a concert elsewhere, but 'only from bitter and sad necessity, to help my poor wife, who has been so long prostrated by sickness, and her poor five children ...' His request to bring his wife to Eszterháza was turned down. Three years later Oliva was given 30 *Metzen* of rye and 6¾ *Eimer* of wine 'in consideration of his many children and until his two sons may be able to earn their own bread, this without further precedence and from an especial act of princely grace ...' At least Oliva had a wife. Johann Hollereider asked for permission to marry in 1778. He was refused, threatened with dismissal and allowed to stay 'if he does not marry and remains single, particularly since there are no quarters available for married couples'. In 1780 Anton Eckhart arrived with a wife in tow, but over other wives she had the estimable advantage of being a singer. Two years later 'Waldhornist Hörmann', whom Salieri would esteem the best horn player in Vienna, was also permitted to bring his wife to Eszterháza, presumably as a means of retaining him.

The influx of new horn players in the second half of the 1770s came after the best horn players, including Franz in 1776, started to drift away from the count's employment when the opera season became the predominant annual fixture. Henceforth singers would be the chief beneficiaries of Haydn's artistry. Later in life, when he travelled in triumph to London, the horn players Haydn encountered were evidently not as gifted as the maestri he had known at home, because the horn parts of his London symphonies are nothing like as dangerous to play. It was for his own Eszterháza musicians in those early years that Haydn wrote his greatest horn music.

When Rafael Kubelík assumed the helm of the Chicago Symphony Orchestra in 1950, he was unfamiliar with the mechanics of horn playing. A member of the public watching a television broadcast of a concert wrote to complain that horn players were pouring water out of their instruments when not playing. The principal horn was Philip Farkas. He recalled being told by Kubelík that the person who wrote in thought it disgusting.

> 'So don't do that,' [the conductor] instructed. 'You mean we're not supposed to take the water out of our horns?' I asked. 'You heard me. Do not take the water out of your horns!' We smiled, and because there was nothing important on the programme except for a lot of loud playing, we simply kept the water in for an hour. By the end of the programme everything we did had a gurgled sound ... As soon as it was over [Kubelík] rushed back and yelled, 'Are you trying to make fun of me? What are you doing with that funny sound?' I said, 'We're not trying to make fun of you, you told us not to take the water out of our horns and that's what we did.' 'What difference does that make?' he snarled. I was mad as hell; I took the slide out of my horn and dumped a teacup of water on his shoe. 'That's the difference,' I told him.

Water. It's a euphemism, of course. The act of puckering your lips and blowing energetically through a tube does not merely produce air. It also produces saliva, or spit. When all's said and done, playing the French horn is spitting with style. While the air comes out of the bell end of the horn, the 'water'/saliva/spit doesn't. It collects in the instrument's nooks and crannies. When enough of it has accumulated, it interrupts the flow of air from mouthpiece to bell. The interruption makes a sound roughly like the distant crackle of sporadic machine-gun fire, or the insistent parping of a faulty moped. It afflicts all brass instruments, but the horn being much the most convoluted and curliest of the brass family, 'water'/saliva/spit is a problem in a way that it isn't for the trombone. Because you have to get it out. And in order to get it out, you have to find it.

The baroque horn players who played for Handel and Bach, for Vivaldi and Telemann, would simply turn their instrument around and around until the spit dribbled out of the mouthpiece. As the instrument became more complex, the liquid was not so easily located somewhere along one long thin conical wrap of tubing. Haydn's horn players used a new-fangled set of detachable curly crooks of varying size. When placed in the lead-pipe it enabled them, depending on its length, to play in an array of different keys. As well as the main body of the horn, the crooks could be pulled out and emptied. In the early nineteenth century, valves were slowly introduced, amid much Luddite protest led by Brahms, who more than fifty years on was still refusing to compose for the valved horn. Valves were a great boon, because they allowed the horn player to vary the length of tubing, and thus the note, at the press of a piston. On the other hand, they introduced three more lengths of tubing in which the spit could get lost. The tubes had slides in them, which could be pulled in or out to alter the tuning, or pulled out altogether to empty water.

In 1897, the year of Brahms's death, the prototype of a double horn was produced. This, in effect, was two horns soldered together like Siamese twins. One tuned in F, the other in B flat, they shared a mouthpiece, a lead-pipe, valves and a bell. Using a fourth valve operated by the thumb, players could switch between them. The advantage of the B flat horn was that it allowed for much greater security in the upper register. The disadvantage was that there were now four more tubes for the spit to get lost in. In the twentieth century, a triple horn was developed – Siamese triplets – incorporating an F horn, a B flat horn and an F alto horn to give the player even more security up in the trumpet's territory. An F alto horn has twelve slides.

Hence the invention of the water-key: a simple, efficient device for extracting saliva through a small opening in the main tubing before it can collect in less accessible places. It's like a fire exit along a long corridor. Except it's a water exit.

I can guess why my horn teacher rather testily recommended buying an instrument with a water-key. Two minutes into a lesson, I would start obsessively hunting for the spit locked inside the horn. Not being very good at the actual playing, this would have been one area where I could do a thoroughly professional job. Swathes of a lesson would be whittled away in a parade of twirling, upending and shaking as I hunted down the offending liquid in the byways of the metal maze. I'd roll the horn round and round and when nothing came out one end, roll and roll it round and round and round the other way. And when that failed, I'd start examining the slides. First the slide for the main body of the horn, which was always the most likely hideout. Then the slide connected to the first valve, followed by the second, and when they yielded not even the faintest dribble, I'd try the third slide, even though I never actually used the third valve apart from those rare occasions when I chanced upon a G sharp.

The spit hunt could also be a party piece. When asked at Christmas to play for my Welsh grandmother, I would make the arcane art of extracting the spit an integral and ritualistic part of the performance.

'What are you doing, Jasper bach?' my grandmother would say. (In Wales use of the suffix 'bach' denotes endearment rather than membership of a clan of German composers.)

'He's emptying the spit on the carpet,' my mother would reply. To her credit, my mother was quick to accept that spitting on the carpet was an indispensable part of the French horn player's performance.

This pantomime is not confined to amateurs. When I see the Chicago Symphony Orchestra perform at Carnegie Hall, I can't take my eyes off Dale Clevenger. If he isn't blowing he is emptying. Where some pros merely up-end a slide to get rid of spit, long years in evening dress have taught Clevenger to be more vigorous, more vexatious. He shakes out each slide as if trying to remove a stubborn bit of sticking plaster from the end of his thumb. For forty years the likes of Georg Solti and Daniel Barenboim must have despaired of this rival arm-waver in the ranks, conducting traffic from his place towards the rear of the platform.

When I got home from Boosey & Hawkes with the Lídl, I lifted the impossibly shiny instrument out of its fur-lined case and noted that it had twice as many slides as I was used to. It turned out that we had purchased a double horn. But contrary to my horn teacher's suggestion, there was no sign of a water-key. I'd have to carry on emptying the hard way.

The young Mozart's fondness for the horn came naturally. Despite his travels across the Holy Roman Empire to Paris and London as a child, then three consecutive sojourns in Italy, the music for hunting horn that he would have been most familiar with as a boy was written by his own father. Leopold composed a concerto for horn, while his Sinfonia da Caccia for four horns nodded to the instrument's roots on the hunting field.

Mozart's partiality may also have been in response to a distaste for the trumpet. Leopold persuaded his friend Schachtner to help the boy overcome his antipathy by blowing loud and sudden trumpet blasts in his presence. 'Scarcely had Wolfgang heard the blaring tones,' Schachtner recalled nearly thirty years later, 'than he turned pale and began to sink down; had I continued any longer he would certainly have suffered a convulsion.' When Professor Samuel Tissot, making a study of the nervous systems of infant geniuses, met the eleven-year-old Mozart, he filed his conclusion to Lausanne's weekly newspaper *Aristide ou le citoyen* that 'wrong, hard or excessively loud sounds bring tears to his eyes'. Perhaps a memory of this reared up when at fifteen Mozart attended a concert in Bologna only for his father to report the occasion 'marred by the dreadful playing of trumpeters imported from Lucca'. His only trumpet concerto, written when he was thirteen, has been lost. Was it lost by the composer?

Mozart was only eight when he wrote his first symphony on the London leg of his first European tour. They had lodgings in the rustic village of Chelsea – 'an hour outside the city' – where his father convalesced after falling gravely ill. He 'lay close to death', recalled Mozart's older sister Nannerl. As he was composing, little Wolfgang said to her, 'Remind me to give the horns something worthwhile to do!' He kept on reminding himself all his life.

The lion's share of Mozart's dealings with other musicians was reserved for singers – the professionals he composed for and the students he taught. Other instrumentalists crop up in his correspondence – flautists, violinists, clarinettists – many of them gentleman amateurs who commissioned works from him. It is only in 1777 when he left for France with his mother – a chaperone foisted upon him by his father even though he was now twenty-two – that his letters make any mention of specific horn players. First there was Punto, one of the travelling wind players for whom he composed a Sinfonia Concertante. 'Tenduci has asked me to write a scena for him – for Sunday – a piece for piano forte, oboe, French horn and bassoon.' Later that year, increasingly concerned about the lack of opportunities afforded by his stay in Paris, he met a distinguished horn player in the royal chapel called Jean Joseph Rodolphe, who had rather more clout than most horn players. 'Rodolphe,' Mozart wrote home, 'has offered me the post of organist at Versailles, if I wish to accept it.'

But the horn player who did Mozart the best turn in Paris was Franz Joseph Haina. The Mozarts met him on their first trip to Paris in 1763, when the prodigy was only seven. Back then Haina was a horn player to various aristocrats, including the royal prince of the blood, Prince de Conti. By the time they met again, Haina had taken up music publishing and supplemented his income by running a small hotel. It was here that mother and son took modest lodgings. While Mozart went out each day to drum up commissions he would abandon his mother, who did not speak French, to their garret for hours at a time. The Hainas showed her every courtesy, inviting her to dine with them and taking her on walks in the Luxembourg Gardens.

Mozart's eye was so intent on seeking employment that when his mother suddenly dwindled towards death in their attic, he was taken entirely by surprise. The night she died – from unknown causes, after three days of delirium – he wrote home to a trusted friend, asking him to prepare Leopold for terrible news. Aside from a nurse, the only other person present when Anna Maria Mozart died was Herr Haina, 'a good friend of ours, whom father knows'. Haina it was who had arranged for a priest to give Extreme Unction three days earlier, and now organised her burial. It would be some years before Mozart thought to compose a concerto for the horn. But is it too sentimental to imagine that the extra-ordinary legacy of horn music Mozart left to posterity, and the foundation stone for the instrument's entire repertoire, owes its existence in part to the kindness at a time of appalling grief of one Bohemian horn-playing hotelier?

Nothing changes. I was embarrassed the day I acquired the Lídl, and as I move through the horn-playing world, I notice a creeping sense of shiftiness whenever the Lídl shuffles into the con-versational spotlight. When I've collared the long-serving prin-cipal horn of some world-class orchestra or other, there is always the moment when they pop the question.

'So what instrument do you play?'

This from Dale Clevenger, forty years the Chicago Symphony Orchestra principal. This from Günter Högner, thirty-five years with the Vienna Philharmonic, from Andrei Gloukhov, thirty-five years with the Leningrad (now St Petersburg) Phil, or Peter Damm, thirty-three years with the Dresden Staatskapelle, or Phil Myers, twenty-five years with the New York Phil. Legends of the French horn, all of them, a veritable Mount Rushmore of horn players, all with the same question on their lips. It's like dogs sniffing one another's parts. This is just what horn players ask.

Makes matter to them, and models. When horn players get together in a dedicated chat room moderated out of the University of Memphis, they are virtually indistinguishable from petrolheads.

They talk about everything under the sun, so long as it's to do with the horn. The possibilities are surprisingly, bewilderingly endless. The merits or otherwise of the detachable bell. Where to snatch a breath in the opening solo of Tchaikovsky's Second Symphony. Performance anxiety: to beta-block or not to beta-block? Tips for travelling by aeroplane with your horn. One day a rather vicious debate breaks out on the subject of fingering on the B flat side of the horn. Slide grease: what works best? (Farkas recommends gun oil. Others suggest sewing-machine oil.) 'Anyone,' someone will write, 'know any good music for horn and flute/lute/organ that I can play with my daughter/wife/mistress?' Tips for finding the right mouthpiece to suit your embouchure. Vitriol flies across cyberspace on the subject of who first played Siegfried's long horn call, and on what instrument. The state of horn playing in China. 'I was wondering,' says someone who is redecorating, 'if anyone had or knew where I could get a horn that has been smashed flat?' The best recordings of Bruckner 4/Mahler 6/Strauss's *Till Eulenspiegel.* Horn jokes. Q. How do you make a trombone sound like a French horn? A. Put your hand in the bell and miss a lot of notes. Q. What's the difference between an orchestra and a bull? A. A bull has horns at the front and an asshole at the back. And of course tips on 'water'/saliva/spit.

But the entry-level enquiry among horn players, the opening foray, is always the same. What do you play? Who made your horn? Hans Hoyer, Kruspe, Rauch, Jiraček, Geyer, Lawson, Engelbert Schmid? Is your Alexander the classic 103? Is your Conn an 8D? That Paxman of yours: you got yourself a double or a triple? And so on and so forth.

In fact all this is a matter of public record. There's a website mastered out of Arizona State University which, among other essential esoterica, lists the horn sections of every major orchestra in the world, and most of the minor ones too. 'Horn section personnel listings for 1,356 orchestras in 63 countries worldwide,' it blares. 'Make sure your section is listed here!' Nearly half those sections are in the USA. Want to know who's playing horn in the Cal-State University Bakersfield Community Band? The Idaho Falls Symphony? The Appalachian Horn Quartet? The Portland

Apostolic Faith Church Symphony Orchestra? It's all here. And then there's abroad. Need to find out who's on horn in the Singapore Armed Forces Band, say, or the Open University Orchestra of Milton Keynes? The Musique-Militaire Grand-Ducale Luxembourg perhaps, or Lima's Orquesta Filarmonica del Colegio Santa Maria Marianistas? Look no further. And they don't just give the names of the 7,500 or so horn players across the globe who are members of these sections. In brackets after each name they also list a make of horn, and often a model. Evidently some orchestras insist on a particular brand. The Berlin Philharmonic horns have let foreigners in, and women in, and foreign women in, but they've never yet let anyone play anything but an Alexander 103, the most famous horn of them all. In the Vienna Philharmonic they play so-called single Viennese F horns, or pumpenhorns, made by Jungwirth. Other sections have clearly benefited from a lorry driving past with its rear door on the latch. The horns of the Hong Kong Youth Wind Philharmonia are all Holtons. The State Simfony Orchestr of Azerbaijan play Yamaha 892s. The Sinfonia São Paulo? Paxmans, a job lot of them.

Interestingly, not a single one of the seven members of the Brno Philharmonic Orchestra plays the home-grown horn.

'Er, it's a Lídl?' I answer when a horn player asks what I play. They nod their heads slowly. A silence fattens between us. They've suddenly realised that they're in the presence of an absolute joker. But most people haven't even heard of my brand of horn.

'A what?' That's what they often say, particularly Americans. 'Did you say a Lada?' At this point in the conversation I usually try to lacquer a bit of glamour on to the brand, a dash of mystery.

'A Josef Lídl. It comes from a country which no longer exists.' That puzzles them. Particularly Americans. You can see them thinking, hell maybe *that* explains why I haven't heard of it. Josef Lídl, born in 1864, was apprenticed to a manufacturer of wind instruments in Brno. He opened his own workshop, where he was an agent for piano and harmonium manufacturers. He also carried out repairs. By 1909 he graduated to making his own instruments, principally brass but also dulcimers, concertinas and pianos, in what was the first factory of its kind in Moravia. The firm soon acquired the title 'Supplier to the Imperial and Royal Household', which in practice meant equipping the army as well as the various court bands of the Empire. The right was also granted to use the Imperial eagle in the sign of the firm.

The family didn't have long to enjoy that status, as the House of Habsburg ceded the archduchy of Austria and the kingdoms of Hungary, Croatia, Bohemia, Galicia and Lodomaria at the end of the First World War. Perhaps the loss of royal patronage was what persuaded Josef to hand over management of the firm to his son Václav that same year. He produced his first French horn in 1924. His first satisfied customer was the principal horn of the Brno Opera. The company's name duly spread as far west as Chicago and east as Siberia. Horns were subsequently improved after meticulous consultations with mathematicians and acousticians, including the rector of Brno's Polytechnic Institute. When Bohemia and Moravia became a Nazi protectorate, production seems to have continued unimpeded. When the Communist party seized power in 1948, the factory was nationalised. Václav Lídl continued in his managerial role until 1957. Doubtless because they were to hand, horn students at Brno's Conservatoire and the Janáček Academy of Music Arts tended to learn on locally produced instruments. In 1966 a Lídl double horn won the gold medal at the International Brno Fair of Commodities, though two years before the Prague Spring, who knows how transparent the judging process was?

No amount of history will spare the Lídl's blushes once people get the thing into their hands. I came across one pro who confessed to having owned a Lídl as a schoolboy. He spoke of it quite wistfully, the way he would about his first tricycle. But he's the exception. 'To be quite honest, Jasper,' says one horn player when I ask him to see if he can explain a buzzing noise the Lídl has started to make, 'and please don't take this the wrong way, but I don't know how you can play this thing.' A student who asks if he can look over the Lídl just bursts out laughing when he feels how heavy it is. And it's true, the Lídl's no bantamweight. 'If you dropped it,' says Dave, 'you'd have to fix the floor.'

I think I must have dropped it at some point, which must

account for the buzzing noise. Certain notes sound like the vibrations of a large, slightly damp rubber band. I can be halfway through the Romanze ('I'm frightfully keen on you') or getting to the exquisite minor passage in the Allegro and suddenly ... Nznznznznznznznznznznznznzn.

'We will find the use of the fourth valve quite tricky!' The parting words of MA Carter, my first teacher at Harrow, the one who thought we'd met before. Lurking discreetly between the lines is a cackle of relief. He knew what I didn't know, that he would not be back next term, that he had no intention of instructing me in the dark arts of the double horn. It would fall to someone else. Who turned out to be rather eminent.

Other people remember John Pigneguy more clearly than I do. Dave, for example. He played alongside Dave in the City of Birmingham Symphony Orchestra. (I'm not entirely convinced they got on.) This was one of the benefits of going to the second most famous school in the country, and possibly the world. Long after the idea of contracting out the upbringing of your children declined in popularity, and boarding schools all over the country started to close, Harrow continued to be oversubscribed. I remember one beak telling me long after I left that only three boys' boarding schools in England had many more applicants than they could possibly accommodate. He listed them. 'Winchester,' he said, 'because it's academically elitist. Eton, because it's socially elitist. And Harrow, because it's on the Metropolitan Line.'

Being on the Metropolitan Line was handy for luring good horn teachers up the hill once a week. It's hard to know how eagerly John Pigneguy made that weekly schlep. Not that eagerly, from the available evidence. 'Jasper can play the horn quite well but his progress is impeded by his lack of attention to detail. He will benefit by being aware of this when practising, and also by turning up to all his lessons.' A barely suppressed rage simmers just below the surface of those well chosen words.

I've no memory of serial absenteeism, but I will own up to settling into a routine of skimping on practice. If the lesson was on a Tuesday, say, I'd obviously not practise the day after. I might think about it on Thursday but, again, it felt a bit too soon. I would certainly blow a few notes on the Friday, just to tide me over for the weekend, when clearly nobody practises, and there wouldn't have been much point in trying to catch up the day before on the Monday, although sometimes I'd give it a go. So I would show up to the next lesson with maybe half an hour's desultory preparation in the bag. I might have practised three times a week a few times, twice a week quite often, once a week very regularly. And sometimes I practised no times.

'Jasper is making progress but still needs to practise more carefully. JJP.'

I have a faint recollection of someone small, trim and beaky, and looking back at the reports I realise why the recollection of John Pigneguy is as faint as it is for all my other horn teachers up until that point. It's not just because I wasn't paying attention, apparently wasn't even turning up. It's also because none of these teachers ever hung around long enough to imprint themselves on my memory. They all scarpered. They downed tools and upped sticks. And my penultimate horn teacher was the same as all the others. After two terms, he'd had a better offer. The only other time I saw him, it was years later, in a photograph with three other horn players and, for some reason, the most famous musician on the planet.

In 1763, when Leopold Mozart was touting his gifted son and daughter around the courts of Europe, he noted in a letter home that one morning tears welled in the eyes of the seven-year-old boy. 'I asked him what was the matter. He said he was so sorry that he could not see his friends, Hagenauer, Wenzl, Spitzeder, Reible, Leitgeb, Vogt, Cajetan, Nazerl, and the rest.'

A young genius rarely forms friendships for himself. Mozart's 'friends' were in fact his father's. But one of them would in due course become his own. The horn player Joseph Ignaz Leutgeb (the Mozarts refer to him in their letters as 'Leitgeb', a phonetic Salzburg spelling) was nearly a quarter of a century older than little Wolfgang. He was born on 8 October 1732 in St Ulrich, a Viennese suburb in which, on 2 November 1760, he married

Barbara Plazzeriani, the daughter of an Italian cheese- and sausage-monger called Blasius. In 1762 a girl called Anna Maria Catharina was born to the Leutgebs. She was named after her godmother, Maria Anna Haydn.

Haydn was also a godfather, but was absent from the christening. In his four-volume biography of Haydn, HC Robbins Landon floats the theory that Haydn's horn concerto written that year, the one for which he confused two orchestral parts and claimed to have written them while asleep, was a christening gift to Leutgeb. There is persuasive evidence for this. Leutgeb's movements across the musical map of Europe are not always clear, but the records show that in the early 1760s he was a frequent soloist at the Burgtheater in Vienna. He played a concerto attributed to Michael Haydn on 2 July 1762, the day before the baptism. 'Concert a joué Le Sieur Leitgeb sur le Cor de Chasse, de la Composition du Sieur Michel Hayde.' It has been plausibly argued that this concerto was in fact by Joseph rather than Michael Haydn.

Leutgeb moved to Salzburg, where he in due course became a family friend of the Mozarts, in 1764. He entered the employment of Count Hieronymus Colloredo, the Prince Archbishop of Salzburg, for whose orchestra he could also scrape a violin. But he was given leave to take his wares abroad. In 1770 he materialised in Paris, where he twice performed at the Concert Spirituel. 'M. Likhgeb,' as the *Mercure de France* referred to him on 1 April, 'of the musique of the Prince Bishop of Salzburg ['Salkbourg'], was given the applause appropriate to the lofty gift with which he played a hunting concerto of his own composing.' A month later the *Mercure de France* went into greater raptures as Leutgeb played not one but two of his own concertos (though uncertainty over the soloist's name continued): 'M. Seikgeb, principal hunting horn player of Monseigneur the Archbishop of Salzburg, performed two concertos with all possible artistry. He draws from his instrument tones which never cease to amaze the connoisseurs who hear them. His particular merit is to sing an adagio as perfectly as the smoothest, most involving and most accurate human voice.' Whether the concertos were actually Leutgeb's own is unknown.

One scholar suspects that in far-away Paris the Austrian horn player may have passed off Haydn's concerto as his own work.

But most sightings of Leutgeb are in the letters of Leopold Mozart and his son. Leutgeb and Haydn's brother Michael, for example, as well as a Salzburg horn player called Drasil, were among the Mozarts' visitors in their lodgings when Leopold took his twelve-year-old son to seek imperial favour in Vienna in 1767. After his success in France in 1770, he returned to Salzburg, but by the end of 1772 he was looking for fresh opportunities and, with Leopold Mozart escorting his son on a third visit to Italy, sought the Mozarts' advice and support as he planned to follow them across the Alps. He first mentioned the idea to Anna Maria Mozart. When she passed news of it on to her husband, his initial response was gruff, even curmudgeonly. He assumed that Leutgeb was fishing for an obbligato part in *Lucio Silla*, the opera Mozart had been commissioned to compose.

'So Herr Leutgeb wants to go to Rome?' wrote Leopold to his wife on 14 November 1772.

And I am to write and tell him whether there is an opening here? That is most difficult! If he were here during the first few days of December, there would be some hope of his being asked to accompany an aria in the opera. But, once they are written, it is too late ... It is not so easy to give a public concert here and it is scarcely any use attempting to do so without special patronage, while even then one is sometimes swindled out of one's profits. Apart from this he would lose nothing and he could live with us and would therefore have no expenses for light and wood. I hear that M. Baudace, the Frenchman, will soon be here with his French horn. Basta! Leutgeb will not lose anything; but he will have to be here in good time if he wants to get work in the opera. So he ought to leave with the mail coach at the very beginning of December, so that he may arrive here in time; for the opera is to be produced on December 26th. What about his leave of absence?

Securing leave of absence from the Prince Archbishop was an abiding problem for Leopold.

The friendship was strong enough for Leopold to offer the horn player free lodging in Milan. Soon the whole family were involved in the Leutgeb's travel plans. Mozart, embroiled in the preparations for *Lucio Silla*, himself wrote two weeks later urging his mother and sister to 'tell Herr Leutgeb to take the plunge and come to Milan, for he will certainly make his mark here'.

Leutgeb dithered. Perhaps the Prince Archbishop was being obstructive. 'I am surprised that Leutgeb did not leave Salzburg sooner,' wrote Leopold on 9 January, 'if he really intended to do so.' Word must have reached them that he was on his way, because two weeks later Mozart declared himself 'vexed that Leutgeb left Salzburg too late to see a performance of my opera; and perhaps he will miss us too, unless we meet on the way'. 'Leutgeb has not yet reached Milan,' noted Leopold on 6 February. In fact he arrived later that day, and turned down the Mozarts' hospitality, unsurprisingly given how much Leopold complained in his letters to Anna Maria of shivering in their lodgings.

'Leutgeb arrived late one evening a week ago,' he wrote a week later,

> and on the following Sunday he came to call on us. I have not seen him for the last two days, for he is staying with the painter Martin Knoller, a good quarter of an hour from this house. He pays nothing for his lodging. So far he has arranged his affairs pretty well and he will make quite a fortune here, for he is extraordinarily popular. If the concert takes place which the courtiers want to arrange for him, I wager that he will get one hundred cigliati on the spot. The Archduke too wants to hear him.

However promising Leutgeb's prospects in Milan, Leopold's optimism proved unfounded. Later that year, back in Salzburg, he found himself lending Leutgeb a sum of money that was still unpaid ten years later.

By 1777 Leutgeb had evidently had enough of stagnating in liveried service. He departed for Vienna, where he took on the running of a cheese shop, presumably his father-in-law's. We do know the address, as a Viennese street directory of 1795 lists a

'Joseph Leutgeb' living at Alt-Lerchenfelder no.32. It was not central. In a letter written five years later Constanze Mozart refers to Leutgeb living 'in an outermost suburb'. It is not clear whether he bought the cheesemonger's outright with Leopold Mozart's loan, or inherited it from his wife's family. It was the disappointed moneylender in Leopold who denounced the shop as 'the size of a snail's shell'. By this time Mozart was in Mannheim, on his way to Paris, with his mother fatefully in tow. '[Leutgeb] wrote to us both after your departure,' wrote Leopold to his son, 'promised to pay me in due course, and asked you for a concerto. But he must know that you are no longer in Salzburg.'

The cheesemonger who asked for a concerto clearly had no intention of renouncing the horn. But it must have been difficult to find a footing in the city of his birth. Martin Rupp, who failed to extract a pay rise out of Prince Esterházy, was one of several well-established horn players plying their trade in the city. Their monopoly on the court posts may explain why Leutgeb needed a tailor-made composition with which to advertise his abilities. However many times he asked, and it must have been more than once, he was obliged to wait until Mozart had brought his own combustible relationship with the Salzburg court to an abrupt terminus. The composer defected four years after Leutgeb. Summoned to Vienna in 1781 to take his place among the prince archbishop's travelling entourage, he baulked at eating with servants and wearing livery, and dismissed himself from service.

Leutgeb met Mozart on the day of his arrival in the city, 16 March. 'Met my old friend Leitgeb on the first day,' he wrote to his father. He will have been thrilled to see a familiar face. Leutgeb must have reminded him of his request for a concerto in that encounter because the surviving manuscript for the Concert Rondo for horn and orchestra is dated 21 March 1781. It was never completed. But Leutgeb and his family stayed in close contact with Mozart. 'Mon trés cher Pére! [*sic*]' Mozart wrote a year later. 'I am sorry that I found out only yesterday that Herr Leitgeb's son was travelling by mail coach to Salzburg; I would have had a great opportunity to send you a lot of things without cost.' While Leutgeb's son waited, he completed the letter and handed over some music, a snuffbox, some watch ribbons and two fashionable Viennese caps for Nannerl, made by Mozart's new bride, Constanze, who even as he wrote added a small crucifix to the bundle. The young Leutgeb stood by as Mozart appealed to his father to render yet more assistance. 'I really recommend the lad to you, my dear father. His father would like to get him into a business house or into the Salzburg printing firm. Please lend him a helping hand.' Leopold may well have tried to help the boy. Having done Leutgeb this favour, it would explain why the creditor attempted to call in his debt again. Two months later Mozart was once more pleading on Leutgeb's behalf. 'Mon trés cher pére!' he wrote on 17 May. 'Please be patient a little longer with poor Leitgeb; if you knew his circumstances and could see how he has to muddle through, I'm sure you would feel sorry for him. I shall have a talk with him, and I know for sure he'll pay you back, little by little.' The circumstances were no doubt pecuniary. There were at least three children, one of them evidently without work, and the entire family was supported by the proceeds of a tiny cheese shop and such horn work as percolated down to Leutgeb from the court. The issue of the loan may explain why the horn player is not mentioned again in Mozart's letters during the five remaining years of his father's life. But that year Leutgeb's circumstances took a turn for the better. He is listed among the personnel of the Hofmusik and National Theatre in the 1782 Theater-Almanach. And Mozart completed his first composition for horn.

Leutgeb was not just a family friend. Mozart must have felt a kindred spirit with a fellow maverick who like him had dared to spurn the continuing patronage of the loathsome Prince Archbishop. That would have counted for nothing if he had not also had great respect for Leutgeb's virtuosity. It was Leutgeb who had singular success with a new horn-playing technique. By placing the right hand in the bell and partly or wholly closing the aperture, it was possible to bend the note downwards by a half or a whole tone, thus extending the range of notes outside the restrictive harmonic series. The technique had been discovered as far back as the 1720s, but was officially codified only in the middle of the century by a Dresden horn player called Anton Hampl. Hampl's other great contribution to the instrument was to give instruction to the young Punto (or Stich as he was known before he escaped from service). The new technique required dexterity of hand and mind, and Leutgeb evidently possessed these in abundance. The exquisite quintet for horn and strings (K407) which Mozart wrote for Leutgeb towards the end of 1782 was without question the most challenging composition yet written for the horn. Leutgeb was equal to it. Mozart referred to the new work as 'das Leit-gebische'. Why a quintet rather than a concerto? Having already abandoned two horn concertos, perhaps Mozart thought he could best assist Leutgeb by writing a piece he knew he could finish. In any event, he had found a soloist for whom he would compose more than for any other.

Within half a year Mozart was inscribing across the autograph score of his first completed concerto for horn and orchestra, '*Wolfgang Amadè Mozart hat sich über den Leitgeb, Esel, Ochs, und Narr erbarmt zu Wien den 27 Maij 1783*' – Wolfgang Amadeus Mozart took pity on Leitgeb, ass, ox and fool, on 27 May 1783. At the top of the score he added, in case the point had not been made, 'Leitgeb Esel' in red crayon. The abusive epithets were terms of crude Austrian endearment. In taking pity on Leutgeb, Mozart meant that he was finally consenting to write the concerto first requested six years earlier.

For the ass Leutgeb, at a time of gathering productivity, Mozart would write two more complete concertos in the next four years. Sadly there is no record of when or where any of Mozart's com-positions for horn may have been first performed. Only in recent years has research established the probable order of the various concertos and fragments of concertos that Mozart composed, or began composing, for Leutgeb. That first concerto, K417, is officially known as his second. Mozart started and failed to finish another some time in 1785 or 1786. On 26 June 1786 he made an entry in a private index of compositions (which he began keeping in 1784) for a completed horn concerto. Known by its catalogue number as K495, the so-called fourth horn concerto was therefore actually his second. The third, K447, seems to be the only correctly numbered concerto in the sequence. Mozart makes no reference to it in his index, so the concerto was always presumed to pre-date it, but scholarly analysis has pinned it down to 1787, if only because it was written on the same paper used for *Don Giovanni*. If so, he wrote it around the time of Leopold's death.

Perhaps the older Leutgeb was a sort of father substitute. But Mozart also seems to have reserved his most playful humour for his horn player. The manuscript of K495, for example, was written in four differently coloured inks: black, blue and a sprightly red and green. It is contested by the more po-faced academics that Mozart used colour-coding to denote the dynamic shading of the piece, but this doesn't explain why he used it only on Leutgeb. Nor why over one particularly difficult passage (in blue ink) Mozart addressed his maestro directly: 'What do you say to that Master Leitgeb?' It seems far more likely that Leutgeb simply brought out the frivolity in Mozart unlike anyone else. This is substantially reflected in the wit and vivacity of the music he wrote for him. A month after completing the second concerto for Leutgeb, Mozart dashed off a set of twelve horn duets. '*Di Wolf-gang Amade Mozart*,' he scribbled on the manuscript, '*mp. Wien den 27 Jullius 1786 untern Kegelscheiben*'. While playing skittles. Leutgeb's presence in the bowling alley can be presumed.

Sometimes, as ever with Mozart, the frivolity went too far. One or two pranks suggest an insolent disregard for the dignity of the older man, and lend credence to the school of thought that Leutgeb was little more than a simpleton. 'Whenever he composed a solo for him,' wrote Mozart's first great biographer, Otto Jahn, 'Leutgeb was obliged to submit to some mock penance. Once, for instance, Mozart threw all the parts of his concertos and symphonies about the room, and Leutgeb had to collect them on all fours and put them in order; as long as this lasted Mozart sat at his writing-table composing. Another time, Leutgeb had to kneel down behind the stove while Mozart wrote.' The portrait of an eminent horn player grovelling in the corner of Mozart's apartment must be treated with circumspection. The five volumes of Jahn's *Biographie Mozarts* were published in instalments between 1856 and 1859, more than sixty-five years after Mozart's death. His source for this story was the librettist and musical archivist Joseph Sonnleithner, who was born in 1776, died in 1835, and therefore must have come across this story at second or more probably third hand. (Sonnleithner is also the source for a suggestion that Leutgeb died in good circumstances, which is certainly not true.)

It seems impossible that these japes – even if they happened as reported – were not underscored by affection. That Mozart was sensitive to Leutgeb's growing frailty is evident from the music he continued to compose for him. From parchment analysis, the two movements of the unfinished 'first' horn concerto are now known to have been written in 1791, when Leutgeb was approaching his sixtieth year. The music itself supports the finding. Mozart was aware that the virtuoso for whom he'd written the quintet nine years earlier didn't quite have the stamina for such pyrotechnics any more, and so he kept the concerto in a narrow range of just over an octave. It was also in the key of D, helpfully a semitone lower than the earlier compositions. On the autograph score Mozart has even scratched out some notes towards the bottom of the range. And although this is the only autograph manuscript of the four horn concertos in which the word 'Leitgeb' does not appear, there is no room for doubt that he was the intended soloist. The private joshing between composer and horn player continues – this time in Italian, which Leutgeb presumably understood from his visit to Milan. Mozart writes '*Adagio*' where the piece is clearly an allegro, and across the top of the music maintains a running commentary for Leutgeb's consumption.

A lei Signor Asino – Animo – presto – sù via – da bravo – coraggio – e finisci già – bestia – o che stonatura – Ahi! – ohimè – bravo poveretto! – Oh seccatura di coglioni! – ah che mi fai ridere! – ajuto – respira un poco! – avanti, avanti! – questo poi va al meglio – e non finisci nemmeno? – ah porco infame! Oh come si grazioso! – Canino! Asinino! hahaha – respire! Ma intone almeno una, cazzo! – bravo, evviva! – e vieni a seccarmi per la quarta, e Dio sia benedetto per l'ultima volta – ah termina, ti prego! Ah maledetto – anche bravura? bravo – ah! trillo di pecore – finisci? grazie al ciel! – basta, basta!

Mozart's relish of foreign swear words is palpable. The ribaldry of his intentions doesn't quite come across in a literal translation of *cazzo* (cock), *porco* (pig) and *coglioni* (balls). Mozart scholars have traditionally been shy of the sheer saltiness of the language. 'Over to you, Signor Ass, take heart – quick – on your way – that's fine – courage – it will soon be over [at the conclusion of the opening statement] – idiot! – Oh! how out of tune! – ouch – alas [at a recurring F sharp] – good work, you poor lad – oh what a fucking pain in the arse! [as the theme recurs] – ah how you make me laugh! – help [at a repeated E flat] – take a short breath [at a pause] – forward – forward! After this bit it'll improve [when the theme once again reappears] – And you can't even bring it to a close? – Oh for fuck's sake! Oh, how delightful you are! – Gorgeous! You little ass! – Breathe! Well, can't you hit at least one note, for fuck's sake? [at a repeated C sharp]. Well done, terrific, go for it! – so here you come to piss me off for the fourth time [at the fourth repeat of the theme] – and God be praised for the last time – oh get it over with, for God's sake! Oh you wretch – you're clever too? [at a short run] – well done – ah! a trill like a bleating sheep – here's the end – Thank heavens! enough, enough!'

Mozart's first English biographer Edward Holmes, whose life was published in London in 1845, was not alone in declining to translate most of these bestialities. But he could see the point of them. 'As all these expressions were faithfully given by the copyist, in writing out the part for performance, the ludicrous effect of such a commentary read by the player, on the execution of each passage, as it occurred, may be well conceived.' All horn players split notes. Mozart was trying to split Leutgeb's sides.

For all his declining powers as a horn player, Leutgeb lived another two decades. Mozart would not see out the year. Like the *Requiem* he left unfinished, K412 would have to be patched together by his student Süssmayr. For much of 1791 Constanze was away in nearby Baden, recovering after her latest confinement. As her husband unwittingly approached his own death, the constant presence in the letters Mozart wrote to her in the last months is his horn player. Mozart couldn't bear to be on his own and frequently stayed with the Leutgebs at Alt-Lerchenfelder no.32. '*Ma trés chére Epouse!*' he wrote on 6 June. '*J'écris cette lettre dans la petite Chambre au Jardin chez Leitgeb ou j'ai couché cette Nuit excellement* ... Madame Leitgeb helped me put on my necktie today; but how! – dear god! – all the while she was helping me, I kept saying: no. she does it this way! – but to no avail.' So the cheese shop boasted a small garden. At some point Mozart took Leutgeb to see *Die Zauberflöte*. In a letter dated 8 and 9 October, Mozart describes going to see it again with Leutgeb, who 'has asked me to take him a second time, and I did'. It seems unarguable that it was his friend's presence in the audience that persuaded the composer to steal backstage and play the Glockenspiel from the wings out of time with the singer playing Papageno onstage. 'Everybody laughed,' he reported. Did anybody laugh louder than Leutgeb?

On 14 October Mozart wrote his last surviving letter. 'Leitgeb and Hofer are here with me right now; – the former will stay and eat with me.' In short, in the final sighting he gives us of himself, Mozart and his horn player are alone together, breaking bread. Mozart died on 5 December. It was Leutgeb who helped the newly widowed Constanze sort out his affairs. He'd had practice, after all. Perhaps, as he shuffled sheets of unfinished music, he could hear Mozart cackling from beyond the grave, ordering him once again to put his papers in order.

Leutgeb retired from playing the following year, presumably after performing the final concerto. But he was still assisting Constanze several years later while she corresponded with Johann Anton André, to whom she granted the right to publish the Mozart archive in her possession. She wrote to the publisher on the last day of May 1800 (it was in this letter that she referred to Leutgeb's home in the suburbs). In a round-up of uncompleted manuscripts both in and out of her possession, she listed a 'Rondo for the horn with jocose inscription. Leitgeb has promised to give me a copy. Nothing of this published, I believe. 12. Rondo for horn with orchestra accompaniment that Leitgeb doesn't know, and he assumes that it isn't fully orchestrated. 14. sketch of a first allegro Leitgeb thinks the same. 15. sketch of a horn concerto also.

Leitgeb doesn't have a copy of anything other than a quintet in D sharp for solo horn, violin, first viola, second viola, violoncello, which you probably have in the original.' Constanze is referring to the quintet in E flat known as 'das Leitgebische'. The Rondo that Leutgeb didn't know about is assumed to be the fragment Mozart started five days after seeing the horn player the day he arrived in Vienna in 1781. It seems highly improbable that Mozart intended it for a different horn player. Either the composer never showed the uncompleted sketch to him, or eighteen years on, the sixty-eight-year-old Leutgeb had simply forgotten about it.

He died in his home on 27 February 1811 at the age of seventy-eight, leaving debts amounting to 1,286 gulden. But there is one last intriguing glimpse of Mozart's horn player. In the only surviving instance of his handwriting, Leutgeb made an addendum to his last will and testament. The Austrian dialect is rough and earthy, as are the sentiments. He goes back on a promise to bequeath a golden clock to his daughter – a previous letter to her on this matter, he says, is *'nula and nichtz'*. The daughter, called Ursula and married to a Herr Pachinger, was presumably the younger sister of the infant christened Anna Maria Catharina in 1762 who could claim Haydn's wife as a godmother. He instructs his widow to sell the clock and give the proceeds to the children of Ernst. Ernst was the Leutgebs' deceased son. Another son, Friedrich ('Fridarich'), is to inherit his father's clothes. His widow is told not to hand them all over at once, but dole them out piecemeal, every six or twelve months. Perhaps Friedrich could not be trusted not to sell them. Either Ernst or Friedrich would have been the young postman who waited to catch the Salzburg coach while the newly married Mozart completed a letter to his father in 1782. Had Leutgeb quarrelled with Ursula? Or did he change his mind about the clock because Ernst had died only recently, and left three mouths to feed? Certainly he takes pity on the three children (*'die trei Könda ... daß seen armenarn'*). 'They are poor fools.' Fools. *Narren.* For three fatherless dependants he uses the same term of affection which Mozart once (and possibly often) used for him.

*

One day I took my usual short cut through Covent Garden and Paxmans had gone. The provocative window display had shut up shop. It fell victim, I discover, to market forces which in the same period drove the more traditional peep shows out of the back alleys of Soho. The landlords swooped, the rents went through the roof, and Paxmans was expelled south of the river. Seeing the window, shorn of its horns, was a bit like hearing about a death in someone else's family. You only found out after, and wouldn't necessarily have gone to the funeral. But still ... And I'd not yet got round to peeping inside.

Paxmans has relocated to a basement of a light-bricked Victorian block in Southwark. 'Paxmans Musical Instruments,' says the street sign hanging outside, although this is a misnomer. You won't find any pianofortes in here, no recorders or even trumpets. Paxmans is a commercial curio, a business devoted entirely to the sale of French horns, French horn recordings, French horn sheet music (solo, duet, trio, quartet, ensemble and orchestral) and all manner of French horn paraphernalia and miscellanea – one-piece mouthpieces, two-piece mouthpieces, mouthpiece pouches, mouthpiece brushes, fixed-bell cases, detachable-bell cases, mute bags, stopping mutes, practice mutes, straight non-transposing mutes, conical tuneable mutes, valve cord, valve springs, valve stops, valve oil, rotor oil, bearing oil, linkage oil, unibal oil, slide wax, slide grease, pull-throughs, microfibre polishing cloths, leather hand-guards, horn sticks, duck's feet, tone blobs. Etc. Etc. I have no idea what most of these things are.

At least in Europe, Paxmans is a neophyte among existing horn manufacturers. Gebrüder Alexander of Mainz opened for business in 1782, the year after Mozart settled in Vienna. Kruspe was established in Erfurt in 1834, a year after the birth of Brahms, and patented the double horn in 1897, the year of his death. Even Josef Lídl was up and running by the end of the nineteenth century, and produced their first horn in 1923. Paxmans turned their hand to French horns at the end of the Second World War.

In the new premises, the window display is no more. There is a window, but it runs along the pavement at ankle-height. I have to ring the bell to be let in, and descend a clanging metal staircase onto the shop floor. Inside, in the well of the shop, is an Aladdin's cave of horns, a cornucopia. A whole alcove under the window is covered in them. There must be forty. To the untrained eye they will look more or less identical, give or take the odd variation in colour – yellow brass, gold brass, silver nickel. To the trained eye, every conceivable incarnation of horn is here – singles, doubles, triples, compensating doubles, compensating triples, descants; spanking new, second-hand, collectors' items. The lion's share of the new horns are Paxmans, but this is also the official British outlet for Alexander, and every other make under the sun is also on sale. You can get your Conns here and Yamahas, your Hans Hoyers and second-hand Geyers. The one make they still don't seem to stock is Josef Lídl.

They also fix horns at Paxmans. There is a roaring trade in the repair end of things. Horns, like top athletes, like thoroughbred horses, like the more temperamental Italian motor cars, need constant monitoring for twinges, glitches, viruses, signs of strain and stress, *Sturm und Drang*. They are exceptionally prone. There's a reason why the leading violinists play on instruments made in the late seventeenth century and horn players play on instruments made in the late twentieth century. And it's not just the advance of technology. Horns break down. They get metal fatigue. They also fall off chairs. In the chat rooms the hottest topic is always horn maintenance. The DIY guys talk querulously to one another across cyberspace about leaks, rotors, lead-pipes, wraps, lacquers. (They're mostly Americans.) They'll strip an instrument down for the pleasure of putting it back together. Q. How many horn players does it take to change a light bulb? Answer A. Just one, but he'll spend two hours checking the bulb for alignment and leaks. Answer B: 100. One to change it, and 99 others to say how much better they could have done it.

I cast an eye down the shopping list of repair and refit options. The Paxmans prices are peculiarly exact. 'Strip, polish and re-lacquer a double horn (does not include dent removal or other repair work)' at £496.25 would seem an extravagance for a horn which once upon a time cost only £3.75 more than that when new. 'Conversion from fixed bell to screw-bell (does not include case)', retailing at £321.72, would be like converting a Lada into a soft-top. Pointless. 'Fit adjustable hand-rest: £46.25' and 'fit adjustable finger-hook: £30.63'? No thanks. I'm intrigued by the 'valve service', possibly a bit steep at £127.50, and the 'pump-through' at an affordable £34.05. I could swear these services are also available in most leading red-light districts. My eye is caught by 'Fit water-key: £28.74'. Hmm. Tempting. But on reflection, a bit late now. Better the spit routine you know after all these years.

'I've got a problem with my horn,' I tell a tall thin young man in a dark blue overall, who like everyone here is a trained horn player himself. He's called Luke. 'It's buzzing. I'm getting this humming, vibrating noise when I practise. Mostly when I play an A flat or a C sharp.'

'Third valve,' says Luke.

'Oh,' I say. 'Oh yes.' I hadn't thought of that. To play A flat or, on the B flat horn, a C sharp, you press down the second and third valves.

'Shall I have a look?'

'It's a Lidl,' I warn him.

I unclip the hard heavy wooden case and hand the horn over. He turns it over in his hands, looking intently at the morass of tubing. In about six seconds I have my diagnosis.

'You've got loose stays. Here, look.' He points to two contiguous areas of tubing. Normally they are glued in place by a two-sided brace, but on one side the tube is detached.

'That's the cause of your buzzing. And there's another bracket loose here.'

I look. So there is. A thin metal arm held across one of the slides is unstuck at one end. It quivers every time I play the instrument.

'Come through to the workshop.'

I'm led down a short corridor into a windowless room. It looks like any other workshop. A large work table in the middle, with workbenches along the walls. Every work surface is covered in tools, tubs, cloths, rags. The French horns look incongruous among all this tool-shed junk, vulnerable even. There is a quantity of them in various states of disrepair, various stages of disassembly.

Luke puts the Lídl into the jaws of a vice and gently clamps it upright.

'Do you want me to re-string your valves too?' ('Re-string valves': £11.48.)

'Er, I don't know. Do I? The valves seem fine to me. Maybe the first one's a bit stiff now and then.'

'How long have you had this horn?'

'Twenty-five years?'

'And when did you last get the valves re-strung?'

'Erm . . . never.'

'And do you want me to get rid of the dents?'

This is getting humiliating. I know about one dent on the bell. It has always struck me as a war wound, a battle scar, the limp of a distinguished veteran. I rather like it. But Luke points out more dents in the tubing.

'I don't know. Do they make any difference to the sound?'

'They do.'

I leave the Lídl with him. Three days later I return to fetch it. Luke unclips the case and hands me the horn. It looks subtly different. I put the mouthpiece in and tentatively blow an arpeggio. No buzzing. Then a scale. No buzzing. The re-strung valves are working a treat.

'Sounds great,' I say. 'Feels great.' I'm in such a good mood I decide to bash out a bit of K447. I settle for the Rondo. Always a tricky moment, this. Playing cold in front of someone else. Naturally I fall at the first hurdle. We are both embarrassed. Luke knows of my ambition to play to the British Horn Society festival. He looks at his shoes.

'I haven't warmed up,' I say.

'Of course.'

I clip the Lídl back into its case and ask for the bill. It comes to £63.27, which strikes me as a bargain for a twenty-five-year overhaul.

'Have you ever considered buying a new horn?' says Luke. I turn to face him.

'Should I?'

'Look, you're going to carry on having problems with your horn. It's not very well made. You'll be throwing good money after bad.' I look around the shop floor. Horns gleam from every wall. They look jolly tempting. The devil gets in me.

'Can I play your most expensive horn?'

He walks across the floor, reaches up for a gold brass instrument and hands it over.

'It's a Paxman triple.' Which explains the weight. I retrieve my mouthpiece, plug it in and blow an arpeggio, a scale, and then the opening bars of the Rondo. It's like exchanging a Lada for a Bentley. You can feel the effortless heft of it, the suave precision-tooled importance. It's a whole new world.

'How much would this set me back?'

'£5,000.' It's nothing. The more expensive violins cost a hundred times as much. Still, a bit too steep for me.

'My concert,' I stutter. 'I have to do it on the Lidl.'

'Of course.' In the brief silence, perhaps he's wondering why on earth I want to give myself such a huge handicap. I know it's what I'm wondering.

'You could always sell your Lidl, you know.'

'Really?'

'On eBay. Someone's bound to buy it.' It's something to think about.

'And how much could I hope to . . . Is it worth anything?'

'You could get, I don't know . . .' I could get what? Is it possible that this instrument which has rapidly become a laughing stock of the horn world could have any intrinsic, residual *value*? As I wait for his considered opinion on the matter, I feel like one of those Middle Englanders who take their antiques to be inspected by tweedy experts on television. Greed flutters hopefully somewhere in the core of my being.

'About £500?' Five hundred quid! It's scarcely credible. If you disregard the vagaries of inflation, Britain's entry into the exchange rate mechanism, the Big Bang, Black Wednesday, the monetary fall-out from our refusal to join the Euro, and various other macro-economic factors that have in the intervening period governed the fluctuating fortunes of the pound sterling, my horn, having spent the better part of its life in one attic or another, is worth exactly the same amount as it was when my father bought it at Boosey & Hawkes a quarter of a century ago. There's some sort of moral in this, some message, though I'm not sure what. When it comes to money, even more than horn playing, I am ox, ass and fool.

6
Hold It Like a Man!

Madame Adélaïde, in particular, had a most insatiable desire to learn; she was taught to play upon all instruments, from the horn (will it be believed!) to the Jew's-harp.
Madame Campan: *Mémoires sur la vie privée de Marie Antoinette*

Horn camp. I've done the jokes already. 'Horn' is a word rich in opportunities for double entendre. So is 'camp'. Put them together and what have you got? An annual course for horn players, actually, in an idyllic lakeside setting in the bosom of New Hampshire.

I get the idea wandering around the internet. Lessons with Dave Lee are going well. With his hand on the tiller, I have managed to navigate a path from 'terrible' to 'tolerable'. But it's slow work. Dave's busy, I'm busy. I practise like crazy. I wrestle with K447, Mozart's third horn concerto, on a daily, an hourly basis. I hum it, sing it, whistle it, play it, mangle it, mostly at home, but sometimes I take the Lidl into town and ride the clanking lift up to the fifth-floor bombsite at the top of the theatre where the Andrew Lloyd Webber musical is still running. The

New Person In My Life says she can hear Mozart wafting high over Shaftesbury Avenue.

'He's taken up the French horn again,' she explains to people in the building.

'Is that the bloke,' asks one wag, 'who looks like he's just been punched in the mouth?'

I take to collaring pianists I know and forcing them to play through the concerto with me. The New Person's mother, who is very fierce, is one volunteer. My conductor pal is another; his wife puts a plastic bucket down in their front room for me to empty my spit into. It's mainly faltering experiences of hooking up the horn part with the orchestral accompaniment that bring it home. I require help. The British Horn Society festival is some way off on the other side of summer, but if I'm to be remotely up to snuff, I am going to need some form of intensive coaching; some shock therapy. Then one day while surfing all the usual horn websites I stumble on a link to something called KBHC. I click, and there it is: the Kendall Betts Horn Camp. It looks perfect. That idyllic lakeside setting, log cabins, greenery, the best professors of horn in the whole of America. And to top it all they've got Hermann Baumann.

Dave is right behind the idea.

'Oh good,' he says at the end of one of our sessions. 'Good. Be a laugh, that.'

'At the end of the week they let you perform to everyone else,' I say. 'I thought it would be good practice.'

'Course. And it'll be good to get the thoughts of other horn players. Instead of just listening to me.'

'Yeah,' I say. 'They've got Hermann Baumann.'

'Hermann the German?' says Dave. 'They can't have.'

'Why not? He's on the website. It says "masterclasses with Hermann Baumann".'

'Well I'll surprised if he turns up.'

'Why?'

'He'll make medical history if he does.'

'How?'

'Cos he's dead!'

'Oh.' Beat. 'Is he? Are you sure, Dave?'

'Yeah, Hermann Baumann had a massive heart attack a few years ago.'

I don't like to doubt Dave's wisdom in horn-related matters. But it seems odd that KBHC has booked a dead man as a visiting maestro. I type the words 'Hermann Baumann + died' into a search engine. Macabre, yes, but the conundrum needs sorting. And there is nothing. Not a single site comes up. According to Google, Hermann Baumann is not in the least bit dead. Dave is exultant when I call him.

'That's wonderful news!' he says. 'Best news I've had all week. Fantastic!'

And we go out for a drink to celebrate the fact that the most eminent European soloist of the last forty years is alive and well and waiting in New Hampshire.

A week before heading for America, I bump into Hugh Seenan, the man who will decide whether or not I perform my solo at the British Horn Society festival. The London Symphony Orchestra is doing Strauss's *Eine Alpensinfonie* one Saturday night. It calls for twenty horn players: eight onstage, twelve off. Other composers have written parts for offstage horn: Mozart, Mahler, Shostakovich, Britten, most notably Wagner with the horn call in *Siegfried*, mimed by the singer playing Siegfried onstage and blown heroically by a horn player in the wings. But the *Alpine Symphony* is the big one. It's a short night's work – the offstage horns are blowing for less than a minute – and therefore popular with freelance pros who fancy getting home, or to the pub, earlier than usual. Horns have been called in from all over town: the opera houses, the other symphony orchestras, the music colleges, the West End. Dave is one of them. He's leased out his desk in the Andrew Lloyd Webber musical for the night.

'You should see this,' he says. 'It's quite a sight.'

In the concrete bowels of the Barbican Centre, I watch an orchestra mustering. My chums from the LSO horn section are all here in their white ties and tails. David 'Positive Visualisation' Pyatt, John 'Run Up The Stairs To Simulate Pre-Performance

Adrenalin' Ryan, Jonathan 'Don't Miss the D' Lipton. For one night only, there are almost as many horn players as violinists. And one of them, unmistakable in bib and tucker, grizzled mane framing an aquiline face, is Hugh Seenan.

It's been a month since I wrote to the chairman of the British Horn Society asking to be allowed to perform in the festival. I haven't had a verdict yet. Here is an unexpected chance to butter him up. Even though I've already met him, I get Dave to introduce me. Dave and Hugh Seenan go back years.

'We met in Southampton,' I tell Hugh, proffering a hand. He's heading towards the bottleneck of musicians queuing to get onstage through the pass door.

'Of course we did. I remember.' Hugh Seenan looks puzzled, distracted. I am out of context. And he is about to clamber up a veritable Alp of the horn repertoire. I give him a better coordinate to lock on to.

'I'm the one who took up the horn last year? I recently wrote to you about playing at this year's festival?' I note the rising inflections in my voice. Jesus, I can hear myself turning into an Australian. I'm not expecting him to give me the nod here and now. No doubt there are protocols and procedures to observe. But I am kind of expecting a more encouraging response than the one I get. Or at least a less enigmatic one.

'You must be mad!' says Hugh Seenan over his shoulder as he follows the orchestral tide flowing towards the concert hall. Do I detect a cackle? I have been around the horn world enough to recognise this as an entry-level horn joke, a variation on the old bumper-sticker riff: 'You don't *have* to be mad to work here ...' Perhaps I should be flattered. Perhaps this is the chairman's way of welcoming me into the worshipful guild of masochists, obsessives and dangerous sports enthusiasts known to the rest of the orchestra as the French horn section. Alternatively, he may just be heading me off at the pass door.

But there isn't time to dwell on this. The LSO, and Hugh Seenan with it, have sallied forth into the public space. Under the low ceiling of the waiting area, only twelve horn players remain (plus, as stipulated by Strauss, two trumpeters and two trombonists), and one very small hunched white-haired figure, who is holding a baton. He shuffles in tiny steps towards the applause waiting for him on the other side of the door. I have to do a double take before I realise that this tiny man is André Previn, famous in this country less for inheriting Frank Sinatra's ex-wife than for being a good sport on *The Morecambe and Wise Christmas Show* at the height of his fame in the 1970s. His destination is the conductor's podium, visible on a large wall-mounted monitor. It takes him an unconscionable time to disappear through the door and reappear on the screen. By the time he does, the horn players (plus additional brass) have gathered in three rows in front of ten or so music stands. Unlike Previn and the LSO, they are dressed in regulation mufti – jeans, shorts, T-shirts, trainers, flip-flops. All but one of them is male. Dave, who has come along in a stripey blazer, seems to be organising them while on the other side of the thick sound-proofed door, the *Alpine Symphony* heaves sepulchrally into life.

Strauss composed the last of his tone poems between 1911 and 1915, inspired to describe in sound a typical day in the mountains near his home in the Bavarian Alps. He doesn't keep the offstage horns waiting for long. The first segment, 'Night', glowers moodily for three and a half minutes, welling up into the brilliant ninety-second fanfare of 'Sunrise'. And then we're straight into 'The Ascent'. After a minute and a half of rising and clambering, the movement reaches some sort of plateau, and in comes the distant chorus of twelve horns (plus two trumpets and two trombones). They conjure up the noise of a passing hunt, galloping joyously in the distance.

At least that's how it will sound to the audience seated plushly in the concert hall, to André Previn, waving a baton only a few yards away on the other side of the pass door. But not if you're standing more or less in the midst of the twelve horns. I'm just behind Dave, who is on first horn, and I'm practically lifted off my feet by a detonation of harmony, an eruption of calls and echoes. This is the sound, I realise, that could have tested the very walls of Jericho, and yet it's indescribably beautiful. I don't think I've ever heard anything quite so overwhelming in my life.

And it's all over in forty-five seconds. Or almost all. After 'The Ascent', the symphony 'Enters the Forest' with a violent surge from the orchestra. It's at this point, cushioned by the door and the wall of noise onstage, that a tradition in horn lore is religiously observed. In the sudden crescendo, the entire offstage horn section lower their instruments and roar at the top of their voices. To the uninitiated – in this case me – it sounds like an act of sonic vandalism.

'We can't be heard onstage,' explains Dave as he hurriedly packs away his horn after, *pro rata*, the best night's pay available to any orchestral musician anywhere. 'Not with all that din.'

It's yet another way in which horn players demonstrate their separateness from the rest of the instrumental community. That separateness is written right there in the score: two trumpets, two trombones, *twelve* horns offstage. No other instrument is so frequently exiled to the wings by the composer. It's the genetic remnant of an earlier exile in forest and field, when all the other instruments were allowed to play indoors. But in addition to this physical symbol of their difference, horn players like to ring-fence themselves in rituals, each designed to make the business of living with such a treacherous mistress that little bit more bearable. This is one of them.

Another, at least in the United Kingdom, is to lead the charge to the pub after the performance. Which we now do.

When I get out of the car at Camp Ogontz, deep in the heart of New Hampshire, it's as if I've stepped back into the *Alpine Symphony*. The womanly contours of the local uplands, the Adirondacks, are hardly as epic as Bavaria, but there's a lot of nature around – a silver lake, a babbling brook, an enveloping forest. And the sound of offstage horns is everywhere. The woods reverberate to them, disembodied, calling and answering across the open glades of the camp. Overhead, a warm sun tilts towards the horizon. Unless I'm very much mistaken, I seem to have died and gone to horn heaven.

The only difference is that once you get into paradise, the

auditioning is over. On arrival in horn camp, the first thing I'm told I have to do is go see Kendall.

'He just wants to get a feel for the level you're at,' they tell me at reception. 'He's right up those steps. But before you do, you need to sign up for a chore.' There's a sheet of A4 along the counter. I look down the list. The choices are mostly in the kitchen or dining room: chopping/laying/washing/drying for breakfast/ lunch/dinner. There is also a 'latrines' option. It occurs to me that if I sign up for toilet duty, then anything else that happens to me in horn camp will be a step up. Including performing Mozart 3. Someone has already had the same idea, because he has put his name down. Jeremy Thal, he's written. He's the only one. Briefly I consider joining him on the dotted line, but there are limits to my masochism. I plump for 'after dinner dishes' and head on up the steps to Kendall's cabin.

Outside on the porch, smashed-up horns hang on the posts holding up the roof. One of them is actually squashed flat. The French horn is evidently not subject to unwavering reverence here at KBHC. I knock on the door. It is opened by a short, blinking man with a high forehead and glasses who looks like a cartoon version of himself.

'How're you doing?' says Kendall Betts. 'I'm real glad you made it.'

Kendall, who was principal horn of the Minnesota Symphony for many years, is the only horn player I come across who somehow seems to have missed out on a career in stand-up. He sounds funny, he looks funny; later in the week he even plays funny. But at this particular juncture he is maybe a tad too serious for my liking.

'I just need to see what you can do so I know what sort of level you're at.' After fifteen hours of travel I'm hot, sticky and knackered, and can't do a whole lot. I release the Lídl from its case after its maiden flight, spew out a scale, an arpeggio and a few notes of the Romanze. It's long past midnight my time, I haven't warmed up, but still I am shocked at how bad the Lídl and I sound.

'Sorry, I don't know what . . .' I stammer. 'It's been a long day.'

'What are you aiming to achieve in the week?' asks Kendall.

'I need performance practice,' I tell him. 'I need to play in the concert at the end of the week.'

'I'm not sure that's a good idea,' he warns.

'Oh. Really?'

'If you crash and burn . . .' I'll be scarred for life? I've just spent somewhere north of fifteen hundred bucks to be here. I'd hate to see that go to waste.

'I'm prepared to take the risk.'

'Well if you want to play in the concert,' concludes Kendall, 'it is up to Hermann. If you're not ready for prime time you're just not going to play. We had incidents in the past when people made fools of themselves. You don't want that to happen, and we don't want to listen to it. Bite off what you can chew. When you play with a pianist Hermann will let you know if you're in over your head. It's called a reality check.'

If I wasn't scared before, I am now.

KBHC's catchment area is the entire American horn-playing community. It's open to all ages from high school kids to pensioners, who come to learn at the feet of *éminences grises* from right across the land of the free, from Wisconsin and Colorado, Iowa and Ohio, Pennsylvania and Massachusetts, New Mexico and of course New Hampshire. College students have flown or driven in from California, Maryland, Texas, Florida. A Canadian has been coming here for the eleven years KBHC has been running. There are just two intruders from the old continent: Hermann Baumann and me.

I am assigned a room in the 'hotel', so called thanks to the existence of walls to go with its low-slung roof. The kids are out in the huts on stilts named after the Adirondacks which instead of walls have roll-down net-cloths. Everyone has to share. When I get to my door, I find a card pinned to it with two names inscribed on it. The other name is Jeremy Thal.

From the far side of the door comes the muffled sound of a delicate horn. I knock. The door is opened by a young man with wild curly hair and silver-rimmed glasses. He is holding a slender instrument.

'Hi,' I say, 'Jeremy Thal, I presume.'

'Hey,' he says. 'You must be from England.'

The camp's self-appointed lavatory attendant is impressively dry, but even he can't quite mask his amazement that earlier that morning I woke up in London. I guess I owe him an explanation. Our room being the size of a railway compartment with couchettes for two, it's not as if we're going to have any other secrets. Right off the bat, I tell him about my quest.

'Sounds kinda cool.' Jeremy's response is temperate. 'What do you want to play for your performance?'

I clip open my horn case, extract from it the sheet music to K447 and place it on Jeremy's music stand. He gets up and peers knowingly at the music.

'My first triumph,' he says.

'How old were you?'

'Fourteen.'

This is becoming a familiar refrain. Almost every horn player I meet started off their performing life with a crack at Mozart 3. After all, it is the – cough – easy one.

'Mind if I have a go?'

'Be my guest.'

Jeremy picks up the horn lying on his bed and proceeds to skip through the first movement. Without the accompaniment it takes about four minutes. The sound he teases out of his horn is soft, deft, subtle. It seems in tune with the stream that trills and descants outside the window of our room. I go through a range of emotions, most of them negative.

'Man, I haven't played this in years,' he says.

'Sounding good,' I say brightly.

'OK if I play the third movement?'

Not really.

'Be my guest.'

Without the accompaniment it takes about two minutes. He completes it at a sophisticated canter.

'Wow.' I don't know what else to say. 'What is that horn anyway?'

'An Alex 103.' I guess I should have guessed.

'I play it louder on mine,' I volunteer. 'Maybe it's the horn.'

'Mind if I try?' I hand over the Lídl and he plays a phrase or two of the Rondo.

'Damn, it *is* louder! What *is* this thing?'

In our railway sleeper, Jeremy and I establish a rapport based on the topsy-turvy reality that while he is fourteen years behind me in age, he is about fourteen years ahead of me in ability. I sense a kindred spirit in a camp full of pros and aspiring pros. A gifted amateur, he's not quite sure where he's heading with the horn. He once threw himself into his horn studies with monomaniacal absorption, but slightly lost his forward momentum when he auditioned in front of Dale Clevenger for an orchestral position in Chicago. He ate bananas beforehand. As an antidote to performance anxiety, bananas have long been established in the music profession as a natural alternative to beta-blockers. Mostly people eat just one. Jeremy had three and, basically, overdosed.

'It was too many,' he says. 'I was *too* relaxed. Clevenger said, "I'm sorry, you made too many mistakes."'

I like him a lot.

It turns out that Hermann Baumann is a sort of Lazarus. He didn't start on the instrument till he was seventeen. After a career as a soloist that scaled all the heights, at the age of sixty he had a debilitating stroke that deprived him of speech and, for a while, his career. In small gradations he returned to playing and teaching, but areas of his memory remain erased. Over supper one evening I try to ask him about his life as a horn player and he looks back with something like affrontedness.

'After se stroke,' he says, '*ich habe alles vergessen!*' He's forgotten the lot.

And yet at seventy-two he looks freakishly young and robust. He has a full head of silver hair, the merest smidgin of a goatee, and a Puckish twinkle lightens a pair of penetrating blue eyes. It's scorching in New Hampshire, and he spends the week in shorts and sandals.

The schedule is so constructed that when you play for Hermann, it's the hottest part of the hot day. In the morning, as the sun torches a heavy deposit of dew on the camp's rolling lawns, you have two lessons with members of the KBHC faculty. Their premises are dotted around the camp: one's in a barn, another in a boathouse, another in a wood cabin, another in a lakeside beach hut. As you commute across the camp, in and out of wooded nooks, along the fringe of the lake, past groups of giggling college students, you feel like you're wandering around inside the imagination of a billionaire children's author. Instead of magic wands, we have horns.

I'm in a group with a retired engineer from New Jersey and a nun from Massachusetts. The classes offer a Babel of advice on everything – warming-up techniques, tuning, developing the lower register, developing the upper register, audition techniques, the psychology of performance preparation. We go away with a reading list that stretches from *Grand Theoretical & Practical Method for the Valve Horn* by Josef Schatt to *The Inner Game of Tennis* by W. Timothy Gallwey.

Midway through the morning we have a session with Kendall in his cabin. Kendall slumps in a high-backed armchair, while we array ourselves on sofas. My classmates, who are two of the most cordial people in the entire American continent, are not quite ready for Kendall. No concessions are made, for example, to the nun from Massachusetts. '"Mummy,"' goes Kendall's favourite joke, '"is it possible to get pregnant with anal sex?" "Why of course it is. How do you think conductors are born?"' I have my sharpest intake of breath all week when he tells that one. The talk in his class is almost exclusively about breathing, and the asininity of conductors. 'Without a good air stream,' he says on day one, 'you're not going to be much of a horn player. To my knowledge,' he adds, 'I'm the only person who teaches this any more.' The nun from Massachusetts, who is in a choir, mentions the breathing technique of singers. 'Don't tell me you're a singer!' he says. 'I'm not interested. The vocalisation of a singer ends here' – he points at his lips – 'Where does yours end? You've got another sixteen feet to work through! Find the sweet spot. If it feels like you're trying to take a crap, that's probably what it'll sound like.'

There's a lot more of this bar-room patter, every morning at the appointed hour. He's street-smart is Kendall. 'Who told you this is easy?' he says to the retired engineer on day three. 'Right, so stop thinking it is.' He's not one for pulling punches or mincing words. 'We are the true outcasts,' he says. 'Write that down.' This *pensée*, I sense, is lobbed in my direction. 'We are doing an old-fashioned thing that takes time. And it can't be done by machine. That's what I tell all these high school students.' We write it down on our lined A4 pads, supplied for just such a purpose. 'Horn playing,' he concludes on day six, 'can teach you a great deal of wisdom.'

But compared to Hermann Baumann, it's Kendall who's the nun. Hermann holds his daily masterclass after lunch every day from one to three in the long log-walled concert hall. This is where people come to audition for the concert. The first day I go up there just to case the joint, sniff the atmosphere. I leave my horn in the railway sleeper, out of temptation's way. Eight or ten people have already mustered. They mostly sit at the back of the hall. Up at the front, next to a piano and pianist, a girl plays Strauss 2 with consummate ease. Hermann sits under her nose in the front row and listens. Occasionally he'll get up and talk. It all seems eminently civilised. When the soloist finishes, people offer desultory applause, and then it's someone else's turn. Eventually it's the turn of a tall, Eeyorish man called Harry, who must be about eighty.

'Vas you are playing?' says Hermann. (Hermann's English is simple but effective. Oddly, it was English that came back to him before German after his stroke deprived him of speech.) Harry, it turns out, is going to play the Romanze. I feel my shoulders hunch in tension. What if he's good? What if my own rendition pales next to his? I wait nervously for him to start. Maybe it's the heat, more probably it's nerves, but whatever the reason, Harry proceeds to drive a ten-ton truck through the movement. I feel an ugly

TOP: Horn-playing youth, aged ten. I was not responsible for the trousers.
ABOVE: 'We are young, we are old': at thirty-nine I play the Hallelujah Chorus with the massed horns of the British Horn Society *(David Wise).*

TOP LEFT: The horn's early prototypes include the Roman cornu seen in bas-relief on Trajan's column *(Scala)*, and, ABOVE, the oliphant as blown aloft in Giotto's *Judas Kiss* in the Cappella Arena, Padua *(Bridgeman Art Library)*. TOP RIGHT: Vittorio Maria Bigari's *Draped Female Figure with a Horn* affords a rare eighteenth-century sighting of a female horn player *(Agnew's)*.

TOP LEFT: Meeting Barry Tuckwell at the pass door. TOP RIGHT: Corridor terror. ABOVE LEFT: Wrestling with Mozart in front of the British Horn Society, accompanied by my last horn teacher, Kevin Amos. ABOVE RIGHT: The End. *(Dillon Bryden)*

CLOCKWISE: Dennis Brain and his single B flat Alexander horn, which was restored after the fatal car crash. I later played it myself, badly *(National Portrait Gallery)*. Recording 'Hey Jude', John Lennon wasn't sure how to hold a horn. Nor was Paul McCartney, with horn quartet after playing 'Sgt Pepper' at Live 8.

Proof that there's no fixed way to pose with a horn. TOP TO BOTTOM: Me, Sarah Willis and the Berlin Phil horns in Salzburg. Some of the Vienna Phil horns are holding Wagner tubas. On the Carnegie Hall stage with Dale Clevenger and his Chicago Symphony Orchestra horns. 'OK, guys. Heldenleben': the mighty Phil Myers and the New York Phil horns blast Strauss.

TOP LEFT: My lessons with Dave Lee were unorthodox *(Dillon Bryden)*. ABOVE: So was my practice routine at horn camp. TOP RIGHT: I managed to stalk the greatest horn players in the world. That's me with Hermann Baumann, Lowell Greer and Vincent DeRosa.

ABOVE: Mozart's autograph score for the Romanze of his concerto for horn in E flat, K447 *(British Library)*.
LEFT: Giovanni Punto, the first internationally renowned horn player *(Bridgeman Art Library)*.

TOP: The horn entered polite society via the hunting field. Trompes de chasse from Jean-Baptiste Oudry's *Hunting in the Forest of Fontainebleau at Franchard (Bridgeman Art Library)*. ABOVE: In Hogarth's *A Rake's Progress*, one of the temptations of the town is hunting, as represented by the rough-looking horn player on the right *(Weidenfield Archive)*.

surge of Darwinian relief. Half the students in camp are half my age, but I'm half Harry's age, and on the horn it's the fittest who survive.

'I don't know what happened yesterday,' says Harry, when I come back the next day, this time with my horn. 'It was a disaster.'

We sit and wait our turn. A woman is wrestling with the Beethoven sonata on a natural horn, and Hermann is getting testy. There is more unnervingly good Strauss, and then someone dances through the so-called Concert Rondo, from one of Mozart's uncompleted concertos for Leutgeb. He finishes, people clap. It's Harry's turn.

'You go ahead,' he tells me. 'It means I'll live a little longer.'

I stumble up to the front with horn and sheet music. To break the ice with Hermann, I tell him how I met Stefan Dohr, co-principal horn of the Berlin Philharmonic, how he said they came from the same village, how he took up the horn when he heard Hermann's Christmas concert.

'Ja, ja,' he says. 'Kettwig.' Kettwig being the name of the village. Hermann doesn't seem to want to pursue the matter.

'Vas you are playing?'

'K447,' I say, and hand my music over to the pianist. 'The Romanze.'

'Gut,' he says. 'Biiig breath.' He expands his arms like a singer and breathes in deeply.

This is the first time I've played to strangers since I was seventeen. I notice at once that my right leg is quivering slightly. It's absurd. There are only four or five people slouched on chairs at the back end of the concert hall, one of whom is Harry, but I am being ambushed by nerves. As a consequence, I miss a lot of the entry notes. The legato phrases of the Romanze all kick off on notes that are just inside the challenging range. The two high Fs, the ardent E flat, the manly D. Even the opening B flat seems to be a problem this afternoon. But after a while I settle down and start to express myself. At one point Hermann even nods appreciatively at a bit of cantabile phrasing. I play through to the end flushed with pride. I have survived, even prospered. The four or five people clap desultorily.

'Gut,' says Hermann. 'Now you come back tomorrow and play the first movement.'

The first movement, the Allegro, is rather more testing than the Romanze. But I've flown to America fired by the ambition to play it in the concert at the end of the week. I've done the Romanze, I reason, even if it was only at my fortieth birthday. I need to see if I can do anything else. With the confidence gained from Hermann's approval, and the many hours of practice I've devoted to it, I calculate that it's scaleable. There are just a couple of unsolved problems with the Allegro. For one, there are a lot of trills in it, most of them inserted by Mozart to liven up long sustained notes at the end of phrases. The best trill sounds like birdsong and is achieved, so I've been given to understand by Dave, by sort of fluttering the lips inside the narrow confines of the mouthpiece. I can't trill. I can't even begin to trill. But that's less of an issue than the second problem. Towards the end of the movement, there is a cadenza. A cadenza, as I'm also given to understand by Dave, is an improvised passage played by the soloist, quoting from and enlarging on themes from the movement. You can't play the first movement without playing a cadenza, and you can't play a cadenza without either (a) learning one or (b) composing one.

Back in the railway sleeper, I decide to compose one. But in a startling and I hope attractive deviation from standard cadenza practice, I work on something which, after a brief nod to Mozart, gradually migrates away into foreign territory: specifically, a lyrical horn solo played by Dave in the Andrew Lloyd Webber musical. In all the spare time I have available in the next twenty-four hours, I graft the Andrew Lloyd Webber musical theme onto the opening statement of the Allegro until such time as I can play it without glitches.

The next day I present myself. The heat is building outside towards some sort of Wagnerian thunderstorm, and Hermann has undone a couple of buttons on his shirt. One of the other people in the hall is Jeremy. He gets there before me and so it's his turn first.

'Vas you are playing?'

'The Rondo, K447.'

Jeremy has been careful to ask me beforehand if it's OK to trespass onto my patch. I huff and puff a bit, but I know the classic repertoire for the French horn isn't the biggest, and it was after all his first triumph, so who am I to deprive him? Plus I'm not planning to play the Rondo in horn camp.

'Be my guest,' I say.

He flawlessly executes the Rondo much as he did that first evening. After he's galloped to the end he looks across at Hermann.

'Very gut,' says Hermann. 'Very very gut.'

'Anything else?' asks Jeremy.

'No,' says Hermann. 'You are your own teacher. Now play the first movement.'

'I haven't practised it,' says Jeremy.

Jeremy looks across at me. Pontifically I nod and Jeremy executes the Allegro much as he did that first evening. When he gets to the cadenza, he unleashes a brilliant blizzard of notes in which the shape of the original is occluded without ever quite disappearing altogether. Jeremy assures me afterwards that it's all made up on the spot. We clap thunderously. Even Hermann claps.

It's my turn. I walk up to the front with a heavier heart than I had anticipated. How the hell do I follow that? My cadenza is going to seem very thin gruel after Jeremy's extempore peacock display. I trudge characterlessly through the Allegro without too many problems, bar the odd split note, until Hermann stops me just as the main theme is recapitulated halfway through the movement.

'Where is the trill?' he says.

'I have no trill,' I answer, embarrassed.

'You must learn to trill.'

'I'll try,' I say.

'OK. Now go on.'

I restart at the recapitulation, and this time I can feel the cadenza looming up ahead of me like a grizzly bear rising onto hind legs. My throat starts to contract as it nears. Tricksy phrases evade my grasp and come out in a clatter of bum notes. It's all going tits up, I think, as suddenly the piano accompaniment grinds to a halt on an expectant chord, a musical colon. I feel as if I'm mounting a scaffold, walking the plank, being fed to the lions. Down at the far end of the hall, the other horn players have mutated into a grim-faced firing squad. I take a gigantic gulp of air and launch myself on the Mozartian part of my new composition. It goes more or less to script until the moment comes to splice on the new section from the alien source. I hadn't noticed before that there's a key change. It sounds horrible. I can feel the Lídl start to judder in my arms, like a steering wheel when you drive over potholed road. My palms begin to run with sweat. As the notes splutter and slip, the mountainous impudence of bolting this deeply unMozartian melody onto the perfection of K447 brings on some sort of hot menopausal flush. It's the musical equivalent of a human ear growing on the back of a rat. I limp home shamefacedly. If anyone claps, I don't hear them. I look at Hermann. For once, he is speechless.

'What did you think of my cadenza, Hermann?' In the ensuing pause, he composes a carefully worded response.

'It's a little bit . . . modern,' he says. I make a mental note never to play it ever again.

Hermann gets up, pads over and, with undisguised weariness, hauls open the bonnet of my interpretation. Pointing to the music, the same sheet music on which Günter Högner spotted all my fingerings, he asks for more dynamics, more legato, more crescendi, more volume.

'Piano means mezzoforte,' he explains. 'Not too soft. This is a solo!'

And I try the opening again.

'No! No! No! Mezzoforte!'

I play the passage over and over again. Hermann's exasperation simmers a few degrees below boiling point. I now know how it feels to drive a ten-tonne truck through K447 with the greatest European soloist of the past fifty years looking on. Eventually we reach an exhausted truce.

'Do you think I can play this at the end of the week?' I ask Hermann as I pack away the Lídl.

'You are not ready to play this,' he says. 'Play the Romanze. This is OK. But the Allegro? Nein. Not so gut.'

Lowell Greer, the great American soloist on the natural horn, is in camp, lumbering around like a giant friendly bear, dispensing bonhomie and CDs of his own making. One of the CDs he hands out has a black-and-white photo of a woman in specs holding a horn. The picture looks as if it was taken before or during the war. 'Helen Kotas Hirsch, French Horn, the Chicago Symphony,' says the cover. The CD has recordings taken from rare 78 rpms, including a crackly memento of a live performance she once gave of K447.

Helen Kotas – the Hirsch came later when she married – was once principal horn of the Chicago Symphony Orchestra. It was extraordinary for a woman to hold such a position in the 1940s. She was only twenty-five when in 1941 she successfully auditioned under the orchestra's long-standing music director Frederick Stock. The desk had become vacant after Philip Farkas left for Cleveland, in pursuit of a higher salary. Stock died a year later, but she continued to thrive under Désiré DeFauw, 'a Belgian conductor,' notes Lowell, 'widely known for his crisp shirts.' In 1947 DeFauw made way for Artur Rodziński, a fifty-five-year-old Polish immigrant with a degree in law from Vienna who had already run the Los Angeles Philharmonic, the Cleveland Orchestra and the New York Philharmonic. When Rodziński took over in Chicago he was featured on the cover of *Time* magazine. He was not the type to be gainsaid. Practically his first move was to lure Farkas back from Cleveland.

Lowell more or less knows how the conversation went, because many years later his teacher was Helen Kotas Hirsch.

'The first day of the new directorship,' he says, 'was marked by a pre-rehearsal chat between Rodziński, Kotas and Farkas, which I understand to have gone as follows. Rodziński: "I'd like to introduce you to Mr Farkas, who is the orchestra's new first horn player. You'll be assistant to him." Kotas: "Hello, Phil. Dr Rodziński, Mr Farkas and I are old friends, we studied with the same teacher, and with all due respect and admiration for Mr

Farkas's work, I'm not sure at this point in my life that I wish to play assistant to anyone." Rodziński: "Then don't. You will sit in the front of the auditorium where I can see you, for every rehearsal and concert during this, your last, season with the Chicago Symphony."'

Rodziński was himself fired after only fifteen weeks by a management who found his high-handed ways insupportable. But he was there long enough to see off Helen Kotas. She moved on to lesser orchestras, and retired from performing in 1965. She was killed in a car crash at the age of eighty-four in 2000, and a number of 78s were found in her basement. Lowell put them on to CD for private distribution. In 2003 he composed a musical memorial to her to be played on *trompes de chasse* and organ entitled *Requiem du Chasseur*. He refers to her as the First Lady of Horn.

Professionally, she undoubtedly was, though other women had taken up the horn before her. A concert in Milan in 1827 featured 'for the first time on the French horn a Tyrolese air with variations' performed by one Madame Vansuest, who claimed on her promotional literature to be the offspring of the 'celebrated Monsieur Mozart', which was a calculated misprint. She was the daughter of one Moysard. The earliest known Englishwoman to play the horn was a Miss Cann, who also played the flute. She died in Paris at the age of nineteen. At a Concert Spirituel in the same city in 1780 a Mademoiselle Beate Pokorny performed one of Punto's innumerable concerti. But there is an earlier instance. A concert was announced in the *Dublin Mercury* for 1 May 1742, to be given by 'Mr Charles, the Hungarian, Master of the French Horn'. Mr Charles was probably Bohemian. His repertoire included horn solos and horn duets, but on those occasions when he was performing a horn trio, he called on the service of his wife, whose name has not come down to us.

When the eight-year-old Mozart first visited Versailles in 1763, he was introduced to the queen and her offspring, among them the portly dauphin who nearly thirty years later would lose the crown, and his head, in the Terror. The dauphin had three unprepossessing sisters. Following the example of their mother, they were passionate about music. Between them they played the violin, the viola da gamba, the clavier, the harp, and one of them, Madame Adélaïde, was a keen horn player. So recalled Madame Campan, Marie Antoinette's first lady of the bedchamber, in a memoir written long after the revolution.

If opportunistic musicians were inspired to compose for her, none of those compositions has survived, so there is no knowing if she truly mastered the instrument. Madame Campan adds that Madame Adélaïde 'was graced for a short time with a charming figure; but never did beauty so quickly vanish'. To go with her lack of looks, she was shrewish. When the fourteen-year-old Marie Antoinette arrived in Versailles from Austria, five years after Mozart, it was Adélaïde who bestowed on her the unlovely nickname '*l'Autrichienne*'. Though its innocent meaning was 'the Austrian woman', its disparaging allusions to the French words for 'ostrich' and 'bitch' were subsequently pounced upon by anti-monarchical cartoonists. Adélaïde had relented by the time she heard of her sister-in-law's execution twenty-three years later. 'What courage and firmness she has shown . . .' she wrote in Rome in 1793. 'How she has talked to these villains . . . If only everything had depended on her!' It's not known if Madame Adélaïde travelled into exile with her horn.

Madame Campan's incredulity at the idea of a female horn player – 'will it be believed!' – echoed down one century and some way into the next. I meet Sarah Willis, the first female horn player to play with the Berlin Philharmonic, in Salzburg. She is English, but has gone so native that her mother tongue comes out with a slight German accent. She was already used to boldly going where no woman had gone before, because fresh out of college ten years earlier, she was the first person of either gender to get an orchestral job on the other side of the newly breached Berlin Wall in the pit of the Staatsoper, where she was also the only woman. Without wishing to sound a sexist note, if Radovan Vlatković wins the Mr Horniverse contest, Sarah walks off with the ladies' crown. She's all eyes and cheekbone and Cupid's bow.

When she took up the instrument, several years after me, there was still an ingrained prejudice to overcome. 'At school they said, "We've got a flute or a clarinet, and we've got a harp." My father said, "Absolutely not, they're too expensive and you always have to carry it." The teacher at school said, "Well we have a horn, but that's not for you because that's something for the boys." So I said I wanted to play that.' The boys have predominated almost up to the present day. In 1999 a CD called *The London Horn Sound*, including arrangements for horn of everything from Wagner's Prelude to *Tristan und Isolde* to Duke Ellington's 'Caravan', was recorded to commemorate the array of remarkable horn-playing talent in London. Dave is one of thirty-two horn players credited in the sleeve notes, not one of whom is a woman. Throughout my travels I don't come across many women in the great horn sections. There are none in the Vienna Philharmonic, the London Philharmonic, the New York Philharmonic, the St Petersburg Philharmonic, the Czech Philharmonic or the Orchestre de Paris. During my horn year the London Symphony Orchestra appoints its first woman horn player. At the Berlin Philharmonic, Sarah had to wait until Gerd Seifert, for thirty-two years the orchestra's principal horn, retired before she got a look-in. 'I would never have got a job if Seifert had still been here. Women were only good for one thing, and it wasn't horn playing. But they don't make me feel like that. Well, apart from having to clean up the horns, polish the shoes and make the tea. But in the next ten or twenty years there are only going to be girls coming into the orchestra because if you look at the conservatories they are full of girl horn players.'

I don't look for girl horn players in conservatories, but I sure as hell notice about six trillion of them when I get to horn camp. Being surrounded by young female horn players for a whole midsummer week might sound superficially like a direct mail shot to someone such as myself. But the more I think about it, and I think about it slightly too much, the more it gnaws away at my intestines. If I'm going to underachieve on this instrument, I reason, I'd rather underachieve in front of my own gender. *So* much less emasculating.

*

Here's some of what I learnt from the faculty in KBHC.

'Playing the French horn is not a high jump competition.'

'It's impossible to have every note in tune.'

'I always thought of Strauss as musical pornography.'

'The diaphragm is a piston which pushes against the lungs and compresses air. The lungs have a capacity of 4,000 cc – four litres – of air. That's a lot of air.'

'This is what I call a trombone exercise, because a trombone has only two dynamics: on, and off.'

'Playing the horn is an athletic event. You are going to burn calories in order to play well.'

'Slurs should be like a doorknob.'

'Barry Tuckwell never warmed up.'

'Society says, "Feel bad about missing a note." You should feel *nothing*. In quantity operations there will be some losses.'

'The tongue is a valve. It opens and closes. Visualise a nozzle of a hose with a trigger. The tongue releases air or stops it.'

'The horn didn't trill outside. I have a theory of how ornamentation arrived in baroque music. When the horn came indoors, the horn player was splitting notes. Everybody said, "Hey, that sounds great!" and started improvising.'

'An "autogenic phrase" will help you deal with performance anxiety. Instead of saying, "Why am I here?" or "You don't have to do this," talk to yourself nicely. "I choose to be here. The audience chooses to be here. Are they here because they want to see me crash and burn?"'

I'm not going to perform it, but I decide there's no harm in finding out what Hermann thinks of my rendition of the third movement, the Rondo. Big mistake. The heat is now intolerable, and Hermann's shirt is entirely unbuttoned. He is evidently hot and bothered. I start to roister through the famous hunting tune. He interrupts me.

'Hold the horn like this. Here. So.' He lifts his arms as if holding a horn proudly, firmly, in front of his upper torso. I imitate him, but I soon slump back into my old droopy, heat-sapped stance. Hermann is not impressed.

'Up!' He reluctantly heaves himself up and walks over. This time he pushes the Lídl in my arms. I let it drop imperceptibly.

'No. So!' I am enfeebled by the heat. The horn slips down again. Hermann is now exasperated.

'Hold it like a man!' he bellows. This is too much. At the back of the hall, apart from Jeremy, I note that everyone seems to be female. I hold up the horn and start again. And now the problem is not my look but my sound. Some way in he raises a hand. I stop, as does the pianist. He rises once more from his seat and starts to prowl in front of me.

'Sing it,' he says.

'I'm sorry?' I say.

'Sing it!' He points at the sheet music. 'From here. Sing.' I'm not sure why this is necessary but I begin to sing the Rondo intro, grudgingly, half-heartedly.

'Sing!' Hermann's voice is now forte. 'You must sing!'

'I understand,' I say.

'No understand!' he shouts. 'You learn!' And he taps his head violently. 'You *learn*! You sing then you play.' It's the end of a fortnight for Hermann. The unrelenting heat has shortened his fuse. He wants to go home to Kettwig. So I sing the Rondo at the top of my voice and for the longest half-minute of my musical life I feel, look and no doubt sound like an utter tit.

'Now,' says Hermann more quietly, placated, 'you start again.' It's at this point that I step over the line and ask a dumb-ass question.

'Where from?'

'Where!' Hermann is incandescent. 'Where!!' He turns and walks down the aisle, throwing his arms in the air. 'Where!!!' And now I'm angry. I am being humiliated three thousand expensive miles from home. In front of an audience of women! Amateur horn players have immense respect for the professionals who agree to share their expertise. They take great exception to any show of disrespect to the maestri of the instrument. These are the virtuosi who have dedicated their lives, and sometimes sacrificed their marriages, to the horn. In the global community of horn players who meet and confer in the French horn chat rooms, they are celebrated, lauded, venerated, prized. And I agree with my fellow amateurs. I am the number one fan of all horn players. I stalk them across continents. I have my picture taken with them. But with Hermann's back turned to me, and in the stifling heat of a moment of insurrectionary madness, I nonetheless do something of which I am immediately and profoundly ashamed.

Reader, I flip Hermann Baumann the bird.

Lowell Greer is a port in a storm. One afternoon I am wandering past the dining hall and he asks me if I want to join his natural horn ensemble. I wander in and Lowell hands me one of his spare horns. He's performed a valvectomy on it. For the next hour eight of us hammer out roistering hunting tunes while up at the front a lavishly perspiring Lowell conducts. I miss about a third of the notes – some achievement given that only a third of all notes are available on a valveless natural horn. But I am back in an ensemble for the first time since playing the Hallelujah Chorus at the British Horn Society festival, and I enjoy myself more than I can say. This, I realise, is what I always liked about the horn. I like being a cog in the machine. I don't like being the whole bloody machine.

I have a private lesson with Lowell. I need a quieter perspective on what I might be doing wrong. As I thrash once again through the first movement of K447 he wears a look of beatific patience on his mellowly bearded face. Occasionally he comments, and if there is criticism, it is delivered quizzically, thoughtfully, subtly. After ten or fifteen minutes of stopping and starting he holds up a hand. I pull up. From a long thin cool-box filled with Dr Peppers floating in water like broken ice floes, he draws two red cans and offers one to me. We crack open and take a life-giving draught of saccharine and gas.

'As a horn player's skills develop,' he says, 'so do their powers of critical observation. If we get to a very unfortunate situation where someone with highly developed critical evaluation is struggling to recapture previous glories of youth, it can be very frustrating, because you are thwarted by your own ability to hear your failures.' He means me. 'And they become larger. If they could give you a pill – a partial lobotomy pastille – then all would fall into place naturally. Part of what we practise as players is confidence. We practise aplomb.'

In other words, stop screaming at yourself in the privacy of your head. Pretend to yourself that you're a good horn player. Easy on the self-flagellation. It makes a lot of sense. Delivered of these well chosen words, Lowell launches himself into a magnificent cadenza of his own about how the jocularity went missing from Mozart's concertos in the po-faced nineteenth century. Lowell thinks people take Mozart's horn concertos way too seriously. He wants me – he wants everyone – to hunt for the levity that underpinned Mozart's friendship with Leutgeb.

'When I listen to the recordings I mostly hear romantic lyricism, phrase after phrase after phrase. Brain, Civil, Tuckwell, the guy in Berlin – Gerd Seifert. Marvellous marvellous players and great musicians but coming from a tradition where a heavily romantic post-Wagnerian breast-pounding lyricism is presumed and thereby superimposed over music that is otherwise much more happy and upbeat. We always hear how Mozart needs to be light and effervescent and simple. And we hear flute players play it and it's light and effervescent and simple and piano players play it and it's light and effervescent and simple and horn players play it and it's a great philosophical statement. "Harry is dead! The kids are dead too! They were killed in a car accident. The funeral is Saturday."'

I leave the lesson floating on a cloud. Now *that*, I tell myself, is worth travelling three thousand miles for.

The funeral is indeed on Saturday. I'm down to play in the last-night concert. Kendall has set up a system in which people playing movements from the same concerto can club together and perform the whole concerto in sequence. After Hermann's extravagant praise – 'You are your own teacher' – Jeremy has put his name down to do the K447 Allegro. I've ducked under the wire and am playing the Romanze. If only we had another horn camper to play the Rondo.

For most of the week, evenings are when campers get to down their horns and listen to entertainment in the concert hall. On faculty night the various professors stand up and do a turn. After the interval it's the turn of Hermann Baumann, who enters to loud applause wearing dapper white slacks and a dark blue shirt. He has elected to play the Glière, as it's known in horn circles. In 1950, at the age of seventy-five, the recently retired chairman of the Union of Soviet Composers Reinhold Glière wrote a concerto for horn for a young horn player called Valery Polekh. It was first heard a year later in the Grand Hall of the Leningrad Philharmonic Society, and has since become a staple of the repertoire. Although Polekh subsequently recorded the concerto with the Bolshoi Orchestra conducted by Glière, it is Hermann Baumann's recording that is now seen as definitive.

It's a soaring, swooning, sweeping piece. Heavily romantic post-Wagnerian breast-pounding lyricism is very much called for. As are a big pair of lungs and lightning-quick fingers. As they say in sport, it's a big ask. The tension in the concert hall is palpable as he takes a 'biiiig breath' and throws himself off the cliff. There are only fifty or so people listening. At least one of us is mere instrumental pond life, but all of us know what it is to pick up a French horn and play. For twenty-two minutes we are witnesses to a performance of quite magnificent charisma. At times it looks like Tarzan grappling with a twelve-foot crocodile. Hermann Baumann, seventy-two, his powers diminished by age and ill health, but his will unimpaired, plays himself onto the highest plinth in the pantheon of gods in my head.

There is mighty applause. When it dies down Hermann cannot stop himself from saying something. It must be pure adrenalin, the shock of having got through it, that makes him address a gathering of Americans in a language they cannot understand.

'Das war das erste Mal in dreizehn Jahre . . .' That was the first time in thirteen years. He has not played the Glière since his stroke.

We file out into the balmy night and I overhear a couple of curmudgeons shaking their heads and muttering that Glière sure as heck didn't write all of those notes. In my mind I flip the bird at the pair of them. The thing I suddenly understand about

Hermann, the thing that he has tried to drum into my skull, is that with the horn there is no alternative to standing up and being counted. You have to have courage to stick out your chest and face down your demons. After nearly dying from a stroke, his demons are far worse than anything I have encountered. But in this country where mesmerising politeness is the lingua franca, it takes a fellow European to give it to me absolutely straight. Be a man!

Saturday comes. All day I feel like a condemned man. To psych myself up, I try to think of some morale-boosting phrases. Sadly, the only ones that spring to mind are 'I suppose I've got to do this', 'I can't wait till it's over' and 'Oh shit'. The guillotine awaits. I've travelled 3,000 miles and spent north of 1,500 dollars for *this*? What was I thinking? That I'd actually enjoy it? As I follow the throng of American horn players and their friends and families up to and into the hubbub of the concert hall, in my right hand there is a horn case, in my left a cool beer. I plan to start drinking the minute this torment is over.

When the concert gets under way with a student soaring through Strauss 1 it becomes apparent that the level of competence is alarmingly high. Even the nun from Massachusetts, newer to this game than me, treads carefully through a folksy American dirge without a hiccup. Jeremy, whom I haven't seen much in the previous twenty-four hours, strides up to the front, looking spruce in trousers filched from my wardrobe, and proceeds to dance and twirl through the first movement of K447. His trilling is immaculate. When he gets to the cadenza, which he has evidently been working on in secret, it's as if he's released hundreds of fluttering doves into the air.

He finishes. Which means it's my turn to stand up. I make a mental note to try to impersonate an air of confidence, but I feel like a dead man walking.

'Is it OK if I blow a couple of notes?' I say to the pianist. He nods. 'The instrument's a bit cold,' I tell the audience. It's a calculated attempt to elicit sympathy, and it's completely transparent. There are maybe seventy people in the room, which means that seven hundred toes curl in embarrassment at my appalling gaucheness as I blow a brief arpeggio. The spell cast by Jeremy's Allegro has been broken.

OK, I think to myself, let's nail this sucker. Raising the Lídl to my lips, I take an epic breath and proceed assertively, powerfully and indeed manfully to split the very first note of the Romanze – the bog-standard B flat – into a dozen pieces. Oh bollocks, I think. That's torn it. Which is exactly what I shouldn't be thinking. I should be thinking *nothing*. The onrush of nerves is not unexpected, but still wholly new. Gradually the easiest movement of the easiest Mozart horn concerto comes spectacularly apart in my hands. It's not that there aren't brief moments of blue sky, but clouds are forever scudding across and darkening the landscape. Every entry is greeted by a distressing inaccuracy. First the pair of high Fs, then the ardent E flat and, for completeness, the manly D. Get a grip, goes a voice in my head. Get a sodding grip, you twerp. Buried somewhere deep beneath the rubble is the occasional felicity. I notice that I need about half the performance to calm down. By the time I get to the passage where Hermann nodded approvingly earlier in the week, I'm past the worst. I enter the home straight somewhat regrouped and start to relax, possibly too much as, in the interests of symmetry, I contrive to split the bog-standard B flat in the final bar too. At least it's over.

To complete the concerto, Kendall Betts has volunteered to step up to the plate and play the third movement. He gallops through it at an exhilarating lick. If he were on horseback, the flying hoofs of his mount would barely touch the turf. Unlike me, he exits spectacularly. The final two bars are all on B flat, one on one quaver, the rest an octave lower: together they should sound like a horse skidding to a halt at the end of the chase. Kendall decides to elaborate. He comes in three bars early and proceeds to rifle through every note in the harmonic series of E flat. It sounds like a horse skidding to a halt while its rider stands in the saddle doing a faultless triple back somersault with double twist.

We take our bow together. Sandwiched between Jeremy and Kendall, I've never felt such a fraud. The applause is generous, but in my case unmerited.

At the end of the concert, with everyone milling around the

hall, Hermann finds me nursing my beer quietly in a seat. He shakes my hand and smiles that puckish smile and pats me on the back.

'You see! You can do it! And next time it will be better!'

A great great man.

7
Without Fear of Death

The solo entered – firm, heroic, and all seemed set for the best of all the wonderful Mozart horn concertos. And then suddenly in the middle of an intricate florid passage, superbly played, it stopped; silence. Dennis shrugged his shoulders and walked off the Jubilee Hall platform.

Benjamin Britten

For work I have to go to Greenland. One morning I sit on a sledge as it's pulled by huskies across a frozen bay somewhere along the complicated east coast. It is cold, of course, and quiet. Cloud is slung low over the fjord. Barely a whisper of wind comes down from the ice cap. The only sounds are of pack dogs panting and sledge runners whooshing across deep snow. Now and then the hush is punctuated by commands from an Inuit musher. In this white wilderness, it is possible to feel utterly at peace. It seems an appropriate moment to listen on the Nomad to Dennis Brain play Mozart's Third Horn Concerto in E flat, K447.

Dennis Brain was in his early thirties and at the pinnacle of his fame when, over three days at Kingsway Hall in London in November 1953, he recorded all four of Mozart's concertos for horn and orchestra. The orchestra that accompanied him was his own, the Philharmonia. The conductor, who since the end of the war had been deNazified and cleared for work, was Herbert von Karajan. The recordings are far more than definitive. If people own a recording of the Mozart concertos, eight times out of ten the soloist is Brain. People who know nothing of French horn soloists have heard of Brain. For a while he was as famous a classical soloist as any in the country, perhaps even the world. On the Memphis horn list I pick up a story in which a keen young student in the 1950s is said to have said to Philip Farkas, 'Oh, Mr Farkas, you must be the best horn player in the world.' Farkas is said to have replied, 'There is a fellow in London who is considered the best. I am considered second best.'

I first came across the name as a child. It would have been Christmas 1975 spent as ever at my grandparents' large house on a hill overlooking the Welsh market town of Carmarthen. I had been a horn player for six months. My mother handed me an LP-shaped wrapping. It confused me. I already had all the LPs I needed. The Sweet's *Biggest Hits. Sweet Fanny Adams* by the Sweet. *Desolation Boulevard* by the Sweet. Suzi Quatro's *Greatest Hits. Band on the Run* by Paul McCartney and Wings. I ripped off the paper. There was a black-and-white picture of a cherubic young man playing a French horn. He had a white bow tie, and the merest hint of a double chin. *The Art of Dennis Brain*, it said. 'Music by Beethoven, Mozart, Dittersdorf, Haydn, Schumann and Dukas (Recorded 1944–1953).' It was one of those presents your parents give you because 'you'll appreciate it in later life'. I certainly didn't appreciate it in earlier life. I slung the record away and moved on to the next present.

Fergus McWilliam was half the age I was then when he saw Brain perform at the Usher Hall in Edinburgh on the last day of August in 1957. 'I was five,' he says. We are in a coffee shop near the Festspielhaus in Salzburg. He is about to play Britten's *Peter Grimes* with the Berlin Philharmonic, with whom he has been second horn for twenty-two years. He was recruited by Karajan. 'Tchaikovsky 6 is what I remember. This is the desperate thing – I have no memories of him at all. But I do remember coming out of the concert and pestering my mother. "Which instrument makes that sound?" And being fascinated by the look, in the gods, second balcony, to see this bright shiny yellow thing, four of them. I thought it was absolutely the bee's knees. "I have to do that."'

One of the four in the Philharmonia's horn section that evening was Alan Civil, who first met Brain during the war. 'Dennis had tremendous energy,' he wrote in the sleeve notes for *The Art of Dennis Brain*, 'and would drive home immediately after recitals and concerts even if it meant travelling several hundred miles.'

At the Edinburgh Festival in 1957 we stood outside the Usher Hall after performing Tchaikovsky's Sixth Symphony with Eugene Ormandy. With the engine of his green (Triumph) sports car ticking over gently he asked me if I would care for a lift back to London. 'You'll be in before the train,' he said.

Declining graciously, I joked that I really must lubricate the instrument with a pint of 'heavy' before catching the sleeper.

'See you Monday morning, Dennis.'

'What's on?'

'Strauss, *Capriccio* with Sawallisch.'

'Anything to play?' he chuckled.

'Yes,' I said. 'Horn concerto from beginning to end, all impossible on Monday morning even for you.'

Dennis Brain died in the early hours of Sunday morning, 1 September. After covering the 400 miles to Barnet, just north of London, his TR2 slid off the road in heavy rain and hit an oak. An inquest was unable to establish the cause of the accident. No doubt poor weather, lack of sleep and his addiction to speed proved a lethal combination. His death was mourned by a wife, two children and a world of admirers. At thirty-six Brain's life ended at the same age as it had for Lord Byron, as it would for Marilyn Monroe, Bob Marley and Diana Princess of Wales; and as it would have for Mozart if he'd hung on a few more weeks. To horn players, if to no one else, Brain merits a place in this pantheon.

Fergus McWilliam remembers hearing the news.

'I didn't understand why everyone else was so upset.'

A couple of weeks after my return from horn camp, emails start to arrive from my new friends in America. 'I don't have the words to express the deep sadness we have regarding today's horrible events. Please know our thoughts, prayers and hearts are with you, your loved ones and your country. Let us know you are okay.' 'I'm worried about you. Please tell me that you and your family are safe and unhurt by the bombings. Let me know, ok?' From Jeremy Thal: 'I know you're probably getting a lot of these emails but I have to ask if you and yours are OK.' And from Lowell Greer: 'Dear Jasper. Are you okay? Concerned in Ohio.'

I am reminded of something Lowell told me in New Hampshire. It's his theory that the world needs the horn more than it knows. Our lives, he says, are beset by difficulty and trauma. There is terror in our cities, there are fresh waves of plague gathering strength among dense, migrant populations, and our addiction to pollutants is spit-roasting the whole goddamn planet. 'We have so much unresolved dissonance,' Lowell says. And music, he argues, has to step in and do something. OK, so it won't fight off armies of invisible bombers or stem the proliferation of bacilli or hold back floods. But it will cheer us up. It will be on our side. It will gird our loins. And nothing, argues Lowell, will cheer us up or be on our side or gird our loins more than the horn.

It seems a tall order for sixteen feet of metal. I ask him to elaborate.

'Everything is a horn,' he says. 'The acoustical shape of the horn exists in the shape of a tree trunk. It exists in the conch shell, it exists in the ram's horn, the cow's horn, the oliphant, the Alphorn. Every shape of a signalling device that mankind has come up with, with the exception of bells. The fire alarm, the police alarm, the air raid alarm – they're all horns. They might have a sound generator but they have the conical form. What that means to me is that the conical sound is so embedded in our memories, in our programmes as human beings, that the sound of the horn will register in the human consciousness in a way that the most brilliant piano player, the most virtuoso violinist will not be able to. Maybe not even singers. Because the horn is the instrument of alarm, but it's also the instrument of repose.'

The horn, he's saying, is more deeply embedded in our DNA than anyone knows. It cuts to the core of things. Its beauty is inextricable from the fact of its sheer age. Lowell is in his stride now, and the cadences of his voice work their charm.

'So horn players,' he goes on, 'have an opportunity and thereby a civic responsibility to furnish their countrymen, their world citizens, with this musical message of tranquillity and resolution of conflict and balance and equity of justice that comes in music. And maybe people only perceive it for the duration of the concert, but for a moment they've been able to forget about the bombs and the diseases and the social unfairness and they were presented with something which was fair and just and balanced and resolved conflict. I've been trying to impress people that horn players regardless of level or achievement are enrolled in a kind of an army. We've got one of the best literatures of any instrument. The fiddle and the piano may be better in numbers, and the music that they play is longer and more involved, but there is something to be said for the brevity and simplicity and the purity of a Mozart concerto.'

I begin to see where Lowell is going with this.

'So,' I say, 'what you're saying is, seeing as how I've returned to the fold after all those years away, I'm now part of this ... this army?'

'You're in the army,' he says cheerfully, as if the choice has been taken away from me. 'You've been drafted.'

'Dear Jasper,'

Another email lands in my inbox a few days later.

Sorry I have not been in touch. I have been in France for the past two weeks. Here is what I suggest. If you could come to the Guildhall School of Music and Drama next week for a horn lesson with me (it is the last week of term), we can have a blow through Mozart 3 with the view to you playing a movement or two with piano at the festival.

Best wishes,
Hugh Seenan

First reaction: relief. I have a response. Second reaction: terror. The nod from the BHS will remove the one and only barrier between me talking about performing at their festival, and performing at their festival. Third reaction: confusion. What does 'with the view to' actually mean? 'A movement or two': is that one movement, or is it two, and is it definitely not three? And when is a lesson actually an audition? It all adds up to an unavoidable conclusion: I'm not in yet. Not by any means.

It was Schubert who first made the connection between the horn, mourning and loss. To mark the first anniversary of Beethoven's death, he took a piece of romantic doggerel called 'Auf dem Strom' by a minor German poet and composed an inexpressibly beautiful trio for piano, voice and horn. It was premiered on 26 March 1828 as part of a private concert in Vienna. It is thought to have been the first significant work composed for valved horn (although there is no conclusive evidence that the soloist, J R Lewy, who also played in Beethoven's Choral Symphony, did not use a valveless horn). Schubert knew he was dying, and within nine months had himself fallen victim to syphilis. At his own request, he was buried next to Beethoven.

It turned out to be a rare moment in the spotlight for the solo horn in the nineteenth century. After Haydn, after Mozart, after Beethoven's sonata for Punto in 1800, itinerant vagabond troubadour horn players had very little new solo material to tout around Europe. For a while the pit at the opera provided a platform for their virtuosity. A poster announcing Spontini's *La Vestale* at the Paris Opéra on 15 December 1807 reserved the largest font for the news that 'M. FREDERIC DUVERNOY EXECUTERA LES SOLOS DE COR'. In England his contemporary equivalent was Signor Puzzi, who would turn up at the Opera 'in immaculate kid gloves, play his important solo, and depart'. It was Rossini who helped to perpetuate the idea of the horn-playing virtuoso. The glorious solos with which he ornamented his overtures were written out of filial devotion. Rossini's father, who impregnated the composer's much younger mother before they were married, was a small-town multi-instrumentalist in Pesaro on the Adriatic coast. He turned his hand to, among others, the horn. The young Gioacchino turned his hand to it too, and wrote a set of duets for them to play together when he was no more than fourteen.

Brahms was also sired by a horn player. As well as dabbling in the double bass, Brahms's father played the horn for the Hamburg militia for thirty-six years. Brahms grew up with the sound of the natural horn in the house, and dismissed its cousin with new-fangled valves as a 'brass viola'. Like Schubert, Brahms would also turn to the instrument for the purposes of lamentation. The death of his mother in 1865 inspired two works: *A German Requiem*, and an inexpressibly beautiful trio for piano, violin and horn. Her life ended in torment. She was seventeen years older than her husband, and in the last year before her death he abandoned her for a younger woman. One morning soon after she died her son was walking in the Black Forest, 'and as I came to this spot,' he wrote in a letter, 'the sun shone out and the subject immediately suggested itself.' In German, the natural horn is known as a *Waldhorn*, a forest horn. Perhaps the use of his father's instrument to mourn his mother's death was a way of effecting some sort of spiritual reunion. Brahms was himself at the keyboard when the trio was first performed, on 28 November 1865 in Zürich. When his father died seven years later, he turned to the horn again and composed ten études for *Waldhorn*, dedicating them to the deceased horn player.

But the greatest horn-playing father was Franz Strauss. Though yet another instrumental polymath (violin, clarinet, trumpet, trombone and guitar), he was altogether more formidable on the horn. For more than four decades he played in the court orchestra in Munich. In this capacity, there was a combustible five-year period between 1865 and 1870 when he was road-testing the most physically gruelling music ever written for the horn or, possibly, any other instrument. He played in the premieres of *Tristan und Isolde* (1865), *Die Meistersinger von Nürnberg* (1868), *Das Rheingold* (1869), and *Die Walküre* (1870); and much later, *Parsifal* (1882). Franz Strauss worshipped at the traditional altar of the Viennese school whose gods were Haydn, Mozart and Beethoven, and took umbrage at the enormous demands made on him by Wagner's interminable operas, and even more interminable rehearsals. In the seventh hour of the twenty-seventh rehearsal for *Die Meistersinger*, under the baton of Hans von Bülow, Strauss 'said bluntly that he could play no more. "Then take your pension!" said the irritated Bülow. Strauss picked up his horn, went to the Intendant, and asked for his pension "at the orders of Herr von Bülow". As he was indispensable, [Intendant Karl von] Perfall had to use all his diplomacy to smooth the trouble out.'

Strauss referred to the composer as 'the Mephisto Richard Wagner'. Richard Strauss recalled an exchange between the pair of them. 'Wagner once went past the horn player, who was sitting in his place in moody silence, and said, "Always gloomy, these horn players," whereupon my father replied, "We have good reason to be."' He was even gloomy on the day after his nemesis died in 1883. The sixty-year-old principal horn refused to stand with the rest of his colleagues in silent tribute to the composer of the *Ring* cycle. He evidently belonged in that rare strain of horn players who are bombastic, dictatorial, vain, monumentally rude and generally insufferable. He once punched an orchestra secretary in the face when told to play *Così Fan Tutte* only twenty-four hours after performing *Der Fliegende Holländer*. 'Strauss is an unbearable, curmudgeonly fellow,' sighed Wagner, 'but when he plays his horn one can say nothing, for it is so beautiful.'

Among Richard Strauss's earliest pieces was a concerto for the horn. It was certainly the first piece he was paid for by his publisher, Eugen Spitzweg, for whom it represented an investment. 'Your shabby little publisher,' Spitzweg joked,

> unfortunately cannot afford to pay you a fee for your Horn Concerto, in view of the material success he has had with your works so far. However, since I want him to be the first to pay you a fee, I have advanced him the sum you have asked for, and told him to act as if it was from him – of course, when publishers are hammering at your door, he will expect you to remember that he was not block-headed or broad-headed, nor was he goat-legged.

In 'block-headed' and 'goat-legged' Spitzweg punned on the names of rival publishers who, he surmised, would one day want to poach his protégé.

As Strauss composed there was perhaps an Oedipal urge at work in his subconscious. The son had already dedicated two murderously difficult chamber pieces to his father at fourteen. When as a nineteen-year-old student he embarked on the concerto, Franz Strauss was in his seventh decade. There is no record of the father ever playing the concerto in public, though he did play it at home. In a letter to Dennis Brain, the composer's sister Johanna recalled that the old man found the piece exhausting.

Where his father's instrument was concerned, Richard Strauss began as he meant to go on. At twenty-four he wrote home during rehearsals for *Don Juan*. 'The orchestra huffed and puffed but did its job famously. One of the horn players sat there out of breath, sweat pouring from his brow, asking, "Good God, in what way have we sinned that you should have sent us this scourge?" We laughed till we cried! Certainly the horns blew without fear of death.' Later, when he began work on *Ein Heldenleben*, Strauss pledged to write for 'lots of horns, which are always a yardstick for heroism'.

In a lifetime of work, Strauss never let the horn out of earshot, even if in the *Alpine Symphony* he let it stray out of sight. It was an instrument for all occasions. A yardstick for heroism in *Ein Heldenleben*, in the opening bars of *Der Rosenkavalier* it was a yardstick for orgasm. As the Marschallin and her young lover (played, for added titillation, by a woman) thrash about in bed behind the curtain during the overture, several sharp phallic blasts on the horn mimic in sound a rampant ejaculatory climax. Strauss was very nearly eighty when his second concerto for the horn was performed for the first time at the Salzburg Festival. The instrument was now a yardstick for nostalgia. Why, after sixty years, did he go back to the solo horn?

The jury has still not come to a conclusive verdict on Strauss's war record. He welcomed the Nazi accession to power in 1933, but for largely non-political reasons: he thought he might have more luck under a dictatorship than he had in the Weimar Republic, whose liberal values he detested, of forcing through a programme of reforms designed to protect serious music in Germany and prolong the copyright of her composers. It was with these goals in mind that he accepted Goebbels's peremptory invitation that same year to become president of the Reichsmusikkammer. In this capacity he frequently had meetings not only with the Reich's propaganda minister but also with Göring and Hitler.

But within two years Strauss had been removed from the post. There was the general provocation of his latest opera, *Die schweigsame Frau*, on which he had been working since 1932 with the playwright Stefan Zweig. The Nazis had private objections to the Jewishness of Strauss's Austrian librettist, but allowed the premiere to take place in Dresden in June 1935. Hitler and Goebbels failed to attend despite assurances that they would. After three more performances the opera was banned. The Gestapo had intercepted a letter to Zweig in which Strauss made disparaging references to the Nazis and Aryanism. Strauss was forced to resign the presidency citing ill health. He wrote a humiliating letter to Hitler in July 1935 explaining away his remarks to Zweig.

> My whole life belongs to German music and to a tireless effort to elevate German culture. I have never been active politically nor even expressed myself in politics. Therefore I believe that I will find understanding from you, the great architect of German social life ... I will devote the few years still granted to me only to the purest and most ideal goals ... I beg you, my Führer, most humbly to receive me for a personal discussion.

He never received a reply. Worse was to follow. Although Strauss grudgingly composed the hymn for the Berlin Olympiad the next year, while more operas flowed from his pen, and his seventy-fifth and eightieth birthdays were publicly celebrated, the war would strip away the comfortable certainties of his old age, both professional and personal. His only son, who was named after his horn-playing grandfather Franz, had married a Jewish woman, Alice, and their two sons were therefore half-Jewish. Franz, bizarrely, was an ardent Nazi, but this did not prevent the Nazis from planning to arrest his wife at the family home in Garmisch in the German Alps on *Kristallnacht* in 1938. Alice was away, so the intruders turned on the two boys and, after roughing them up, took them to the town square and forced them to spit on

Jews. These attacks were evidently *ad hominem*. 'Unfortunately we still need him,' Goebbels wrote of Germany's greatest living composer in his diary soon after the Nazi party's accession, 'but one day we shall have our own music and then we shall have no further need of this decadent neurotic.'

Strauss was able to secure protection for his family by moving them to Vienna, where he could rely on the city's new gauleiter, Baldur von Schirach, a former head of the Hitler Youth, who was an admirer. But Alice's extended family, who came from Prague, were beyond his help. One day, driving to Dresden, Strauss passed Terezín (Theresienstadt), the concentration camp in occupied Czechoslovakia in which the regime imprisoned Jewish scholars, musicians and artists and which it attempted to present to the International Red Cross as the humane face of internment. According to Alice, Strauss 'wanted to visit my grandmother. He went to the camp gate and said, "My name is Richard Strauss, I want to see Frau Neumann." The SS guards thought he was a lunatic and sent him packing. We did not discover what went on in the camps until after the war.' More than half the prisoners of Terezín ended up in Auschwitz. In all, twenty-six members of Alice's family died in the Holocaust.

In February 1942 Zweig and his wife took poison in Brazil. In a suicide note he expressed the hope that his friends might live to witness a new dawn. 'Being too impatient, I go before them.' That same month Strauss was summoned to meet Goebbels for a strategic dressing-down. The minister was already irritated by the views on German music that Strauss was putting into his letters. 'I whisper a few sweet nothings into Strauss's ear on the subject of his insolent letters,' he wrote in his diary the previous year. 'Next time I shall give him something to think about.' In a letter Strauss had circulated to other composers, he scoffed at Lehár, whose light operettas he despised, and suggested that 'it is not for Dr Goebbels to interfere'. The recipients of the letter, also summoned to the ante-room to Goebbels's office, heard the propaganda minister screaming at Strauss. When they were ushered in for their own carpeting, Goebbels read out the letter and shouted at him, 'Be quiet! You have no conception of who you are, or of

who I am! . . . Stop your claptrap about the importance of serious
music, once and for all. Tomorrow's art is different from yesterday's. You, Herr Strauss, belong to yesterday!'

It was with this philistine message thundering in his ears that
Strauss returned after sixty years to his father's instrument. Musically he took Goebbels at his word, and composed a concerto that
reached back to his own distant past. *Capriccio*, his final opera,
was premiered in Munich on 28 October of that year. A month
later he completed his second horn concerto. 'My life's work is at
an end with *Capriccio*,' he later wrote, 'and the music that I go
on scribbling for the benefit of my heirs, exercises for my
wrists . . . , has no significance whatever from the standpoint of
musical history . . . I do it only to dispel the boredom of idle
hours.'

He didn't mean it. The concerto's first soloist was Gottfried
von Freiberg, principal horn of the Vienna Philharmonic, who
were conducted by Karl Böhm at the Salzburg Festival on 11 August
1943. Freiberg was descended from Schubert on his mother's side
and Jewish on his father's side. He could rely on the protection of
Goebbels because he had written a quartet for horn entitled 'The
Horst Wessel Fanfare', in commemoration of the Nazis' most
famous political martyr. At times lyrical and full of longing but
also defiantly cheerful and flamboyant, the horn concerto that
Freiberg now performed contrived to obliterate the sheer ugliness
and banality of life under the madmen whose imperial pretensions
had provoked the hailstorm of bombs falling on the concert
halls and opera houses in which Strauss had spent his long and
profitable life.

'It reveals a mind wholly detached from the world as it had
become,' wrote Norman Del Mar, a horn player turned conductor,
in his three-volume critical commentary on Strauss. 'Music of this
kind had not been composed, except possibly as a stylistic exercise,
for at least half a century . . . Strauss had managed to sever all
artistic connection with a society he despised and to compose
happily for himself alone music which belonged to the beloved
world of his youth.'

So it must have seemed to the Salzburgers in the audience as

Freiberg, a famously daring player who split notes with riotous abandon and was later fired by the Vienna Philharmonic, launched himself into the fiendishly difficult concerto. During the depths of war the old instrument preached a musical message of tranquillity and resolution of conflict.

I had been playing the horn for five years. It would have been apparent to anyone who heard me that I was not, and was never going to be, out of the top drawer of musical prodigies. Or even the second drawer. Over half a decade of dilettantism and half a dozen teachers, I had lurched and stumbled towards competence. Competence meant no more than not letting the side down, not lowering the tone, when the school wind band performed on Speech Day.

Not that there was much tone to lower. The school wind band is a traditional repository for the musical conscript. Most of them were on clarinet, an instrument which, in the hands of a Harrovian, sounds like a dromedary in the later stages of cervical dilation. They make a sort of anti-music. There are rows of them, pressganged woodwinders with absolutely no feel for a tune. Where there is harmony, the school wind band with its fleet air arm of clarinettists fills the skies with the buzz and quack of chaos.

One Speech Day, when the parents and sisters of Harrovians descended on the school for an annual afternoon of picnicking and cricket and oratory, the Harrow School wind band wearing its black tailcoats and parked out on the gravel terrace in front of the library launched itself into *The Dambusters March*. *The Dambusters* famously told the story of Barnes Wallis's devilishly canny bouncing bomb which helped to flood the industrial heartland of Germany during the war. The raids by 617 Squadron in their Lancaster bombers took place in May 1943, three months before the premiere of Strauss's second horn concerto. In the hands of the wind band, Eric Coates's iconic march had more bomb than bounce. It didn't so much bust dams as split atoms. The fathers in their bespoke summer suits, the mothers and teenage sisters in their fluttering cotton print dresses could only stand and politely listen as this famous tune on this breezy summer afternoon on a hill near London formed a mushroom cloud of white noise in the jasmine-scented air. The clarinettists, carrying the tune, were the worst offenders, though I accept my share of blame for the atrocity.

I was fifteen by now, and finally they sent me a horn teacher I could do business with. As usual no one had told me his predecessor was leaving. I pushed my way through the inner and outer door of the small practice room in the music schools where horn lessons were held, to be greeted by a small wiry man, with hair over his collar and a beard that hovered on the cusp of ginger.

'Hello,' he said, 'I'm Kevin. Kevin Amos.'

Unlike all his predecessors, Kevin dressed as if paying some sort of lip service to the times. He certainly didn't wear a tie, and was evidently not much older than I was. I wasn't aware that he ever did much horn playing. He worked in theatre a lot and most weeks brought in stories of rubbing shoulders with the stars on major musicals. He also composed on the side. One day he sat at the upright piano and played a fill-in fanfare he'd been commissioned to write for the television broadcast of Miss World. He said it had to be exactly nine seconds long. I was impressed.

It seems he was too. 'Jasper maintains a sensible approach to horn playing,' Kevin wrote at the end of his first term. 'I am confident that by the end of his school career his playing will have reached a very high standard.' I must have been improving because I was finally introduced to some real music. One day in the second term of our collaboration, Kevin came in with four books of sheet music, one orange, another pink, and two light green.

'It's about time you tackled a Mozart concerto,' said Kevin. The words sounded like a threat. I didn't know anything about any Mozart concertos. Up till now I'd never really had to grapple with *composers*. 'I think we'll try this one first.' Fishing out one of the green books, Kevin produced from inside a four-page sheaf of paper with a lot of notes on it. 'The third horn concerto's a good place to start. Let's have a go at the second movement.' He placed the music on the stand of the upright piano. 'The Romanze.'

The first bar looked simple enough. A dotted crotchet on the

C, slurring up to a tough F quaver, then down to the safety zone for couple of crotchets on A. I started to play.

'That's a B flat,' said Kevin.

'No it's not,' I said. 'It's a C.'

'The key is E flat, not F, which means that that's a B flat, not a C.' To me this sentence sounded like radio crackle.

'But it's a C.' There was an affronted edge to my voice. 'Why write a C if it's not a C?'

'You need to play a note down from the written note.'

'But if it's a B flat, why is there a C written?' Music has always had the capacity to bring out my inner moron.

'Are you sure you've not talked about this with your previous teacher?'

'He never mentioned a thing.'

So it fell to Kevin to explain the unique lot of the horn player. In its infancy the instrument was restricted to the sixteen notes of the harmonic series – spaced out at the bottom end of the register, crammed together at the top. By altering the length of tubing, it was possible to change the key of those notes. This was achieved by alternating between so-called crooks of varying length. All but one of the Mozart concertos were written in the key of E flat. The composers of the period thought it simplest to write their horn parts in the key of C stipulating at the top of the part which key the instrument was to be set up in and therefore which crook the player was to use. This also meant that the players of the day avoided the need to transpose. As the horn's middle register lies at the lower end of the treble clef this system had the added advantage of allowing the composer to avoid the continual use of ledger lines off the bottom or above the top of the staves.

'But I still don't get why they don't write it as you're meant to play it,' I complained.

'Tradition's part of it,' said Kevin. By the second quarter of the nineteenth century, he continued, when the invention of valves was making it possible to play in any key without changing crooks, F had become the standard key for instruments to be built in. By that time there existed already over a hundred years of repertoire written for instruments of the old style. Rather than demanding a complete reprint of the instrument's catalogue, players of the new valved instruments in F just got used to transposing. So what was once done to make things easier for horns was now precisely the opposite: harder. Horn payers take great pride, he said, in being able to transpose from every key.

'But E flat's easy,' Kevin added. 'Just play a tone down from what's written. You'll get the hang of it.'

It took a while. I faltered my way in, translating Cs into B flats, Fs into E flats and As into Gs. It was rough work, but by the end of Kevin's first term I had more or less wrestled the Romanze to the floor.

You have to laugh. On the horn list there is an online discussion about the increased difficulty in a climate of global insecurity of carrying your horn onto planes (which was never easy in the first place). 'Anybody know how many terrorists they have caught carrying French horns?' someone asks. Kendall Betts replies from New Hampshire. 'None. The ones I know only carry batons.'

Dennis Brain's single B flat Alexander 103 was severely damaged in the fatal car crash in Barnet. His horn was retrieved from the wreckage and restored by Paxmans. For many years it stood in the window of the Paxmans shop in Covent Garden. I meet one American horn player, now retired, who remembers going in there as a young man and being asked if he'd like to 'have a blow on Dennis's horn'. He turned down the offer. It seemed to him to be sacrilege. This was the same horn Brain is playing in the photograph on the cover of the album I was given one Christmas in my grandparents' house in Wales.

Since 2002 the instrument has been behind glass at the Royal Academy of Music. Brain's genealogy is laid out right there in the cabinet. Next to his Alexander is the Alexander 'with adaptations by Sansone' played by his uncle Alfred, and the horn made 'by Labbaye with Périnet valves by Brown' played by his father Aubrey. Alfred and Aubrey were the sons of AE Brain, who played fourth horn in the first-ever Prom in 1895. Alf spent much of his professional life in Los Angeles. Aubrey, eight years his junior, was principal horn of the inaugural BBC Symphony Orchestra and in 1927 became the first person to record a Mozart horn concerto. Dennis was taught by his father at the Academy, and made his professional debut alongside him at seventeen. They played the first Brandenburg Concerto. 'The famous family keeps up its traditions in the representative of the new generation,' wrote the *Daily Telegraph*. 'Son seconded father with a smoothness and certainty worthy of his name.' But Dennis was to be spared an Oedipal confrontation of his own. On Christmas Day of 1940, during a blackout in Bristol where the BBC Symphony Orchestra was based during the war, Aubrey had a bad fall slipping on ice. He was never the same player again. By the end of the war he had retired as a soloist.

Britain went to war soon after Dennis's eighteenth birthday. He joined the Royal Air Force and wore military uniform but, as principal horn of the RAF Central Band, and then the RAF Symphony Orchestra, his contribution to the war effort was largely musical, give or take the odd spell on guard duty. A fixture at the National Gallery's morale-boosting lunchtime concerts, he performed Brahms's horn trio there no fewer than six times. In the eighteen years of his professional life, he managed almost single-handedly to put the solo instrument back on the map for the first time since the death of Mozart, spurring a succession of composers to respond to his virtuosity, and the purity of his sound. Benjamin Britten, returning as a conscientious objector from American exile in 1942 with his companion Peter Pears, was the first major composer provoked into enlarging the literature for Brain. 'I first met Dennis in the early summer of 1942,' Britten recalled.

I was writing incidental music for a series of radio commentaries on war-time England which were being broadcast weekly to America at the ungodly hour of 3 am. The orchestra was that of the RAF, in which he was the first horn. I well remember being approached by him at one of the rehearsals, over, I think, some technical point in a solo passage. (Needless to say, having heard his playing in the first programme of the series I took every opportunity to write elaborate horn solos into each subsequent score!) We soon became friends.

On that first meeting Brain asked Britten to compose a concerto for the horn. Britten countered with enquiries about the horn's technical possibilities – particularly whether it was possible for a horn player to enter on a stratospherically high C, which Brain proceeded to demonstrate there and then. Britten's *Serenade for Tenor, Horn and Strings*, written while working on *Peter Grimes*, took up the baton from Schubert's 'Auf dem Strom'. Bookended by two mournful horn calls, including an entry for the horn on high C, the *Serenade* set to music six English poems in a hypnotic dialogue. Britten wrote no horn part for the sixth poem in order to give the soloist time enough to walk offstage and play the final muffled horn call from some distant corner of the building. Brain was only twenty-two when it was premiered on 15 October 1943 at Wigmore Hall in London. Britten described the event in a letter to a friend in America:

> I wrote a Serenade (words from Cotton, Tennyson, Blake, Jonson, Keats etc.) in 6, or seven pieces for Horn & Tenor & strings. There is a wonderful young horn player called Dennis Brain, who plays as flexibly and accurately as most clarinettists, & is a sweet & intelligent person as well. He did the first performance; I leave you to guess who did the singing! – and we had a lovely show with wonderful enthusiasm and lovely notices.

Brain also did the second performance, in Euston on a foggy night in January 1944, though he was booked to play at the Albert Hall the same evening. 'Just as Dennis came off the platform a man came along in a car in Euston Road and Ben stopped him and asked if he was going anywhere near the Albert Hall, and he said no, the nearest he was going was Marble Arch. So Ben said, "That's better than nothing" – and they bundled Dennis in ...' No musician has ever made more strenuous effort to be in two places at once than Brain did for his entire career.

Before the end of the war Brain's fame was already spreading around the globe. The RAF Symphony Orchestra visited America, where he turned down an offer from Leopold Stokowski to join the Philadelphia Orchestra. Two months after the war ended the RAF Symphony Orchestra performed at the Potsdam conference. A year later Richard Strauss visited London to conduct Brain and the Philharmonia in *Ein Heldenleben*. In 1948 Brain flew to Vienna to become the third man – and the first non-Austrian – to play Strauss's second horn concerto. Two years later he travelled to Baden-Baden to perform a horn concerto written especially for him by the German composer Paul Hindemith. Hindemith had gone into exile in Switzerland in 1938, soon after an exhibition on 'Degenerate Music' made explicit reference to his wife's Jewish roots. In 1946 he took American citizenship. The horn concerto was the first new work of Hindemith's to be premiered in his home country after the war. A former horn player himself, he wrote it after hearing Brain play a Mozart concerto the previous year. He presented Brain with a copy of the score. 'To the unsurpassed original performer of this work,' he inscribed. 'A grateful composer.'

The reviews offered never-ending praise. In 1946: 'Was anything like such horn-playing known a generation ago?' In 1948: 'Dennis Brain's horn playing – so expressive, so finely shaded and always of a brightness which puts it in a different class from the safe but dull German horn playing – verged on the miraculous.' 1951: 'It is difficult to say anything of Dennis Brain's performance, except that he was an alchemist, turning copper into gold. Anyone who plays the horn at all is to be honoured, but when a phenomenon like Brain appears, whose artistic and technical capacities seem limitless, one can only write (like Haydn) "Laus Deo".' His Midas touch extended as far as the Himalayas in 1953, where James Morris was covering the British ascent of Everest for *The Times*. 'Marching through Sherpa country,' Morris subsequently recorded , 'it did not in the least surprise me listening on the radio one day to Dennis Brain playing a Mozart horn concerto to find a whole posse of film men bursting through the tent flap to hear him too.' The day the news reached London that Everest had been conquered, Brain was playing in Westminster Abbey at the coronation of Queen Elizabeth II.

His other interest was in cars. When he recorded the Mozart concertos with Karajan he played from memory and, instead of the sheet music, had a copy of *Autocar* on his music stand. He was the only member of the Philharmonia whom Karajan, also a lover of cars, addressed by his Christian name. In one recording Brain split the opening note. Karajan put down his baton and quietly gave thanks to God. The prodigy was human after all.

Brain was a slave to his own genius. He was in such heavy demand that he missed his father's funeral in 1955. He also expedited his own. His addiction to speed was no doubt of a piece with the tolerance of risk that helped to make him the ideal horn player. The Philharmonia played three concerts at the Edinburgh Festival on the last three days of August in 1957. Brain fell asleep at the rehearsal for the first of them. During a break in rehearsal on the morning of the third concert, he approached Eugene Ormandy to discuss Strauss's second horn concerto, which he was due to play in Edinburgh the following Friday. He was planning to spend the week in London. The conductor couldn't help but notice how shattered he looked, and urged him to slow down. Brain smiled and shrugged. He did a lecture-recital that afternoon and fitted in a catnap before the concert.

On Monday morning, at the recording of Strauss's *Capriccio* at Kingsway Hall in London, the news of Brain's death was broken to the Philharmonia. Alan Civil, who had turned down the lift to London, shifted up into the newly vacated seat of principal horn. At the Prom in the Albert Hall that evening, the audience was asked not to applaud the Royal Philharmonic's performance of Tchaikovsky's Sixth, which Brain had played only forty-eight hours earlier in Edinburgh. At the festival on the Friday, when Brain should have played Strauss 2, they scheduled instead a performance of Schubert's Unfinished Symphony. For his own memorial, Britten turned to the sixth poem of the *Serenade* he wrote for Brain, where the horn is silent as the soloist walks into the wings. He began incorporating it into a piece for four horns and orchestra, but never completed it.

*

'So how's it been going?' Hugh Seenan has a cheery Glaswegian accent. It is unbelievably hot and airless. I have been summoned to the Guildhall School of Music and Drama, where Hugh is professor of horn. I am sweating at every pore. It's here, in this very building, that the twenty-fifth festival of the British Horn Society will be held in four months' time.

This is my 'lesson', but we both know it is an audition. I tell him how it's been going: about taking up the horn, about meeting famous horn players, about my lessons with Dave Lee and practising my arse off, about horn camp and Hermann Baumann; I tell him about wanting to play at the British Horn Society festival in four months' time.

'Good,' says Hugh. 'So you want to play a movement from Mozart 3.' I actually want to play three movements from Mozart 3, but at this stage settle for getting my foot in the door. 'Which movement?'

I've thought about this. If I'm going to be confined to a single movement, it seems logical to play the longest one: at seven minutes, the Allegro is twice as long as the Romanze and the Rondo, or the same length as both of them put together. It's also the hardest one. It calls for a cadenza, and an ability to lip-trill, but there are still four months to work them up.

'The first movement,' I say. 'The Allegro.'

'Right,' says Hugh, 'so why don't you play me a bit? In your own time.'

I have warmed up, but I blow my traditional scale and arpeggio just for good measure. And then I address the music in front of me, starting with the strange leap from F to D, the weird interval of a sixth ('And now' from 'My Way', 'The lord's my shepherd'). Hit the D, I tell myself. If it's the last thing you do, hit the bloody D. If you miss it, you fail the audition. And then the end really will be near.

There is no piano to keep me company, so I'm on my own. I take in my maximum litrage of breath, and embark. The good news is I hit the D, bang in the middle. It's a bull's-eye: the lord is my shepherd after all. I feel a surge of confidence and sail on into the movement, gliding up to the top of phrases and sliding down the other side in furious concentration. I botch the odd note, but my ordeal with Hermann Baumann has clearly paid off, because nothing will ever be quite as intimidating ever again. I'm just cantering in a lordly way towards the middle of the first page, with a rapid descent down the scale from high F to a long held note on the G. Technically the G should be trilled, but as I haven't crossed that bridge yet, I just hit the G, count to four and nestle into the F.

'OK, let's stop there.' Hugh has intervened. This can't be good. 'Can you play a trill?'

'Er, not yet,' I say, squirming.

'To play this you need to be able to lip-trill.'

'Yes I know. I . . .' I can feel my confidence draining through some imperceptible plughole. I've not passed the audition. The quest is over. I'm done. I'm dusted. I can put the Lídl back in its case and put the case back in the attic, where it belongs.

'Put the horn down.'

'Should I just play a bit m—'

'You've got some issues with your embouchure that we need to have a look at.'

'Oh. But did I . . . was it . . .' I am giving way to a rising panic. Hugh can hear it, and kindly puts my mind at rest.

'You can definitely play in the festival. Don't worry about that. You're much better than I was expecting you to be.'

My heart does a cartwheel. I've passed. I've passed the 'lesson'. Eight months after I first hatched the plan of playing a solo at the British Horn Society festival, they've finally agreed to let me under the wire. This is incredible. My heart does another cartwheel. I'm in. And another. I'm in! I can feel a monumental burden rising from my shoulders as I . . .

'We've got some work to do.' Hugh stops my private exaltation in its tracks. 'Let me see your embouchure without the horn.' I obediently form the horn player's moue and face him.

'You've got lovely thin lips,' he says. 'Perfect for horn playing. Not like mine.' He pouts fleshily. 'Nightmare lips for playing the horn. Now show me where you place the horn on the embouchure.'

For the next hour I have a tutorial in embouchure formation and mouthpiece placement from the Guildhall School of Music and Drama's professor of horn. It is thrillingly technical, amazingly useful and entirely specialist. Towards the end we get round to lip-trilling. Hugh gives me his theory on achieving a workable trill. He talks at some length about vibrations and oscillations, about air flow and throat manoeuvre. I lob it into the pot with all the other advice I've picked up on the lip-trill. In all I asked about six professors of horn in horn camp how to trill. They all had a different answer. One of them even managed to flog me a book on the subject. Cost me 20 bucks. Lowell's is the most colourful advice. 'It's actually Tuckwell's way,' he says. 'He was doing a class and trilling brilliantly and young ladies asked him. "Can you tell us how to trill?" He said, "It's as if I were a bunny rabbit chewing a carrot." And when he said that, I went, "It's a jaw trill." I went home and started practising moving my jaw and suddenly I had the most reliable trill in the world.'

Dave's theory is the simplest. 'Start slurring slowly between the note and the note above, and gradually speed up until the movement between the two notes is so fast it sounds like a trill.' I ask him how long it takes.

'Took me about six years,' he says, and laughs his head off.

But I'm in. That's the main thing.

There was a musicians' barrack in the gulag at Magadan, at the eastern end of Siberia. 'Individual bunks were neatly covered by blankets,' wrote one eyewitness, marvelling at the relative comfort granted to the camp orchestra. 'Mattresses and pillowcases were filled with straw. Instruments hung on the walls – a tuba, a French horn, a trombone, trumpet, etc. About half the musicians were criminals. All of them held soft jobs – the cook, the barber, the bath manager, the accountants, etc.'

In the Soviet Union, as much as in Nazi Germany, the ingrained reverence for music was kneaded and pummelled by inflexible ideology. One way of surviving and even prospering under communism was to be a classical musician. Horn players have a habit of occupying a desk the way some long-reigning monarchs occupy thrones, or dictators keep a grip of the reins of power. Thirty years is not an unusual tenure for a principal horn. But the natural longevity of horn players was exaggerated to an almost absurd degree in Leningrad, which only had two principal horns between the Russian Revolution and the fall of the Berlin Wall. Mikhail Buyanovsky began his long tenure in 1919. His son Vitali succeeded him in 1956, the year of the Hungarian uprising. Andrei Gloukhov took over only in 1989. I meet him and his horn section one afternoon when they are passing through London. The rest of the section were all taught and recruited by him, just as he was taught and recruited by Vitali Buyanovsky, who in turn owed everything to his father. The system is entirely dynastic and hierarchical.

'We never had any difficulties with travel,' Andrei says. 'We toured all over the world.' Nor did they play on instruments from their side of the Iron Curtain – Josef Lídls, for example, manufactured in the fraternal democracy of Czechoslovakia. In the Leningrad Conservatory where the Buyanovskys and Andrei Gloukhov were successively professors of horn, the students were supplied with Hans Hoyers shipped in from what was known after the war as the Federal Republic of Germany. Elsewhere under totalitarianism, musicians were similarly privileged. Peter Damm, who was principal horn of the Dresden Staatskapelle for thirty-three years, travelled extensively in the West. Fergus McWilliam remembers doing a masterclass with him in America in 1976.

Other East German horn players took the chance to move permanently over the border to the West on the night the Democratic Republic of Germany stretched barbed wire across the heart of the city on 13 August 1961. Several horn players who lived in West Berlin had desks in the pit of the Staatsoper in the Soviet sector of the city. They would commute unimpeded between the capitalist and communist halves of the city. But once the Wall went up, they were cut off from their jobs overnight. Karajan seized the moment and doubled the size of the horn section of the Berlin Philharmonic, which was in the British sector. 'There have been eight horns since 1961,' says Fergus. 'Karajan loved to double the wind and brass. Certainly he seemed never to get enough of us. Usually he wanted us to really crack it out.' No doubt so they could hear him on the other side of the Wall. Or even bring it down. It was breached four months after his death.

I have in my hands the horn of Dennis Brain. His single B flat Alexander. The horn mangled in the car crash. The horn on which he recorded the Mozart concertos with Karajan, on which the five-year-old Fergus McWilliam saw him play his last-ever notes, which he is playing on the cover of the album I was given at the age of ten. I have spent much of my year as a horn player feeling like an impostor, but this moment really caps it.

Photographs exist of the instrument when it was retrieved from the wreckage of Brain's Triumph. The damage seems irreparable. It looks like the squashed-flat horn hanging outside Kendall Betts's cabin in New Hampshire. The horn has nonetheless been repaired. I scour the bell and the main tubing for evidence of the accident. If you hold it to the light, tiny interruptions of the smooth surface can just about be discerned. Otherwise the restoration is astonishing.

My companion this morning is Andrew Clark, the principal horn of the Orchestra of the Age of Enlightenment, which performs on period instruments. One of the world's great natural horn players, Andrew happens to be the owner of Dennis Brain's other instrument, a French piston-valve horn in F made in 1818 by Raoux, a firm of horn manufacturers established in Paris in the eighteenth century. It was made a decade before the invention of valves, so it was of course a natural horn. Detachable valves were added in the early part of the twentieth century, some time before it was presented to Brain as a student by his father Aubrey. Horn players are practical, often unsentimental types, and none, it seems, more than Andrew. 'I was tipped off by a colleague that the Raoux was going to be for sale. I know some would be interested in it because of its provenance, but I was more interested in it because I thought it would be a good natural horn.'

Dennis Brain switched from the thinner sweeter sound of the

Raoux to the more robust German sound of the Alexander in the early 1950s. At the Royal Academy of Music it has been temporarily displaced by an exhibition of Scottish violins, so I have asked if I can see it. We are wearing white gloves to keep our paw prints from sullying the holy relic. Andrew – studious, bespectacled and extremely knowledgeable – starts to talk in great depth about the reconstructed instrument I turn over in my hands. As he talks his gloved forefinger points to various features – the thickness of the metal, the extra tubing to put the instrument into the key of A, the old-fashioned water-key. He talks about the gusset, the pretty, the chemise, the sleeve, the bore, the mouthpiece, the sharp angle of the curve, the silver nickel guard around the hoop, the lead-pipe. The lead-pipe is the straight stem into which the mouthpiece is inserted. 'A lot of discussion went on as to how to repair it,' he says. 'One of the things that the repairman wanted to do – because it's standard practice – is replace the lead-pipe, but Mrs Brain was very keen that the instrument should not have replacement parts if at all possible. That's very interesting because the lead-pipe is a customised version for Dennis Brain. He wanted it to feel more like the old-fashioned piston horn, which has a narrower bore. It should make the sound more contained, a bit smaller. Dennis Brain was never known for being the biggest blower in London. He was known for his lightness of touch and his accuracy and his musicality.'

It's time for someone to play it. I hand the horn over. Andrew tests the valves, which have not been oiled, and declares them noisy. 'If you waggle the bearing from side to side the rotor is not a good fit in there. It's worn for one reason or another. It may be that the rotor got squashed. I don't expect this horn to play as well as it did when it was first made.' With that disclaimer, Andrew inserts a mouthpiece into the lead-pipe, raises the instrument, and blows. A flurry of scales and arpeggios rushes out of the bell. It sounds splendid to me. He stops and looks quizzically at the horn.

'What do you think?'

'It feels slightly like a leaky instrument to me. It's all right.' He is making an effort to sound undisappointed. 'For me it's a slightly old horn. I'd probably say, "Let's replace the first valve" but obviously that's never going to happen. It's got a brighter sound than I expected. Alexanders are known for being quite bright but not quite as bright as that. But it feels like it would be a nice responsive instrument.'

He hands the horn back. It's my turn to play Dennis Brain's beautifully restored single B flat Alexander, perhaps the most illustrious wind instrument in the world. I am, it goes without saying, not worthy. It should be someone else doing this. But I am here and there will never be another chance. I take the thin sharp mouthpiece out of the horn case, attach it to the lead-pipe, and lift the horn towards my lips. I am struck by how light it is, and say so.

'You've got that old Lídl, haven't you?' says Andrew.

The thing about the old Lídl is I'm used to it. I'm a bit thrown by the fact that the horn stands in B flat. My double horn stands in F and is put into B flat by pressing down what Americans call the trigger, or thumb valve. I have a go at the Romanze. It's a bit of a botched job. Absurdly I can't remember the fingering. I try the Rondo instead. It doesn't sound much better. Unlike Andrew, who has extracted a very presentable sound from it, I can't blame the air leaking out of the valves. I can only blame myself. This is as good a practical demonstration as could ever be staged that when it comes to horns, the sound is made not by the instrument. It's made by the person holding the instrument. And the person holding the horn is in the grip of a severe dose of vertigo.

'I waited till the Sunday morning before Katrina struck before making a decision to evacuate. My neighbours and I were watching the TV and the storm was still moving west and it was 125 miles south of New Orleans. I said, "This could miss us and go on to Texas." About three hours later we noticed on the Weather Channel it made the north turn. We said, "That's not good. It's going to go right over us." So we commenced to load our cars with whatever we could, we wished each other Godspeed, and left.'

The month after the London bombings, the levees break on

the Mississippi in Louisiana and the city of New Orleans is flooded. Among the many made homeless by the disaster is the Louisiana Philharmonic Orchestra, the only American orchestra owned by its own musicians. All of a sudden there is nothing to own. CNN picks up a story about the orchestra's fourth horn evacuating his collection of forty horns. He uses them in an act called Howard Pink and his Musical Garden Hoses.

It was Dennis Brain who famously used to demonstrate the musical properties of the garden hose by fixing a mouthpiece in one end and a funnel in the other. He even performed Leopold Mozart's concerto with a hose. In a BBC recording you can hear him rather stiffly explaining the science of an air column's passage through a conical tube, and then demonstrating on a hose. But Howard's collection, built up over twenty years, runs to more than hoses.

'I took my cow's horns, conch shells, ram's horns, kudu horns, which are about four feet. I took my three Alphorns in three different keys. My original one was an E horn. I got it from a man in Idaho who holds the record for the world's longest Alphorn of 154 feet eight inches. I took my four natural horns. One of them is a valvectomy horn I got from Lowell Greer. I took my four-inch posthorn wrapped in leather, and the world's smallest hunting horn, which is about as big as a recorder.'

He also took the Reynolds Chambers horn he plays as fourth horn in the Louisiana Phil, and he has brought it to New York. The orchestra is in town to participate in a benefit concert with the New York Philharmonic in Avery Fisher Hall. I meet Howard in a bar in the Lincoln Center. He is short and fully bearded, with a gnarled look. He has been fourth horn in New Orleans for thirty-two years. (A colleague on second has been there for thirty-eight.)

'I went back a week after the storm to recover legal papers, diaries that I've written for my daughter, family photos. The mould and mildew had already started to form. My house hadn't been flooded. The neighbours' across the street did because they back up to a canal. But a tornado ripped off all my roof shingles, my tar paper and my attic vents, and so the rain from Katrina was able to enter from the top of my house, completely soak the insulation, go down the walls, through the ceiling. The parquet floors upstairs were all buckled six to eight inches. I had to rip some of that out to open my daughter's closet. And when I looked through the crack I realised I was looking at the sky. Downstairs my whole kitchen ceiling had caved in to the floor from the weight of water that had leaked in. The carpets in the dining room were totally soaked. The wallpaper and paint was blistering off the walls. Three of my eighty-foot pines were down in the yard – root-ball and all. The walls of my shed had literally been lifted off the foundation and tossed sixty feet away. And so I just packed some more stuff in the car and stuff from my garden hose show and closed the doors. I left the air conditioner on at about 85 degrees, left some ceiling fans on so that when the electricity came back there would be some air circulating.'

When I meet Howard, he has yet to have his meeting on site with his insurer. 'I hear the going price to replace a roof is about $20,000. We don't even make that much money in a year. The insurance guy was pretty adamant. "You better get down there and mitigate the damages." I said, "You don't seem to understand, I'm going to New York to play with the New York Philharmonic, then the following week I've got a chamber music job in Bloomington Indiana." He said, "How about if I offer you another $2,500?" I said, "Are you bribing me not to go to work? I'm the only horn player in my section that plays fourth horn. You can't just pick up somebody and expect them to play a concert." He said, "Well you know I can disallow your claim."'

Howard has relocated to Nashville, where he repaid the many kindnesses from the Red Cross and the Jewish Community Center by giving free performances of his Musical Hoses act to children. CNN are more interested in the plight of the orchestra, but the local media in Nashville descending on Howard all have the same question. With his life more or less in ruins, how can he manage to put on a show? And the answer is the expected one.

'Playing the horn,' he says, 'is a relief.'

*

At the end of the summer my parents, the three sons, the three partners and the six grandchildren muster in a house rented for one week on the north coast of Somerset. Wales, the land of our fathers, shimmers in the haze a few miles across the Bristol Channel. The idea is to gather the family under one roof. It's like Noah's Ark, without the animals. I take the Lídl.

None of them will be there for my performance at the British Horn Society festival. So I decide to perform the concerto for them all in Somerset. There's a handy outhouse with a washing machine and a freezer. I set up shop in there and do my Farkas warm-ups. My niece, who is nine and learning the horn, now and then pokes her head round the door to listen for a bit.

People spend the day of my performance playing beach games, board games. There is harmony in the air. It's a beautiful late summer late afternoon. All is at peace in this little corner of the world. A rich full sun slumps towards a high horizon, spraying oranges and pinks along a tangle of peninsular valleys. It'll be good, I tell myself, to get the horn back to its natural habitat. On the terrace, in front of the front door, I set up a semicircle of sturdy garden chairs in two rows, enough for an audience of thirteen. At the edge of the terrace, where the paving stones meet a sloping lawn, I wheel a stand-up barbecue into position. This will double as my music stand and sound system desk. I place the Nomad and its mini-speakers on the domed lid of the barbecue and balance the sheet music of K447 on top of that. The arrangement is not ideal – the music is at waist height – but it'll have to do.

On the advice of Dave, I've been playing along to recordings for a while now. From Paxmans it is possible to buy a recording of the orchestral accompaniment to the Mozart concertos without the horn track for about thirty quid. I go for the cheaper option. I've got half a dozen recordings programmed into the Nomad to choose from, including Barry Tuckwell, Hermann Baumann, Alan Civil, Peter Damm, Radovan Vlatković and Lowell Greer (my recordings of Vitali Buyanovsky, Gerd Seifert and Günter Högner are on LP) and I could even plump for the First Lady of Horn,

Helen Kotas Hirsch. But for this performance, my concert debut, I decide to play along to the recording made by Dennis Brain. My hope is that if I play loud enough, no one will hear the maestro.

The New Person rounds people up. Tall and small, united under one surname, they start to dribble through the French windows and on to the chairs I've laid out. My older brother and sister-in-law, whose daughter is learning the horn, decline despite repeated entreaties to attend, for reasons I fail to put my finger on. Perhaps they hate the horn. Whatever the reason, it affords me a unique opportunity to find out what it must have felt like to be Franz Strauss, playing his way through Wagner while simmering with rage. It also ensures that the balance of my audience is underage. It's stupid, but I'm nervous. This is without question the least judgemental crowd any horn soloist can ever face. But it's the first time I will have played the whole concerto all the way through in something like performance conditions. It has to be done.

I press 'play' and we listen together to Karajan conducting the Philharmonia over fifty years ago. Before the start of the solo, Mozart – no doubt to give the ageing Leutgeb a gentle entry – asked the horn to join the accompaniment for a couple of bars. As I launch into three descending minims of the Allegro – B flat, F, B flat – I feel the music loosen the tight fist of terror coiled somewhere around my diaphragm.

There are mistakes galore. I'm not entirely convinced that most of this audience – particularly the nippers – will spot a mistake, so just to let them know that I know I've boobed, I find myself frowning at every cracked note, every interrupted phrase, every infelicity. Afterwards the New Person says it looks terrible, and makes the audience nervous. The smaller children stare at me impassively throughout, somehow aware that they are witnessing something slightly different. The only truly embarrassing moment is the cadenza. I can't play along to Dennis Brain, so for a brief moment the audience is privileged to listen to the greatest horn player the world has ever known.

Normal service is resumed. The Romanze is presentable, but

the best movement is the Rondo. This seems to be the pattern. It takes me half a performance to conquer my fear of death, and only by the end am I relaxed. The notes of the hunting tune gallop out of the horn and into the open air with coltish abandon. I almost feel like a horn player, and chase towards the finish with a mixture of relief and elation. As I bash out a pedal B flat to finish, my relatives explode into applause, rising from their heavy garden chairs to shout and cheer. My father claps longest and loudest, and carries everyone along in his slipstream. In my shorts and T-shirt and bare feet, I step in front of the barbecue and bow awkwardly to my family.

8
Holly Wouldn't

I used to love listening to classical music to hear the horns and whenever I heard them I felt kind of proud because I felt it had something to do with me. Or I had something to do with it.

Ewan McGregor

There is a famous sequence in a famous film. A colonel – who is an out-and-out psychotic – wants to secure a particular beachhead from the Vietcong. He's heard the surfing's good. Someone should enjoy it, and 'Charlie', as he explains, 'don't surf'. Cut to a marauding fleet of American choppers as they swarm the clear skies over a blameless Vietnamese village. From strategically placed loudspeakers the colonel unleashes the terrifying triumphalist anthem that is 'The Ride of the Valkyries'.

Thus it is that eight French horns have the honour of accompanying an airborne division of the US army into battle. With horns to gird their loins, they wreak hell, sow slaughter. The colonel is asked about the point of this novelty musical tactic. Over a cacophony of whirring blades and strident Wagner, he has his answer primed. 'It scares the shit out of them.'

Here was a military man who knew his horn history.

The Internet Movie Database is a goldmine. It tells you everything about the film and television industry. *Everything.* Need to know who was the colour consultant on *Guys and Dolls*, the second assistant director (second unit) on *American Beauty*? Who was the gaffer on *The Diary of Anne Frank*? The additional dialogue recordist on *The Incredibles*? The good people at imdb.com have total recall.

They've even got Mozart on there: his full name (Johannes Chrysostomus Wolfgangus Theophilus etc.), place and date of birth, place and date of death (and reason for: renal failure). They've got his height, in imperial and metric (5'4"/1.63 m). And they've got a list of all the films on which his music has in some shape or form occurred on the soundtrack. At the time of writing, the list stands at 816 appearances for Mozart's music in the movies. It goes back as far as 1921 and *Mozarts Leben, Lieben und Leiden.* From *The Magic Flute* to *Meet the Fockers*, it's all there. Among classical composers, he is way out in front, whupping Wagner on 722 into second place and Beethoven on 601 into third. Of the also-rans, Verdi is on 514, Mendelssohn on 484 and Rossini on 465. Bach is 409, Tchaikovsky 407, Schubert 381, Puccini 377. Brahms is on 279, pipping Johann Strauss and Vivaldi, who are twelfth equal on 274. Handel, Richard Strauss, Haydn, Donizetti, Prokofiev, Shostakovich and Mahler are all under the 200 mark.

Mozart's four horn concertos, according to their records, have been used a total of six times, most of them in recent years. Concerto no. 1, K412, can be heard on *Stealing Beauty* and *The Truman Show.* The second, K417, crops up on *JFK*; the fourth, K495, on *Sour Grapes* and *Wedding Crashers.* According to imdb, Mozart's third horn concerto, K447, is used just once, on the 1998 underwater action thriller *Sphere* (tagline: 'Terror can fill any space').

The Internet Movie Database is remarkable that way. But it turns out to be fallible. In 1997 a low-budget British family comedy called *Remember Me?* included a subplot in which a teenage boy attempts to perfect the Romanze of K447. The film sank without trace. The only reason I know about it is because I'm told about it by Dave Lee. And the only reason Dave knows about it is because that's him playing on the soundtrack.

It was a novelty booking for a professional musician. 'Basically,' says Dave, 'I had to play badly. I had to invent various ways, that you'll recognise, of fucking up scales and practice routines.' The booking went against the grain in an additional way. 'We recorded all the Mozart bits that were going to be used with an orchestra,' Dave recalls. 'Then the producer, bless him, decided that his favourite bit of Mozart was the slow movement of the bassoon concerto. Presumably because it was the only Mozart that he knew. So I had to do the slow movement of the bassoon concerto as well. But on the horn.'

There are forty-four David Lees and seven Dave Lees listed on imdb. Actors, directors, composers, editors, producers, miscellaneous crew, David/Dave Lees in the camera and electrical department, the sound department, visual effects. None of them is a French horn player. Even Dave will concede that this is a minor omission compared to the result that comes up when you enter in the site's search engine the following name: Vincent DeRosa. There are two credits, twenty-nine years apart, for *Days of Wine and Roses* in 1962 and *The Last Boy Scout* in 1991. It's a rather sketchy résumé for a man who has been playing the French horn in Hollywood since 1936.

You know the work of Vincent DeRosa. You just don't know you know it. There aren't ways of measuring these things, but he is almost certainly the most widely recorded musician on the planet. In any genre. Music is ruthlessly deployed by filmmakers to steer the emotions of their worldwide audience. In its most overt form, an instrument will step forward into a starring role on camera. Movies such as *The Piano, The Pianist* and *Shine*, a film about a piano player, all prospered at the Oscars. The horn has confined itself to more enigmatic, Hitchcockian cameos. Off-screen is another story. The instrument the great film composers – Bernard Herrmann, Alfred Newman, Maurice Jarre, John Williams – have all instinctively turned to first is, yes, the horn. The instrument can do the heroic stuff and the romantic stuff. It can be athletic and cathartic. It can soothe, swoon, soar, scream and, in that sequence in *Apocalypse Now*, scare the shit out of film-goers of every age, race and creed. So it's possible to state that Vincent DeRosa, who for four decades played on pretty much every major movie soundtrack recorded in Hollywood, has tugged at the heart strings, lifted the spirits, set the pulse racing, soundtracked the back-row romance of just about everybody who has ever seen a Hollywood movie. If you measure success purely in terms of how many lives a musician touches, he is the most successful unamplified musician in history.

By the time I shake Vincent DeRosa's hand, he is eighty-five. He shuffles to the door of his home on a long low single-storey house in La Canada, a quiet neighbourhood in the suburban hills of Los Angeles. Medium height, medium-to-solid build, with a hint of a quiff and dark pointy eyes, he looks every inch the southern Italian middleweight, which may explain why Frank Sinatra used him from the war 'up until he couldn't sing any more', says Vince. 'He liked me,' he adds as he leads me into a large main room. 'He was very nice to me.' Sinatra wasn't the only one. A framed tribute from John Williams, Steven Spielberg's composer, stands on a side table. When Williams was nominated for his forty-fifth Academy Award, he finally equalled the bench-mark set by Newman. 'Vince DeRosa's contribution to American music can't be overstated,' it says. 'He was the premier first horn player on virtually every recording to come out of Hollywood for over 40 years. He represented the pinnacle of instrumental performance and I can honestly say that what I know about writing for the French horn I learnt from him. He was an inspiration for at least two generations of composers in Hollywood and beyond. He is respected worldwide and universally regarded as one of the greatest instrumentalists of his generation. It's been a privilege to have worked with him all these many years.'

The other side of the long sliding window is a swimming pool and a view of the neighbouring hills. There are Conn 8Ds slung around the soft furnishings. They aren't just for decoration. Vince still nips into town to play the incidental music on *The Simpsons*.

'I like to go to be with the fellas,' he says, 'and I play well enough to get by. I don't practise any more, I don't have any technique or tongue. But I can play.'

The inspiration of at least two generations of composers in Hollywood and beyond offers me tea and *Sachertorte*. We sit at a round table in the kitchen and talk over the chatter of a pink parrot installed in a cage. Vince DeRosa arrived in Los Angeles at fifteen after the death of his father turned him into the family's breadwinner. He started working at once. He had the good fortune to fall into the orbit of Alfred Brain. Older brother of Aubrey and uncle of Dennis, Alf emigrated to New York in 1922, when his nephew was only one, moved to Los Angeles a year later and took US citizenship in 1930, a year after the introduction of the talkies. Alongside a productive orchestral career, he played first for MGM, then for Fox. He went to America partly to flee his first wife, a former Tiller Girl whom he was in the process of divorcing.

'Whew,' says Vince, who met her. 'She was really a piece of work, that one.' Alfred was the most outgoing of the Brains. When he returned from service in the First World War, he snaffled the principal horn desks in three leading London orchestras, squeezing Aubrey into the sidelines. The brothers were not close. Alf's flight from a tempestuous marriage made room for his younger brother to advance. 'His brother from what I can gather was kind of jealous of Alf,' says Vince. 'Dennis was quoted as saying the horn player in the Brain family is Alfred. Which is true. Neither one of them could touch him. He was just phenomenal. In every respect.'

Alf Brain died in 1966, having spent much of his later life running a chicken farm with his second wife, but forty years on his protégé still finds it hard not to refer to him as Mr Brain. In the absence of his own father, it seems the younger player found a father figure in a hard-drinking, hard-playing English expatriate. Vince was born in the same year as Dennis Brain, but the paths of two most influential horn players of the twentieth century never crossed. They might just have met during the war when the RAF Symphony Orchestra's American goodwill tour brought Dennis to Los Angeles. 'Mr Brain wanted the two of us to meet,'

Vince remembers. 'But I was in the service. I was busy, and I missed him.'

By the time he was thirty Vince DeRosa was a leading orchestral musician employed on a constant round of broadcasts and recordings for classical and jazz artists at the hub of the entertainment industry. Then in 1951 Alfred Newman, who was head of the music department at Fox and composed its iconic anthem, asked him to join the studio orchestra on a contractual basis.

'He was like the man upstairs in the music business. I told him that I really liked what I was doing and I was making a lot of money. I was making *a lot*. So I told him, "Whatever the top salary is in the orchestra, I don't want more, but I want your top salary." He said, "You got it."' The other major studios each had their own orchestra. But Vince rapidly established a reputation as the best horn player in town. When the studio system started to collapse later in the decade, every other studio suddenly wanted him as their principal horn too. Now he found himself bartering not for his own gain but on behalf of studio horn players he'd put out of a job.

'I worked for every conductor there and I worked for every studio. I was in demand all over so evidently they wanted me for some reason. I'd ask, "If I go there you've got to pay the first horn his money." And they would do that.'

Coming from hard-working immigrant stock, he took bookings day and night. When not playing on major film recordings or fulfilling commitments to Sinatra and other singers, he would accept a block booking of B movies and do seven in a week. 'They were all three-hour calls. You go in with a whole book of music and you start recording and at the end of three hours you stop. We did them like TV shows. I would do those when things were not too busy.' He also did a lot of TV shows, including the biggest TV show of them all, in the pit at the Academy Awards.

'I did forty of them and then I said, "That's it." I hated every one of them. Oh it was *boring*. You'd just sit around all week. The music was junk. But I had to do it. It was part of the industry. I just had to be there. And I didn't like that at all.'

The work was constant, and constantly new. Unlike orchestral musicians, film musicians never play the same thing twice. And for the most part, Vince has never heard any of it again. He played on all the Herrmann scores for Hitchcock and Newman's soundtracks from *All About Eve* through to *Airport*, as well as all Williams's scores recorded in Los Angeles, and there were thousands of others. I run by him a list of some of the greatest films ever made and ask if he played on them. He has no idea. 'A lot of times we'd make a movie and all we'd have was just a number. Unless it was a big production by Newman where we had 100 people in the orchestra and sixty-five-piece chorus, and everything was live, so then you'd remember. *The Diary of Anne Frank* and things like that. My wife would say, "Well what movie are you working on?" I'd say, "You know? I don't know." And no I did not go see them. When I had a night off I wouldn't go to the movies. Last thing in the world I would do.'

One Thursday afternoon in the September before my sixteenth birthday, I sauntered down to the Music Schools for my first-ever orchestra rehearsal. It hadn't occurred to me, until I walked through the door and heard the whinge of sawing strings, that the concert room would be heaving with violins and cellos. I'd only ever played with wind instruments before. I must have looked vaguely lost.

'You're over there, Jasper,' said an impossibly tall man, pointing with a thin stick to an empty chair in the corner at the back. Our conductor. It was the first time a beak had ever called me by my first name. He was the nicest man imaginable, but no one in the two years that followed would make me anywhere near as unhappy.

'Schumann,' he explained over the buzzing throng as I made my way to the back, 'said the horn was the soul of the orchestra.'

I smiled thinly and sat down to the right of a nerd with black curly hair from which dandruff fluttered like snowflakes in a paperweight. He was holding a horn. I nodded, unclipped my horn case and glanced at the sheet music on the stand in front of me. Second horn. Something by Schubert. Didn't look too difficult, give or take the odd flurry of squiggles. I blew a few desultory notes on the Lídl.

The impossibly tall conductor made his opening address – something about Schubert's Ninth Symphony being actually his Seventh, mostly known as 'the Great C major' . . . his last finished symphony . . . the composer never heard any of them performed etc. etc. I wasn't really listening. Numbers, letters, facts. Not interested, thanks. I looked around the room and noticed that it was absolutely teeming with girls. There were definitely at least five of them. Including an unbelievably beautiful one on the cello desk. She looked roughly my age. Was it just me, or did she look startlingly like the new bride of the heir to the throne? She caught me staring at her. I looked away and pretended to study the second horn part.

The nerd said something which I didn't hear.

'Rees,' he said again.

'Hm?'

'We're starting.'

'Oh. Right.'

I looked at the music again and saw that the second horn part kicks in with a few gentle notes in the upper part of the register. Of my register, anyway. A C first off: not so very easy to hit, but not impossible. I'll play quietly, I told myself, skirt along the edge of the noise, keep out of harm's way. The impossibly tall conductor raised his baton. He counted in a bar. On the first beat I lifted the Lídl. By the second it was safely on my lips. On the third beat I noticed that no one else in the entire room seemed to be making ready to play their instrument. No one else apart from the nerd on my left. By the fourth beat I was having a minor coronary episode. The 'Great C major', it turned out, begins with a solo for horns.

It would have been nice if someone had mentioned this before, I thought. The nerd on my left was playing, but I had pulled my mouthpiece away from my lips. A look of profound mystification had settled on my face. The impossibly tall conductor tapped his baton.

'What happened to the second horn?' I blushed, instantly and profusely.

'I don't . . . I'm not sure, sir.'

'Let's have another go after four,' and he sang the first bar. A ghost of a smirk played across the nerd's face as we were counted in again and this time I went for the high C, almost hit it, just about found it, and then began a wobbly progress towards the end of the bar. C minim, D crotchet, E crotchet. New bar. Dotted crotchet on A, B quaver, C minim. I noticed that the nerd seemed to be playing something different, something lower. We were in time, but not in tune. Didn't sound too great, to be frank, but who am I, I thought, to argue with Schubert?

The impossibly tall conductor tapped his baton. I looked up, wondering if there was a problem.

'It's in C major, Jasper.'

'What?' I blushed, instantly and profusely.

'The part is written in C major.'

'Oh. I . . .'

'You'll need to transpose it.'

'Pardon, sir? . . . Not sure I, er . . .' Muffled giggles scurried around the room. I deflected the white heat of my humiliation onto the nerd.

'Transpose to what?' I whispered aggressively, as if it was his fault.

'The C is really a G,' he whispered back. 'You drop every note by a fourth.'

I looked down the page. An entire sheet of music had suddenly morphed into incomprehensible hieroglyphs. It might as well have been a jar of tadpoles thrown randomly onto the page. I might as well have been a chimpanzee holding this instrument. I dredged up a memory of my teacher, Kevin Amos, explaining to me why horn players have to learn to transpose from more or less every key. I could transpose from E flat, because all that involved was playing one tone down from the written note. But four?

All music not written in the key of F on a horn player's sheet music needs, in effect, to be translated. There are two ways of transposing. Either the publisher can avoid a lot of fuss and bother and do it before printing the music so that when it reaches the horn player the part is already safely in F and everyone's happy. Or the horn player can do it there and then on the spot. Unfortunately, a precedent was established in the nineteenth century that meant horn players would just have to lump it. Some of them actually love it. It accentuates their separateness from all other musicians that they have this extra mountain to climb. Even at fifteen I knew that this was a reality of horn-playing life. You just never think it's going to happen to you, and in the middle of a roomful of nerds, creeps, boffins, spods and at least five girls who comprised the Harrow School orchestra.

As ever, Kevin looked on the bright side. 'Another excellent term for Jasper. He has made great advances, both technically and musically and by all accounts is also turning into a very stable ensemble player. I look forward to more exciting progress next term!'

I'd spend the week in dread of those looming Thursday afternoons. Rehearsals passed in a pit of despair. The start of each term was the worst. Across twelve weeks with the Great C major I haltingly worked out how to transpose four notes down. By the end of term, playing in the vast complex organism of an orchestra became bearable, even enjoyable and then, come the concert, actually uplifting, joyous, thrilling. There would be nothing like it for sheer exhilaration. But that term ended, and there was no guarantee that I'd ever see C again. I'd pitch up for the first rehearsal of the new term not knowing what fresh key I'd have to transpose from. It could be G (up one tone from the written note), or D (down three semitones), or A (up two tones) or E (down a semitone).

And then there was the counting. The horn is a busier instrument than, say, the trombone. It's often supplying fills, fattening out an orchestral chord, providing additional colour and now and then taking on the tune. However, there is an awful lot of resting too. But resting is of course a misnomer. Actually what you're doing in 103 bars of rest is counting down to your next entrance. If it's four beats to a bar, that's a count of 412. Is it any wonder people get lost? I got lost as a matter of course. Sometimes I just let the nerd do the counting. He was good with figures.

But after a year the nerd disappeared to read maths at university, rendering me the only horn player in the whole school who was remotely good enough for the orchestra. Kevin was optimistic. 'Jasper has now started on some of the more demanding works of the repertoire. The Mozart concerto which he is at present working on will be a worthwhile challenge. He will make a very useful first horn in orchestra next term.'

The exposed passages were the worst. That first time in the nerd's seat, I had an attack of acute innumeracy. I'd been counting for what felt like half my lifetime through a slow rising crescendo of strings and woodwind. Eventually, about midway into the count, I lost my place. I was dimly aware that at some random point in the future I had a semibreve to play, leading into a short rising phrase. It was marked fortissimo with diminuendo. Probably one of those fat orchestral chords, I told myself. If I'm not there, no one will notice. So after what felt like the appropriate amount of time I lifted the Lidl and, pasting an unconfused look across my face, prepared to pretend to play. All of a sudden the whole orchestra ground to a halt.

'HORN!' yelled the impossibly tall conductor. 'Where are you?'

Silence. Tumbleweed. The heads of forty nerds, jerks, boffins, spods and girls turned to stare.

'Er, I lost count, sir. Sorry.' Sniggers. Smirks. As I smarted under this onslaught from a roomful of hoity-toity prodigies, I privately wondered whether Schumann didn't leave out a syllable. The horn, I felt certain he meant to say, is the arsehole of the orchestra. I was just thinking this when, from the cello section, the spitting image of the wife of the heir to the throne gave me a look of doe-eyed sympathy. Furtively, I smiled back.

Just as one in twenty people is said to be gay, one in however many hundred or thousand people learns to play the horn. I don't have an exact figure, or even an inexact one. But I do bump into fellow travellers. '*I* used to play the horn!' I hear this a lot in the course of my year. Maybe as many as seven times. A theatre director who gave up after he didn't get into the Royal Marines band. A music producer who gave up after his face was smashed in at rugby. Andrew Lloyd Webber, who gave up at fourteen because, he tells me, 'I just couldn't get on with the Hindemith horn sonata.'

'Such a beautiful instrument,' says Holly Hunter wistfully. Holly Hunter, who did all her own playing in her Academy Award-winning performance in *The Piano*, learned the horn for three years as a teenager. We meet in the deserted bar of the Old Vic, the famous London theatre. She looks away into the middle distance, as if transported back to the farm in Georgia where she grew up, the youngest of seven. 'I *love* the French horn.' The deep-southern vowels writhe and curl on her palate, the sibilants splash on her tongue. 'I played for four years in high school. I played trumpet too but I much preferred the French horn.'

We're here to talk about her acting. But this seems a promising lead. Here is a Hollywood star who once played the Hollywood instrument. Maybe she'll have some piercing insights. She is in town to perform in a play. The New Person In My Life is producing it, so there will be bags of access to her. I decide to ask for a formal interview. I accept that there's nothing in it for Holly, and that interview requests with Hollywood stars should normally go through the proper chains of command, the publicists, representatives, handlers, gofers, personal assistants, impersonal assistants, the armour-plated, iron-fisted, bullet-tongued tiers and cordons and phalanxes of people. But I don't want to talk to Holly's team in Los Angeles. I want to talk to Holly in London, where she is currently on the payroll of the New Person, in a theatre 200 yards from her office. Surely a polite letter will suffice. I write Holly a polite letter and leave it at the stage door. Would Holly, it basically says, like to talk horn?

The play begins its run. I leave Holly to it for the moment. The play continues its run, with no word from Holly. After a while the play ends its run and still no word from Holly. Holly leaves town and takes a holiday in Paris. At this point Holly is no longer on the New Person's payroll, but nonetheless the New Person gets a call from Holly. She is desperate to get into a performance of *Otello* at the Paris Opéra. It's sold out and she can't lay a hand on a ticket for love nor money nor special superstar pleading. She's tried every avenue going. The New Person calls me, who calls his friend at the Royal Opera House, who calls the Paris Opéra, who call my friend at the Royal Opera House, who calls me, who calls Holly.

'*Allo?*' Holly, on holiday in France, is pretending to be French.

'Holly, it's Jasper. I've organised your tickets for *Otello* tonight.'

'Wow!' Holly reverts to English. 'That's great, man!'

'You need to pick them up from the box office. They're in your name.'

Holly knows about my request to talk horn. And I know that she knows. And she knows that I know she knows. Et cetera. There is a pregnant silence, and it's filled with an unspoken question. Would Holly talk about the Hollywood instrument? Would Holly talk horn? Would Holly?

I badly need a cadenza, and I need it fast. Without a cadenza, I can't perform the first movement of K447 at the British Horn Society festival, or indeed anywhere else. So I must learn one, or compose one. Learning one is out, because when I listen to, for example, Dennis Brain's cadenza, it's just too difficult. Plus it's Dennis Brain's. I am reminded of something Phil Myers, the principal horn of the New York Philharmonic, told me. When I met him in New York, he was just back from performing Mozart 3 in South Korea.

'For the first twenty years of my career I just did the Brain cadenzas,' he says. 'I got embarrassed after a while that I was just so goddamn lazy. I started thinking I really just should try writing a cadenza, even if it sounds like shit. Just to do it.' And he sings it to me. It doesn't sound like shit at all. It sounds like him: witty, and surprisingly soulful. My understanding is that a cadenza is meant to be just that: an expression of the soloist's musical personality. However, my first attempt at a cadenza, in horn camp, revealed the musical personality of someone with a bipolar disorder. Clearly I want to inflict something slightly more har-monious on any future victims. So for a week I stop all practice on the actual concerto, and try to work up something more meaningfully Mozartian.

It's hard graft, but after a few days I have cobbled together a series of quotations from the whole of the concerto. There's a bit of lyricism in there from the Romanze, some jocularity from the Allegro and a spot of up-tempo riffing from the Rondo. It's less a home-made quilt, more a stretch of crazy paving. I'm quite pleased with it, and I play it to the New Person with maximum expression, slowing and speeding, rising and falling. At the end I lower the Lídl and look at her expectantly.

'It's a bit long, isn't it?' she says.

'Is it?'

'How long are cadenzas meant to be?'

'I dunno. A minute?'

'Tell you what. Let me time it.'

I play it again against the stopwatch on her phone. At the end I lower the Lídl.

'How long?'

She looks at me a bit ruefully.

'One minute and forty-three seconds.'

'Jesus.'

I decide to measure all the K447 cadenzas in my collection. It's a pleasant hour's work. Barry Tuckwell breasts the tape first at 29 seconds, just in front of Lowell Greer on 31 and Dennis Brain on 33 seconds. There's a bit of a wait for Günter Högner to come in on 44 seconds, Helen Kotas on 48 seconds, Alan Civil on 49, while the Slavs, Vitali Buyanovsky and Radovan Vlatković, both duck in under the minute on 52. Somehow I'm not surprised that it's the Germans bringing up the rear. On the natural horn Hermann Baumann crosses the line at one minute and 16; he's three seconds slower with valves, while Gerd Seifert and Peter Damm stroll in last at one minute and 22. In other words, in its current incarnation my cadenza limps home a full 21 seconds after the slowest of the other runners and riders. I am more long-winded than the most long-winded soloist in my collection. Somehow, I need to cut myself down to size.

I have a basic structural problem to surmount. The cadenza is the composer's invitation to the soloist – in this case Mozart's to Leutgeb – to extemporise. It's a platform to show off. The obvious difficulty is that I'm not good enough to show off to a roomful of horn players. My musical personality will be pretty obvious to anyone sitting in the audience. 'You're joking,' people say when I tell them about taking up the horn after a twenty-two-year lay-off and playing it in front of a paying audience. 'You're not serious.' Maybe that's just it. Maybe I *am* joking. I am a musical joke. My cadenza should in some way embody that. If I can't do anything else, I can at least make people laugh.

I go back to square one.

Film composers are extraordinarily rich. One afternoon I penetrate the inner sanctum of Studio One in Abbey Road, where an orchestra of freelance musicians is recording the soundtrack to a movie by Tim Burton. Up at the front, on the conductor's podium, is Danny Elfman. At the back, in the horn section, are the principal horn of the Royal Philharmonic Orchestra, the principal horn of the Philharmonia Orchestra, the principal horn of the English Chamber Orchestra and the Aubrey Brain professor of horn at the Royal Academy of Music. I sit behind them and listen as, like naughty schoolboys, they work out how much Elfman must be worth. As the composer of the theme tune of *The Simpsons*, he gets a cheque every time his music is played anywhere in the world. The horn section loses count. But it runs into many many many millions of dollars. Per annum.

There is no real money in horn playing. When Dennis Brain died he left £30,109 in his will. It included a £10,000 insurance policy on his lips. In 1957 it was a tidy sum, commensurate with the deceased's status as one of the most sought-after soloists in the world. But he was the exception to the orchestral rule. The only place there is any guarantee of remuneration in horn playing is Los Angeles.

They seem to know this at my Beverly Hills hotel. A monstrous complex of concrete at the intersection of Wilshire Boulevard and Rodeo Drive, it looks more like a small city state than a place to kip. But I feel at home the minute I walk into the foyer and notice two tapestries hanging on opposite walls above twin reception desks. They depict identical French hunting scenes from the seventeenth century, and slap in the middle of each of them is a man in livery blowing on a *trompe de chasse*. Truly the horn is everywhere. Despite crippling jetlag, it puts me in an excellent mood. Maybe the City of Angels is not entirely given over to Mammon.

As you would expect of Tinseltown's principal horn, Vincent DeRosa is the richest horn player in the world. At the height of his career, in the days before synthesisers, he was making more than the major league baseball players. Reaping the reward of more or less inventing the big and beautiful Los Angeles sound with the stoutly flared bell of his Conn 8D, he sank his earnings into bricks and mortar. He began buying real estate in the 1960s, at the start of the Californian property boom when the dollar went a lot further, and bought homes up and down the state.

But there was a trade-off. I get my first inkling of this when I go to see the film version of *The Phantom of the Opera* at a gala premiere in Leicester Square. Soaring over the soundtrack in great arcs of brave Brucknerian splendour is my mate Dave. He is Andrew Lloyd Webber's chosen horn player, and the film's orchestrations work him incredibly hard. For the listener the rewards are rich. For Dave the rewards are monetary. I hang around at the end of the gala premiere looking for his name, but can't seem to spot it. Outraged on Dave's behalf, I feel the urge to take up cudgels. Music, and usually horn playing, is part of the backbone of pretty much every major motion picture you've ever seen. But if you loiter among the shards of popcorn and spent buckets of carbonated tooth-rot after everyone else has left, to find out who is playing in the orchestra, you will be wasting your time. In the movies, they tell you who was key grip, best boy, focus puller, artist responsible for Mr Cruise's lifts and assistant to Mr Spielberg's assistant personal assistant. They even, heaven help us, tell you who the publicist was. But do they tell you who is playing that exquisitely plaintive horn solo at the end of *War of the Worlds* when the invading Martians have been vanquished and the camera pans across a ravaged landscape aglow in a russety thermonuclear haze? Do they tell you who's playing? Do they hell.

He's called James Thatcher.

'Well I hope it sounded OK,' says Jim. Don't bother looking Jim up on imdb.com. There are just three entries – for *Sleepers* in 1996 and *Amistad* in 1997, and in 2005 for re-recording the soundtrack on a 1926 silent movie called *The Temptress*. I am sitting in his living room one evening, not far from Vince DeRosa's house in La Canada – or Mr DeRosa, to Jim. Tinseltown's principal horn turns out to be a scrupulously polite and self-effacing man with small blue eyes in his early fifties. Hollywood, I discover, has pretty much the same dynastic arrangement for horn players as they had in Soviet Leningrad. The top job is handed down once every thirty-five years or so from one generation to the next. Just as Vince DeRosa was Alfred Brain's protégé and successor, Jim Thatcher is the creation of Vince DeRosa. Born and raised in California, he first noticed the horn on a movie soundtrack when he went to see *How the West Was Won* at the Warners Cinerama in Hollywood as a thirteen-year-old.

'It was an Alfred Newman score. I was just mesmerised by what the horn players were doing there. I didn't even know who Vincent DeRosa was when I listened to it. It wasn't until I was well into my high school years when I went down to a music store and was listening to a couple of older fellas and the subject of studio horn players came up. This one guy just told me how the finest players around play in the studios, but no one really knew them. We all knew of Philip Farkas and Dennis Brain and the famous horn players in the major symphonies. Even here on the West Coast the studio players were pretty anonymous. But when I found what the studio horn players made compared to the symphony horn players I thought, Wow, this'll be something very comfortable to get into if one could do it. The remuneration is on a very high plane.'

How high a plane? High enough to buy a plane. Earlier in the day Jim has just nipped over to Vegas in his. That's not something you can say of many other horn players. In fact you can say it of only two other horn players in the world, and they both play in Jim's section in Los Angeles.

'We began flying about twenty years ago,' he explains, 'so that we would have something to talk about besides music. And it's been good therapy, it really has.'

Jim Thatcher began playing in Hollywood studios in 1979, initially at the side of Vince DeRosa but latterly as principal horn. He has long since lost count of the number of movie soundtracks he's appeared on.

'It could be twelve to eighteen hundred,' he says. 'On top of that there are many many television shows and recording dates with Frank Sinatra and Barbra Streisand. Sinatra was just a few times. Very imposing man. Kinda scary, even at eighty-three years old. I remember that he walked out of Capitol Records when we finished recording and he turned around and said, "If anybody hits you guys, call me." Still very much the boss.'

The Faustian pact could not be more simple or stark. No credit in the film: good credit at the bank. Well off: not well known. In return for signing away their right to any form of acclaim, Jim and his fellow Hollywood musicians receive residual payments for the afterlife of the movie. Some soundtracks can have quite an afterlife. That was Jim, for example, matching Celine Dion note for note in 'My Heart Will Go On', the mega-blockbuster written by James Horner to play out over the end credits to *Titanic*.

'The horn and the vocalist were doing this wordless quasi-Irish theme,' he recalls. 'She's already put down the tracks. In her singing she had little inflections so I had to listen to what she had done and put the inflections in as she did them. She'd lift something sometimes or put in a little ornament here or there or be ahead or behind the beat as singers are apt to do. My job was to ghost that. I had to mesh in with her style and make it so it sounded like one.'

Did he like the song?

'Sure,' he says. 'I like everything about people who hire me and pay me.' It seems rude to ask exactly how much he is paid but he is happy to divulge how much more he is paid than he would be if he had spent his career in a symphony orchestra. 'I probably make at least three times as much as a principal horn in a major symphony,' he says. 'And that also includes a residual payment which is a very fine retirement if I ever chose to just leave the instrument. That residual is still more than what most principal horn players make. I'm an independent contractor, one could say. I'm like a plumber or electrician. Someone needs the horn? I have an answer and exchange and they call me.'

'Jasper continues to work well and achieve the progress he deserves. He has recently started working on another Mozart concerto which I am sure he will find a satisfying challenge.'

Kevin was my final horn teacher. His school reports are, without exception, raves.

'An excellent term, and indeed year's work. Jasper now handles difficult pieces with a good sense of style and high standard of musicianship. He contrives to maintain an intelligent, mature attitude towards music. I look forward to his next year's progress!'

They just don't tally with my memory of struggling with transposition and sight-reading. I don't ever remember being able to play the horn particularly well. I decide to track Kevin down and ask him. We meet in the West End, in a private members club of which neither of us is a member. The beard has gone, as has the hair over the collar. But the really big change is that Kevin no longer plays the horn. He sold his Paxman, he tells me, to pay the taxman, and now works as a musical director and pianist in theatre. Otherwise he is just the same. We sit down at a table with a bottle of white wine. After a few re-introductory exchanges, I whip out my school reports and flop them on the table.

'Have a look at those,' I say. Kevin picks up the top one and starts to read an encomium he wrote twenty-five years ago. I've put them in chronological order. He reads another, and another, before putting them down. He's got the gist.

'Was I any good, Kevin?' I ask him.

'Yes,' he says.

'But that's not my memory.'

'I seem to remember you were very good.'

'What about the nerd with dandruff? What was he like?'

'I don't remember him,' he says. I don't get it. How can he

remember my playing if he doesn't even remember his only other presentable pupil? I read out one of the reports.

'Another excellent term for Jasper, who continues to develop musically and technically.' I suggest to Kevin that there is a credibility gap between his words and my music, that I never did any practice, was catatonically afraid of the orchestra and found Mozart hard uphill work. I further put it to him that, in the manner of school teachers covering their arses up and down the land, his end-of-term reports praise me beyond my deserts, perhaps because he liked me more than the nerd, possibly because I liked listening to his stories of rubbing shoulders with the stars, but mostly because we just sort of hit it off. As we are hitting it off again. He skims another report and looks up at me.

'Maybe there's a bit of that going on,' he concedes. Now we're getting somewhere. He puts down the report. I collect them all up and return them to my bag. It's good to clear that up.

'But I think that if you'd persevered and worked hard there's no reason why you couldn't have got into music college.'

I practically spit out my white wine. Kevin is evidently in the vice-like grip of false memory syndrome. I was never never never ever that good. I just know I wasn't. It's that simple. But I do like Kevin's optimism. He is delighted, for example, that I have taken up the old instrument again, and intrigued that I have been accepted as a soloist at the British Horn Society festival. He asks me if I'd like to come round to his house and bash through Mozart's third horn concerto with him on the piano. I'd be thrilled.

A week later, Kevin ushers me straight into a beautiful room at the back of the ground floor of his house. It contains a Yamaha grand and nothing else. I unclip and warm up, and hear the walls singing back at me. The acoustic is mind-blowing. I give Kevin the sheet music, and we begin. By the end of an hour I've asked Kevin to be my accompanist at the British Horn Society festival. And he has accepted.

Holly wouldn't, but Obi Wan Kenobi will.

'I was sent to play in the regional orchestra in Perthshire,' Ewan McGregor tells me, 'because I was good enough to be in it.'

The most famous lapsed horn player in the world is taller than I am expecting. We are sitting in the basement dressing room of a theatre in the West End. Ewan, who is in a show, is talking to me before curtain-up. It turns out that the star of *Star Wars*, the biggest and most heavily marketed movie franchise in Hollywood history, plastic models of whom decorate boys' bedrooms in every corner of the globe, dreaded orchestra rehearsals as much as I did. If not more. And for the same gamut of reasons.

'It was like being driven to the gallows. It was a Friday night and it was a twenty-five- or thirty-minute drive to Perth, just before the Highlands, so it was usually raining. And dark. I remember it always being really dark. My mum would go off and I would climb those stone stairs to this huge hall. Because I went to the same school in Crieff all my life I didn't have any skills for meeting new people. I didn't know anybody. It was a seventy-piece youth orchestra and I felt like there were sixty-nine people who were really good friends and me who no one liked. I was completely swamped with fear. I sat at the back and I couldn't hear what I was playing and sight-reading wasn't ever one of my strong points. It was literally, "There's the music. Get on with it." My biggest problem was that you had to transpose everything as you played. I thought, why don't they print it in the right key? And they just scoffed at me and went, "Because it's the horn." I just remember feeling awfully out of place and I hated it. I must have done it for three terms until I just couldn't do it any more.'

Ewan took up the horn at the age of ten, partly because there was a spare horn in his primary school, partly because 'Everyone kept telling me it was difficult, so I just thought that's the one for me'. His father was the school's PE teacher, but music and art were the only things that interested him. 'Eventually they wouldn't let me do both: you were only allowed to do one or the other or you're copping out of the corporate society.' He got to grade seven standard on the horn, and remembers being much more comfortable in front of an audience playing solos with a piano. 'You could hear the fruits of your labour. And I've always found any kind of performance is a very good way to get girls.'

Eventually he was talent-spotted by Grampian TV, the regional independent television station, and invited onto a programme featuring young musicians. He played the Rondo from Mozart's fourth horn concerto, K495. His performance was preserved in the televisual archives and inevitably cropped up, after he was famous, on a programme called *Before They Were Famous*. The sixteen-year-old Ewan McGregor has spiky hair and a thickly knotted school tie and, given the circumstances, plays with great fortitude.

'I played with their accompanist,' he recalls, 'which threw me a little bit. He wasn't quite as good as mine, I don't think. He was a bit rumpty tumpty.' His nerves manifested themselves in a not particularly telegenic visual tic. 'Every time there was a rest period in the piece, I'd do a lot of wiping of my nose, because I thought it looked kind of cool. But of course on television it just looks like you've got a bogey up there that you can't get out.' He left school that year and gave up the instrument. His horn is in a cupboard in the bedroom at home.

'I could never get rid of it. It's not a very good horn. I don't think it's even as good as that one.' He points at the Lídl, which I've brought along. He asks if he can play it. Despite the fact that he has a streaming cold, I hand my horn and mouthpiece to one of the most celebrated actors on the planet and watch him blow his first notes for the first time in years. After a scale or two, Ewan goes back to the Rondo he played on Scottish television, feeling through his fingers for the famous sequence of notes. It sounds approximately as bad as I did when I first tried to play Mozart again after twenty-two years off. After a couple of minutes he puts the horn down.

'How did you get back into it?' he says. 'Did you go back to *A Tune a Day*?' I tell him about the restart, and Dave, and horn camp, and the concert. 'It's nice to have a little blow. I'm sure you'll have inspired me to dig mine out.' Ewan McGregor hands back the Lídl. 'On a film set I spend so much time sitting in a trailer it would be a good thing to do.' He gets up. He has a musical to perform. My time on planet Hollywood has drawn to a close. 'Maybe you'll bring my midlife crisis forward a few years.'

*

Not all Hollywood film scores are recorded in Los Angeles.

'I remember turning up at Anvil Studios in Denham outside London,' says Terry Johns, who in the mid-1970s was principal horn of the London Symphony Orchestra. He has a strong Welsh accent, though lives in Scotland. 'The place was empty. I asked a colleague on the horn desk what we were playing. "Some fucking space thing," he said.'

The LSO made their first appearance on a soundtrack in 1935. Down the years the most recorded orchestra in the world has been heard on *Raiders of the Lost Ark, Aliens, Braveheart, Notting Hill* and a couple of *Harry Potters*. But the biggest feather in the LSO's cap is playing on the original *Star Wars* movies. With his faith in the instrument bolstered by half a lifetime of composing for Vincent DeRosa, needless to say John Williams gave the horns a lot to do. There were eight horns used on the original *Stars Wars*, nine on *The Empire Strikes Back*, six on *Return of the Jedi*.

'During Darth Vader's funeral, when they burn him like a Viking,' says Terry, 'there's a horn solo, and that's me. So that makes me the most famous horn player in the world. If people say, "What have you done?" I say, "I've played at Darth Vader's funeral."' I spool forward to chapter 47 on the DVD and there Terry is, playing a beautiful, haunting dirge as crackling flames devour the infamous helmet.

When the LSO got the gig again for George Lucas's trilogy of so-called prequels, Williams scored for eight horns on *The Phantom Menace*, nine on *Attack of the Clones* and a whopping fourteen on *Revenge of the Sith*. The most successful movie franchise of all time may have starred Ewan McGregor, but in a very real sense it also starred the principal horn of the London Symphony Orchestra, in front of whom I am standing, Lídl in hand, in a room at the Royal Academy of Music.

It was David Pyatt who told me, many months earlier, that I need to practise performing in front of an audience. 'Positive visualisation,' he said. Live the dream, he might well have added. Feel the force. I am taking him at his word. He is holding a horn masterclass, and I've invited myself along. Outside it is a greyish afternoon in early autumn. This is the very building to which my grandmother came up from Dolgellau to study the piano just after the First World War. She was barely twenty. There are a dozen or so horn students in here too. Not one of them would have been born when I gave up the horn. They amount to a rather more imposing audience than the one consisting largely of daughters, nephews and nieces with whom I previously stepped into the ring. These people actually know what they're listening to. An array of performances has dazzled and daunted: the usual outing for Strauss, some fiercely complicated Messiaen, a pair of students speeding fleet-footed through Haydn's concerto for two horns. The masterclass would not be complete without someone – and just to make it worse, a girl – playing some Mozart with intimidating freshness and certainty. She asks what brings me here. I explain about taking up the horn at thirty-nine and three-quarters.

'I suppose it's better than buying a motorbike,' she says witheringly.

To think Kevin thinks I might once have been good enough to join their ranks. Bless him, but it's absurd. They all hope for a career in horn playing. I merely hope for the next ten minutes to be free of incident. My performance is now only a few weeks away. By rights I ought to be swelling in confidence. I have had two sessions with Kevin and his Yamaha, and they have gone well. Playing to a piano accompaniment is utterly thrilling, especially with the fabulous acoustic of Kevin's music room. I am starting to sound like a horn player. Nonetheless, I have taken the pre-caution, after the jitters I suffered when performing in front of my family, of bringing a banana. Not three, as my horn camp pal Jeremy Thal did when auditioning in Chicago, with terrible consequences. Just one. I don't actually like bananas very much, so this can be taken as a yardstick of the sacrifices I'm prepared to make for the furtherance of my playing. Only I'm not quite sure when to take it. How long does a banana need to storm the stomach and ruthlessly quash a gang of renegade butterflies? Take it too early and the effects might wear off. Too late and you will be relaxed enough to perform only after you have actually performed. I unpeel my banana during the break, halfway through the masterclass. By the time everyone musters for the second half, about ten minutes have sprinted by.

'Who wants to be next?' David Pyatt looks inquisitively towards the small gathering of twenty-year-old horn players, and me. I stick up my hand. My banana must have taken effect. Only when I get up and walk the plank to the front do I discover that it has had no discernible impact. Terror can fill any space, and it suddenly floods my head. I'd like to say the fear is irrational. In fact it's all too rational. I am an impostor. I am a pretender. I should not be here. Maybe I should have eaten two bananas. Or even three. Maybe I shouldn't have chosen this particular occasion to premiere my freshly composed cadenza.

The playing itself, measured on the catastrophometer scale from 'could do better' to 'train wreck, no survivors', is no worse than 'piss-poor'. The notes are knocked over like skittles. The lip-trills on which I've been half-heartedly working are – shall we be polite? – strikingly pedestrian. But I do settle. The clouds clear here and there. The Mozartian swoops and glides are attempted, and I keep Lowell Greer's advice about the Allegro in the back of my mind: make 'em cry, but also make 'em laugh. I'm not convinced I make 'em do any of these things as and when intended, but I give it my best shot.

I work my way along each line, and down to the next, over the page, past the recapitulation and on towards the finale of the movement. The moment is drawing inexorably nearer when the pianist, who now I come to think of it is a bit rumpty tumpty, will cease to play, and I will have to go on without him. But there's no stopping now. *Courage, mon brave.* Unsheathe your light sabre and confront your demons.

A positive thought springs into my head. If anyone is going to understand my cadenza, it's going to be this audience. Why? As things stand, I will be playing only the Allegro at the British Horn Society festival, so into my cadenza I have decided to jumble up and compress a succession of romantic phrases from the Romanze and rousing horn calls from the Rondo. I also quote from pieces I've played and pieces I'll never play: the three-note fanfare from Strauss's first horn concerto; Mendelssohn's Nocturne for four horns is in there; the Great C major which, in a backwards nod to my problems with transposition, I play in the wrong key before oh-so-wittily realigning into the right one. It's a bunch of jokes, basically. Towards the end, I thud down onto a pedal F which I discovered by accident one day, lurking there unnoticed at the bottom of my range, then clamber up through three-and-a-half octaves to a top B flat I've been squeezing out with increasing certainty during my Farkas warm-ups. I never got anywhere near either as a student, but with a following wind I now frequently can. To round off I slip across to the more famous Rondo from K495, nodding in the direction of Flanders and Swann's comic song about the French horn. Where Michael Flanders sang 'I found my horn was a bit of a devil to play', I play the matching notes, ending on a trill.

That's the plan anyway. That's the piece I've spent hours practising each day. And they do get the jokes. There's the odd nasal exhalation, one or two titters. When I can tear my gaze away from David Pyatt's laser-blue eyes, I think I spot the ghost of a smirk. But the reality is that one banana is no defence against paralysis. It's difficult to give a sense of the existential loneliness that washes over a horn player in the middle of a cadenza that's going wrong. You are on the high wire without a paddle. You are up shit's creek without a leg to stand on. You are marooned in space. There is absolutely nowhere to run, or hide, or go, except onwards into the unknown.

The co-principal horn of the LSO, the co-star of *Revenge of the Sith*, rises from his seat, walks over and stands next to me.

'What does every horn player have to know how to do?'

'Er ...'

'Anyone?' He looks out at the dozen students sitting in front of us. About six of them speak at once.

'Breathe.'

'Exactly,' says David Pyatt. 'Your problem is very simple. You don't breathe properly. You need to breathe in slowly two full beats before your entry. You shouldn't snatch a breath with half a beat to go. You'll be amazed by how much easier it is if you breathe properly.'

That is all he says. It seems sound advice. When I try the first page again, I am grateful to note an improvement. Perhaps the banana is now working its magic. It was worth putting myself through this hoop of fire. I must breathe in such a way that everyone knows I'm breathing. I must breathe emphatically, sonorously. I must breathe in a manner that leaves no doubt that breathing is what I am doing. My breathing must mimic, in brief, the signature technique of the Dark Lord of the Sith, Darth Vader.

Only I don't want to be playing at my own funeral.

9

The Act You've Known for All These Years

I had a note that actually was just out of the range of the French horn. And you get these great musicians that give you sort of a look and they go, 'Um, surely this is, um, um.' And you give them a little look like 'Can you do it?' And they give you a little look like 'Yes I can.' It's really a great moment. It ruins it for all the other horn players who can't do it, but the greats will always go that little extra.
Paul McCartney

I'd say we're in about row 67, the New Person In My Life and me. Not as near to the front as all that, but a good third of a mile closer than the unfortunates to the rear. From where they're standing on tiptoe, even the faces of megastars on the tennis-court-sized video relay screens, the dukes of riff and divas of rhythm and the leathery gerontocrats of rock, are pinpricks.

A human sea at high tide has flooded this royal park in the green heart of London. They say there are over 200,000 of us at the very largest, the very longest concert ever mounted. By row 67, I mean that standing in a direct line between our little patch of park and the nearest point of the stage there would probably be something like sixty-six people. It is two in the afternoon. The

New Person and I will not abandon this tiny territorial redoubt until absolutely the last encore of 'Hey Jude' has been na-na-na-naahed. That'll be around midnight. Not for food, not for drink, not for bodily functions of any category. Over the next ten hours, loud music will perform the biggest conjuring trick ever attempted: to make poverty history.

'It was twenty years ago today ...' In the absence of John, George and Ringo, Sir Paul makes his entry with an Irish band I never liked even before I went off rock music. '... Sgt Pepper taught the band to play.' They crack straight into the title track of an album near universally regarded as the greatest ever. 'They've been going in and out of style ...' After I went classical, I kept a place in my heart for the Fab Four. '... but they're guaranteed to raise a smile.' The song has never before been performed live by the man who wrote it. 'So may I introduce to you ...' My favourite Beatle. '... the act you've known for all these years ...'

'Look!' says the New Person. She grabs my arm. 'Look! Quick!'

I've been watching the tennis-court-sized screen and missed their entry.

'Sgt Pepper's Lonely Hearts Club Baa-aa-aand!'

Four young men are standing downstage right. You can't miss them. They are garbed in the day-glo marching-band outfits worn by the Beatles on the iconic album cover: bright pink, bright orange, bright blue, bright lime. But they are not brandishing guitars, or saxophones, or even trumpets. Unless one's eyes are deceived, they are all ... no, it can't be. But it can. The first instrumental solo of the biggest gig of all time, in front of the eyes of billions, falls to a quartet of French horns!

'We're Sgt Pepper's Lonely Hearts Club Band!'

The New Person shouts in my ear, 'What the hell are four horns doing up there?'

'We hope you will enjoy the show!'

'What?'

'I said what the hell are four ...'

'We're Sgt Pepper's Lonely Hearts Club Band!'

'What? I can't hear you.'

'Sit back and let the evening go!'

'You must be so excited!'

In the space of a few brassy bars, four boys in Beatles moptops and moustaches have become the most visible and indeed audible players in the entire history of the instrument.

I am so excited.

At Paxmans, the French horn shop, the walls that aren't plastered with horns are plastered with photographs. There are well over a hundred. Horn soloists, horn sections, horn professors – snaps of every major British player of the last fifty years, and most major international ones. One day, when I'm having more work done on the Lídl, I wander around the room, counting how many of them I've stalked. It's an impressive number, though dwarfed by the number I haven't. My eye is caught by a small photograph behind the cash desk. Five men stand in a row. All of them, apart from the one on the left, are holding horns. The man in the middle, wearing a check shirt and brandishing a shiny instrument, is the greatest living composer of popular music.

What, my favourite Beatle? With a horn? And a horn quartet? An optical illusion, surely. I peer more closely and recognise the solid form of one of the horn players. It's Mike Thompson, who conducted the massed horn blow at the British Horn Society festival, the one where I took up the instrument again and played the Hallelujah Chorus with all those other horns. He looks a few years younger here. I ask Luke, who works at Paxmans, to identify the rest of the quartet.

'That's Richard Bissill,' he says. Richard Bissill is principal horn of the London Philharmonic Orchestra. 'And that's Richard Watkins.' Richard Watkins is the Dennis Brain professor of horn at the Royal Academy of Music. I know these two by reputation.

'And who's that one on the left? The one not holding a horn.' He looks slightly older, and is wearing a crazy pullover.

'That's John Pigneguy.' John Pigneguy is my old horn teacher, the last but one. I have no strong memory of him but his slightly beaky face, now that I'm looking at it, does ring a distant bell. He taught me at the age of fourteen or fifteen for two terms. Then he disappeared. A quarter of a century later, now I can see why.

He had slightly bigger fish to fry. Presumably when the picture was taken, someone suggested that for this historic photo opportunity Paul McCartney ought to be holding a horn. My old horn teacher must have drawn the short straw, and handed his over. Could the instrument in the hands of my favourite Beatle be the same one my old horn teacher brought to lessons? I'd like to think so.

But bigger questions remain unanswered. Paul McCartney. Four horns. What? When? Where? Why?

On the evening of 19 May 1966, Alan Civil entered Studio Two at Abbey Road in St John's Wood. He was indisputably the country's greatest living horn player. Two years earlier he had been offered the post of principal horn with Karajan's Berlin Philharmonic, the first non-German musician ever approached by the orchestra. He turned them down to stay with the Philharmonia in London, where he had been first horn since the day after Brain's car crash. In 1966 he defected to the BBC Symphony Orchestra, where he would remain till his retirement in 1988. He died a year later, aged fifty-nine.

The Beatles had spent the day in the neighbouring Studio One shooting a promotional film to accompany the release of 'Paperback Writer'. The next day they would continue filming among the blooming wisteria and budding greenhouses of Chiswick House. Their career as a live act was all but done. On the first day of the month they performed for the last time in Britain at the New Musical Express Poll Winners' Show at the Empire Pool, Wembley. That same week in an interview in the *Evening Standard* John Lennon uttered his 'Bigger than Jesus' remark which made that summer's third and final tour of America a dispiriting ordeal. As they renounced live performance, the prototype video of their new single would be sent out in their stead to television stations all over the world. Henceforth, Abbey Road became their bunker and their laboratory.

In the process of the Beatles' transmogrification, an album track on side two of *Revolver* assumed a significance out of proportion to the two minutes' traffic of its playing time. It's not simply that 'For No One' was the first Beatles song in which both John Lennon and George Harrison would have no involvement. ('Yesterday' was recorded the previous year with McCartney's vocal and guitar accompanied by a string quartet, but the rest of the Beatles would subsequently play a guitar version of the song on tour.) It also marked the first solo on a Beatles recording by an orchestral instrument. That instrument was the French horn.

McCartney wrote 'For No One' in March while on a skiing holiday with his girlfriend Jane Asher in the Swiss resort of Klosters. He had learnt to ski while shooting *Help!*, and fancied another go. The melody and bitter-sweet lyric about a woman coldly turning away from her lover came to him in their rented chalet. If he and Asher had argued, as McCartney has subsequently suggested, it would explain why he was sequestered in the bathroom when it was composed. McCartney's own relationship did not yet mirror the 'love that should have lasted years' portrayed in the song: he and Asher would not become engaged until the following year.

The Beatles were enjoying a three-month break, much their longest since 1962, so McCartney didn't get round to recording the backing track until 9 May. Nine different takes were made of him playing one of his signature descending progressions on the piano, while Ringo Starr supplied the drums. For the tenth take the piano was overdubbed with a clavichord; Starr added maraca and tambourine. On 16 May McCartney recorded his vocal. All that was needed was an instrumental solo.

Why the horn? 'For No One' was not the horn's debut with a ground-breaking 1960s group. On 10 March, at a studio in Hollywood, the instrumental track of 'God Only Knows' was recorded with an ensemble of orchestral musicians. The opening bars of the song were ornamented with a simple, expressive horn solo. Brian Wilson envisioned *Pet Sounds*, the Beach Boys album on which the song appeared, as a response to the mushrooming ambition of the Beatles' *Rubber Soul*. In a year's time the Beatles' riposte to the technical brilliance of *Pet Sounds* took the form of *Sgt Pepper's Lonely Hearts Club Band*. But when they were recording *Revolver* in the spring of 1966, they didn't yet know they were in a transatlantic dialogue. *Pet Sounds* was released on 16 May, the same day as McCartney recorded his vocal for 'For No One' and three days before Civil came to Abbey Road. It seems unlikely that the horn intro to 'God Only Knows' was the spur to hiring Alan Civil. In which case, whose idea was it?

'I honestly don't remember,' says Sir George Martin. Forty years later I am sitting in Abbey Road with the producer who steered the Beatles into uncharted musical waters. 'I think probably it was me.' In the early part of his ninth decade, with lanky white hair flopping like two awnings over his hearing aids, he is the Methuselah of the recording studio. 'Yes I'm sure it was me, because Paul in those days would say, "What can we use here? What classical instrument can we use?" And I probably suggested the horn because I quite like the horn as a solo instrument.'

The official McCartney account, as recounted in *The Beatles Anthology*, is slightly different. 'Occasionally we'd have an idea for some new kind of instrumentation, particularly for solos. On "You've Got to Hide Your Love Away" John had wanted a flute. On "For No One" I was interested in the French horn, because it was an instrument I'd always loved from when I was a kid. It's a beautiful sound, so I went to George Martin and said, "How can we go about this?" And he said, "Well, let me get the very finest."'

Sir George began his recording career in the classical sphere and had used Dennis Brain as part of the London Baroque Ensemble. 'He had to play some difficult stuff. But he also used to play on a Latin American mock-up I recorded called Roberto Inglez and his Orchestra. In fact Roberto Inglez was really Bob Ingles from Acton. He used to do very simple arrangements with strings and French horn and rhythm which sold particularly well in South America. I went up to Dennis one day and said, "Why do you play this stuff?" He put away his copy of *Autocar* and said, "I always get a nice tune to play, and I get paid for it."'

Alan Civil was similarly pragmatic about supplementing his orchestral income. This was his third three-hour session of the day. Thanks to a rogue full stop on his call sheet, which referred to his booking as 'For No. One', he assumed he would be playing on a first symphony by an unnamed composer. When he arrived at the recording studio, he was greeted by Martin and McCartney.

'That was one of the great things about George,' says McCartney. 'He knew how to obtain the best musicians and would suggest getting them. On this occasion he suggested Alan Civil, who, like all these great blokes, looks quite ordinary at the session – but plays like an angel.'

There are varying accounts of who actually wrote the solo. According to *Revolution in the Head*, Ian MacDonald's definitive critical account of every Beatles recording, Civil composed it himself. Martin remembers McCartney singing the tune to him while, as usual, Martin translated the tune into notes on the page. 'He hummed it and I think I was still writing it when Alan was coming in.' According to McCartney's account, the devil got into him. 'When we were getting the piece down for Alan to play,' he recalls, 'George explained to me the range of the instrument: "Well, it goes from here to this top E," and I said, "What if we ask him to play an F?" George saw the joke and joined in the conspiracy.'

Martin claims responsibility for taking the solo to the outer edge of its range. 'Alan looked at it and winced. He was a fantastic player, but I have a reputation in my scores, I'm afraid, for writing rather high parts for French horn. And I wrote a very high part for Alan Civil.' In another interview McCartney recalls Civil's consternation. 'Alan looked up from his bit of paper: "Eh, George? I think there's a mistake here – you've got a high F written down." Then George and I said, "Yeah," and smiled back at him, and he knew what we were up to and played it. These great players will do it. Even though it's officially off the end of their instrument, they can do it, and they're quite into it occasionally.'

When Civil listened to the backing track he noticed that the key fell, as he later put it, 'in the crack' between B natural and B flat. 'It was probably because we recorded on this clavichord which we tuned ourselves,' says Martin. The clavichord was Martin's own, brought from his home for the occasion. 'I remember him having to tune a bit, but that was part and parcel of any instrument when they overdubbed in those days. They had to get used to it.'

Civil recorded the piping, trumpety solo, with lashings of immaculately slurred notes, in a single take. 'We got the performance that you hear on the record. And I thought, "Fantastic, that's bloody marvellous." And Paul pressed the intercom and said, "That's pretty nice, Alan, but I think we can do better, don't you?" Alan by this time was very red in the face. I turned to Paul and said, "You've just listened to one of the greatest performances of a horn that I think is possible!" He said, "He can do better than that, can't he?" He had no concept of how difficult it was.'

Alan Civil left without bettering his first take. Dave Lee, who in later years found himself sitting next to Civil on recording sessions, tells me that Civil claimed he was offered a royalty in lieu of a fee. According to Dave, Civil's response was 'Fuck off, how does a thousand pounds sound?' It's a good story, but not entirely plausible. Civil was famous in the horn world as a rambunctious saloon-bar anecdotalist with a Falstaffian appetite for beer, food and tall tales. To illustrate the abrasive side of his personality, his obituary in the *Daily Telegraph* picked a story in which he was on a train to Leeds. 'He sat opposite a young girl who was wearing headphones from which hissed a sound unacceptable for a long journey. When asked to turn the volume down she refused, adding that it was a free country. Alan proceeded to take his horn from its case and to play Mozart loudly. The girl then left the carriage to the applause of the other occupants.'

I run the story of Civil's royalty offer by Sir George Martin.

'No, that would never have happened,' says the fifth Beatle. 'Impossible. That would have meant the Beatles were giving up something. And they were *mean* bastards.'

I ask around the horn world until eventually another veteran of the session circuit, Terry Johns, confirms that rather than being offered a royalty, Civil actually asked for one. 'Alan was quite shrewd,' says Terry. 'He was mega-famous as a horn player. He would have asked for the minimum you could get: a farthing per record. But they wouldn't have anything to do with that. They refused. And he eventually got a fiver out of them.'

I was now the undisputed principal horn of the Harrow School orchestra. Undisputed, that is, until the concert came around at the end of term, when the impossibly tall conductor would bring someone in to beef up the section. He was usually a music college student, or maybe a young pro.

'It's quite hard, this piece,' I'd warn my temporary colleague. 'I've been having a bit of trouble hitting that note,' I'd add, pointing at some lofty peak in the first horn part of the Mozart or Schubert we were performing.

'That's an F,' the incomer would say.

'Yes. It's pretty high. How high can you play?'

'Oh I can usually bang out a top C.'

'What?!?' In all my years of horn study I had never heard of such a note. 'A C above the F? Are you kidding?' He raised his horn to his lips and played an arpeggio up to a glass-shatteringly, dog-summoningly high note. The highest I'd ever played was a G, five distant semitones below. There seemed to be only one appropriate response. 'I think we'd better swap seats.' Gratefully I resumed my old role as second horn of the Harrow School orchestra.

At seventeen, I was now overdosing on self-belief in every other area of my life. Ancient boarding schools are organised to breed such feelings in young males as they swagger towards adulthood. The school that produced Sheridan and Byron, Churchill and Nehru, that produced Mark Thatcher, did not fail in its task. An anachronism evolved over generations, the system existed to purvey to nation and empire a rolling supply of plummy young gentlemen oiled in the unimagining ways of the establishment. We were custom-tooled to go forth and occupy the important postings in Her Majesty's Forces, Her Majesty's Government and, for several of the more raffish white-collar adventurers among us, Her Majesty's Prisons. I did not escape the side-effects of this training. By my final year I thought I was pretty wonderful. I was brimming with knowledge and acumen, discernment and taste. Teachers had enjoyed the pleasure of teaching me. Literature and languages had had the privilege of being studied by me. I really was quite the thing. I could even escort the girl cellist off the hill to Andrew Lloyd Webber's *Cats* without having to untie my tongue.

The only time I never felt ten feet tall was when I had the Lídl in my hands. I consequently had no particular incentive to put my name down for the school's competition for instrumental soloists. Each year the gifted musicians, most already in the National Youth Orchestra, would tough it out for the top gong. A distinguished professional would be invited along to sit in judgement and anoint a winner. I had always given the annual face-off a wide berth.

'You should enter this year,' said the impossibly tall conductor. A bunch of trumpeters had left. I could feel myself being leaned on. Most of the gifted musicians were woodwinders. They clearly needed someone to make up the numbers in the brass section of the competition. I consulted Kevin Amos, my horn teacher.

'You should do it,' he said. 'Why not?'

'Because it'll be terrifying.'

'No it won't. It'll be fun.'

I bowed to Kevin's perennial optimism. We plumped for the Romanze from Mozart's third horn concerto as the safest bet for a public performance. I could more or less play this. The more I practised, the more I thought I might just be able to snatch victory in the brass section from the jaws of my own defeatism. After the clear-out of trumpeters, the opposition looked weak. The threat posed by a squit on trombone could be discounted, which meant that there was only a fifteen-year-old on trumpet to beat. I privately assumed that it would not be possible to lose to someone two years my junior, even if his father was Cabinet Secretary in Mrs Thatcher's government. That sort of thing didn't happen in a hierarchical environment. Juniors had to wait their turn.

'I'm playing in the music competition this Sunday.' I rang my parents. 'Do you want to come and watch?' My mother answered.

'Oh.' My parents never came to London on a Sunday. 'It's a Sunday.' They always came up on a Monday.

'Oh.'

'If it was in the week . . .'

'Maybe they should have consulted your diary before they scheduled the competition!' I was going through a violently sarcastic phase. I slammed down the phone.

On the eve of battle I went to a rehearsal in the school's concert hall. My accompanist was a short round music teacher, one of those brilliant dysfunctional types who can play a sonata backwards and blindfolded but are less competent on the shirt-buttoning front. The purity of his immersion in the parallel universe of music intimidated the hell out of me. After I had shunted and stalled through the Romanze, he explained with as much twinkly civility as he could muster that it would not be possible to stop and actually apologise for mistakes made during the performance itself.

'But I'm having problems with those high Fs, sir,' I explained.

'You'll just have to hope,' he said, 'that all will be tickety-boo as I believe they say, on the night.'

A day later I stood behind the pass door leading onto the raised stage of the concert hall, crisis-managing the urge to vomit on the blue parquet flooring. Through the door came the muffled sound of the fifteen-year-old son of Mrs Thatcher's Cabinet Secretary blowing his trumpet in a flawless display of smug insurrection. This isn't happening, I told myself. He can't be playing this well. It's impossible. He's two years my junior. I'm *taller* than him. There are *rules*. In due course the trumpeting stopped and the clapping started. The sound flared sharply as the pass door burst open and there framed in the doorway stood the trumpeter triumphant.

'Good luck, Rees.'

I stepped fractionally aside to let him pass. Then, with the Lídl in my right hand, K447 in my left, I loped out to join the short round accompanist seated at a grand piano. The audience consisted mostly of gifted woodwinders and their beaming parents. It was the first time I had faced one on my own since attempting to play 'Abide With Me' to my fellow fourth-formers at the age of ten. At my feet, on his own at a table covered in paperwork, sat the distinguished professional, a concert pianist I had not at this point heard of called Murray Perahia. I spotted my parents sitting near the back on the far side. They had fallen on their swords and made the pilgrimage. My mother looked pensive, my father impassive.

The performance had the scope and scale of a natural disaster.

The Romanze opens with an entirely doable B flat, but I landed on an altogether different note, and flailed and thrashed through the rest of the opening phrase like a drowning three-year-old. After four bars my intimidating accompanist decided that there was no real point in hoping for some kind of overlap between the key I was playing in and the key he was playing in. He pulled his fingers away from the keyboard and, looking enquiringly over his shoulder, sounded a discreet B flat.

'Shall we start again?' I wanted to die. I will say no more than that. I would have welcomed the guillotine, the noose, I would have welcomed the chair, if it meant never again – never, *ever* – having to grapple with this booby trap, this serpent, this metal hex. But the *coup de grâce* was not an option. In three minutes' time I could consign the instrument to the dustbin of history, but for now I ruefully stumbled back into the movement. The testing high F entry at the top of a cascading legato phrase was predictably and morale-sappingly missed. I felt like a rock climber reaching blindly up for a crumbling handhold. It was missed again when the phrase was repeated. I tripped and stumbled and clattered through the delicate stockade of semiquavers and barrelled on through the rest of the assault course towards the end. Pain-wise, it was the closest I'll ever get to giving birth. It passed. It happened. The agony in due course subsided, leaving behind the ghost of a memory of a public disembowelling.

The audience's polite response was tinged with relief. I bowed with as much dignity as I could muster. Beneath me Murray Perahia scribbled something briefly. I assumed it was 'shit'. Out in the audience my mother clapped supportively and my father grimly. I could see him thinking: 'We came up to London on a Sunday for *this*? I've paid for lessons for seven years for *this*?'

'Jasper has had yet another good term,' wrote Kevin at the end of my last term as a schoolboy. 'That he has not won a prize for his playing is a matter I feel more of misfortune than a reflection of his ability. I am sure that in the future his progress of the last two years will be realised as a worthy investment. I hope he continues this musical interest throughout his university life.'

I didn't play the horn again for twenty-two years.

*

I am standing on the conductor's podium in the West End theatre which, more than a year after opening, remains home to the Andrew Lloyd Webber musical. In the pit, seated at an electric piano, is Kevin. Far away at the back of the stalls is Dave. It is late on Saturday afternoon. The matinee has been and gone, the evening performance is more than an hour away. To an audience of 1,200 empty seats rising in tiers to the distant ceiling, I am driving another articulated lorry through K447.

My performance at the British Horn Society festival is no longer months or even weeks away. Now it's a matter of days, and I can count those days on the fingers of three hands. After barely surviving my previous public outing, at the David Pyatt masterclass at the Royal Academy of Music, I direly need more performance practice.

So a week before the festival I have decided to play the whole concerto to the dutiful friends who attended my fortieth birthday party nearly a year ago. Andrew Lloyd Webber has kindly granted use of the conservatory of his company's offices. But before my practice performance, I need to practise performing, which is why I am standing on the conductor's podium while Dave prowls the back of the stalls near the sound desk. A sound operator is checking cues for the evening performance. The noise of wind, church bells, a babbling brook and twittering songbirds randomly punctuate the jitter and judder of my playing.

It goes without saying that back at home, in the privacy of my own front room, I can now play this sucker with remarkable aplomb. After a year at the coalface, you'd scarcely fit cigarette paper between my rendition and a professional's. Even round at Kevin's place, in his piano room, I can do a presentable impression of someone who knows his way, if not entirely round the horn, then round Mozart's third horn concerto. If they could only hear me when I'm playing as well as I know I can, people would think good things, kind things, nice things. Unfortunately I'm not the same person when playing in front of people.

This is the first time I've played the whole concerto through in front of Dave. David Pyatt's injunction to breathe like Darth

Vader has been entirely forgotten as I systematically lay waste to the first movement, the Allegro, raping and pillaging anything across my path. I grind on with remorseless inefficiency, glumly aware as I recapitulate the main theme that any minute, any second now I must finally unleash my excuse for a cadenza on Dave. We've laughed about it in the pub, about its comical medley of in-jokes and one-liners. But this is no longer the pub. In a three-bar rest I look up and note that Dave is looking more serious than I've ever seen him. His arms are folded, his brows knitted, his whole body is knotted in excruciation.

I'm about to hurl myself into my so-called composition when a deafening, disembodied wail ricochets around the vast chasm of the auditorium.

'NOOOOOOOOOOOOOOOO!!'

It's one of the sound effects from the show. We all laugh – Kevin nervously, Dave uproariously, me hollowly.

'You've got two weeks,' says Dave at the end. 'What you need now is a structured period where we work on specific things.' Let's make the best of a bad job, he's saying. 'You've tried to pick up in a year what most people spend years learning.'

I go home to my first horn-related sleepless night.

'I'm relieved you're spooked,' says the New Person. 'It was all sounding too easy.' Was it? I wasn't aware that it was. Her retort is crushing. 'You don't want to be Eddie the Eagle.'

In 1995 Mike Thompson was invited to participate in a charity concert at St James's Palace hosted by the Prince of Wales to raise money for the Royal College of Music. Paul McCartney was going to perform 'For No One' live for the first time, thirty years after he recorded it with Alan Civil's solo. He needed a horn player. 'I said I'd love to,' says Mike. 'They said, "Do you want us to send you the music for the horn part?" I said, "Probably not necessary because I kind of grew up with it. Send it anyway, why not?" Very glad they did because when it came through it was a tone higher than I was expecting. The difference is between squeaking up to a top D or a top E. Ds are kind of high but doable. But Es just seem to be above the tree line. Eventually they came back and said, "The confusion seems to be apparently if you actually play the LP at exactly the correct speed it comes out in B major," which is not the key that people would have recorded in from choice. So it clearly was in B flat or C. No one could remember. George Martin couldn't remember. The bottom line was "Paul currently finds it a bit more comfortable to sing in C than B flat". Obviously there wasn't really any argument with that.

'I practised like mad, turned up for the rehearsal and got it 95 per cent right. Paul said, "Yeah I think that's going to be OK," looking a bit nervous. We did the sound check at the Palace in the afternoon and I got it about 97 per cent right and Paul said, "Is that going to be all right tonight?" And I said, "I'm really sorry about this but this is life as a horn player. I have no idea." He said, "I suppose it's my fault for writing stuff that's so high." I said, "Well I didn't say that but ..."

'I remember going for a walk in St James's Park before the concert and, not for the first time in my life, just thinking this is the loneliest feeling on earth. It's a bit like being a stuntman. Paul was the star of the show. All I had to do was play about eight bars and not screw it up. Of course as horn players, especially if you're playing top Es, we know it's not quite as simple as that. I went back in. The gods were obviously smiling, and I nailed it. It was 100 per cent. Huge sigh of relief. Paul came up, gave me a huge hug and said, "You were just messing. You were just teasing."'

Mike's reward followed soon after. McCartney's people phoned to say he had written a piece for a horn quartet. Mike rounded up the horn quartet pictured on the wall in Paxmans and went down to McCartney's recording studio in East Sussex. 'When we were about to leave I said to him, "It's been a really nice day, really enjoyable. Why don't you write some more horn quartet stuff?" He kind of laughed and said, "Yeah, nice try."' Not long afterwards McCartney's people were on the phone again. Two more movements had been written. The quartet went back down to East Sussex. Then there was another call. McCartney wanted to record it with the bigger acoustic of Abbey Road Studio One. 'We were halfway through the recording and just breaking for a cup of tea to rest the lip and Richard Bissill said to me, "God this is high! It would be so much more comfortable just down a tone." Paul said, "OK, I'll get the copyists to write it out." And we said, "You don't need to do that. We're horn players." He was terribly impressed.'

The piece was given the name of 'Stately Horn'. It was utterly McCartneyesque, bouncy, rhythmic, tonal, melodic: the horn solo on 'For No One' writ large. After re-recording it twice in 1997, the Michael Thompson Horn Quartet was swiftly invited to perform 'Stately Horn' at the Royal Albert Hall and, following the success of that concert, at Carnegie Hall in New York. Mike remembers 'standing in the wings ready to open the concert when the place just erupted. Paul and Linda had just come in and taken their seats. It was like a Beatles concert, people shouting and screaming "We love you", and it went on for minutes and minutes. The guy standing next to us was putting the house lights down and just trying to get people to settle down and be quiet. They weren't having any of it. Eventually he said to the four of us, "I can't get them to settle down. You're just going to have to go on." So the four of us walked on to the biggest, noisiest, most enthusiastic standing ovation I've ever experienced in my life. Which immediately died. You could almost hear the whole audience thinking, "Who the *hell* are these guys?"'

Some horn players thought the same of the Beatles.

'The Beatles didn't mean a thing to us musically speaking. We were getting peanuts – six pounds ten shillings or something. It was just another session.' So says Maurice 'Mo' Miller, now pushing eighty, who converted to the horn in his late thirties from the trumpet. He is hazy about the title of the Beatles song he was booked to play on. 'Was it "Walrus something"?'

The horn appears on eleven Beatles tracks altogether. On six of them, the names of the players are known and recorded in the various discographies and Fabologies compiled for a greedy global army of nerds, anoraks and trainspotters. But the identity of other horn players has been lost: one played on 'Good Morning Good Morning', two on 'Hey Jude', and four on 'Golden Slumbers' 'Carry That Weight' and 'The End', McCartney's medley of songs on *Abbey Road*. And who played horn on 'Good Night', their solo soaring beatifically over the strings in the final notes of the final track on *The White Album*? Nobody knows. The horn players themselves are either dead, or they're old and they've forgotten.

'Playing with the Beatles,' says Tony Tunstall, 'is undoubtedly the least interesting moment in my entire career.' Tunstall, who for many years was principal horn in the orchestra of the Royal Opera House and thus knew his way around the prodigiously challenging horn-writing of Wagner, was sitting next to Mo Miller on 'I Am the Walrus'. (He was also the lone horn on 'Martha My Dear', one of McCartney's music-hall-tinged compositions.) 'They had fish and chips delivered on silver salvers. When we took a break, as we were allowed to according to union rules, the conductor on the podium shouted, "Call yourself musicians? We were just getting going!"'

'I remember I was bloody awkward,' says Mo Miller. 'A wrong note had been written in by one of them and I insisted on playing it knowing full well it sounded wrong. They spent maybe twenty-four hours round the clock working out something and we would play what was written in front of us. Eventually I said, "I think you want a B flat rather than a B natural." We didn't think we were making history. I still don't think much of it. To me there's no comparison musically speaking with some of the things that were written by proper composers.'

The antipathy felt by some orchestral musicians towards the Beatles is part aesthetic, part monetary. The classical musicians of the 1960s had not grown up with pop music. The sight of trained musicologists swooning over the chord sequences of 'Yesterday' or 'God Only Knows' was a thing of the future. The Beatles were making mountains of money, and although from 1967 they began employing sizeable orchestras to augment their sound and in some cases help compose their music, they weren't seen to be sharing it out. On 'Hey Jude' the session musicians were at least paid double for not only playing but also providing handclaps and singing the na-na-na-naaahs in the outro. All but one of the thirty-six-strong orchestra consented. A lone refusenik packed away his instrument and harrumphed out of Trident Studios saying, 'I'm not going to clap my hands and sing Paul McCartney's bloody song!' Tony Tunstall insists it wasn't him.

However, a fee was still a fee. Alan Civil was back at Abbey Road nine months after recording his solo on 'For No One' to play in the unscored atonal orchestral crescendo of 'A Day in the Life'. This time he and Neil Sanders, a colleague from the Philharmonia horn section who also played the horn fills on 'I Am the Walrus', were part of a forty-one piece orchestra, the first such ensemble to be gathered on a Beatles recording. It was an unconventional day in the life of a horn player. The musicians and George Martin were asked to come in evening dress. A variety of comedy hats were pressed on them by the Beatles and their guests – among them Mick Jagger, Keith Richards, Marianne Faithfull, Donovan and Mike Nesmith of the Monkees. 'It was quite a chaotic session,' Civil later recalled. 'Such a big orchestra, playing with very little music. And the Beatle chaps were wandering around with rather expensive cameras, like new toys, photographing everything.' This was a remnant of a costly notion they had conjured up of making a mini-movie for each song on the album.

Pictures from the 'A Day in the Life' session capture John Lennon in full hippy garb seigneurially holding either Civil's or Sanders's horn. In some of them he is blowing on it, but with his right hand under the bell rather than in it. His fingers aren't on the valves either (though his embouchure looks correct enough). The image suggests an interest in orchestration that doesn't tally with George Martin's memory. 'Paul was very keen on having orchestral instruments on the record,' he says. 'John couldn't be bothered. When we did "I Am the Walrus" he said, "I want you to put some musicians on this." I said, "What you want then, John?" He said, "A bit of brass, a bit of cello – you know, your usual stuff." I said, "Do you want to sit with me and work it out?" He said, "That's your job."' A horn was still in Lennon's hands for its iconic appearance on Peter Blake's famous pop art cover design for *Sgt Pepper*. He holds it upturned under his right arm. In a discarded image from the session Lennon's horn is balanced on top of the bass drum in front of the band. McCartney got to hold the cor anglais.

Neil Sanders returned within a month as part of a horn quartet booked to play on the album's title track. Civil must have been busy with the BBC Symphony Orchestra. Two of the other horn players were old pros. James W Buck, better known as Jim Buck One because his son Jim Buck Two also plied his trade on the horn, was a session veteran in his sixties. John Burden was taught by Aubrey Brain and often duetted with Dennis Brain, his exact contemporary, when they were both students at the Royal Academy of Music. He was made principal horn of the London Symphony Orchestra from 1948, but in protest at the orchestra's poor administration left in 1955 with most of the other principals to form the Sinfonia of London. The fourth horn player was a young Welsh freelance called Tony Randall, who took a more positive view of the Beatles' musicianship than his older peers.

'I was booked by Neil Sanders,' he recalls. 'He didn't tell me what it was at the time. When I got there I was delighted that it was the Beatles. The word was out that they were using classical music. To me they are fellow musicians.' Four decades on his memory of the rest of the quartet is foggy. 'Was it Tony Tunstall playing on it?'

Now entirely studio-bound, the Beatles were toying with the notion of inventing a fictitious band. It was McCartney's idea and lasted only as far as the title track and its segue into 'With a Little Help from My Friends'. The horn quartet, however, were unwitting participants in the concept. 'By the time we recorded the actual song,' recalls Sir George, 'we were convinced that we had to provide a band called Sgt Pepper to perform in lieu of the Beatles. A quartet of horns was the natural thing to have for something that was going to be like the opening of a show. We wanted something slightly declamatory, slightly brass-bandish, because it was like a street band.'

There is a photograph of McCartney sitting opposite the four horns and smoking a cigarette as he explains to them what he wants. Another photograph shows him conducting the horns because 'he wanted to get a photograph of himself conducting', says Sir George. 'He didn't actually do it.' John Burden once noted in an interview that all the Beatles were present in the studio 'but only Paul took an active interest in our overdub'. In fact Lennon took more interest than anyone realised. He asked the tape operator to record the conversation between McCartney, Martin and the horn quartet. At the end of the session he took the tape home.

The tape will have borne witness to a haphazard creative process. Tony Randall remembers McCartney 'coming down the steps from the actual recording box and playing something to us on the guitar and asking us if we could reproduce that on the horns. We wrote it into the horn parts and played.' 'I was the principal horn in that little quartet,' recalls John Burden, now eighty-five. 'They picked our brains, mostly mine. They were very nice but they didn't know what the horn was all about. They wanted some sort of tune so I made up a tune to fit the script. I wrote out phrases for them based on what Paul McCartney was humming to us. It was very easy.' As a result of the creative negotiation, the quartet divided into pairs and played two criss-crossing melodies which chase each other through a few bars of a rousing fanfare.

According to one source they all collected the Beatles' autographs. Tony Randall thinks this highly unlikely. 'We got £6 10s for a session at the time. That was the rate for the job. It was a gig as far as we were concerned.'

Has John Burden ever heard the song since?

'Not for a long time. I think we've got a record of it within my store of records.' It's probably the most frequently played recording by a horn ever made, I tell him.

'It's time somebody gave me some royalties then, isn't it?'

The conservatory of Andrew Lloyd Webber's London offices has high glass walls and a grey-tiled floor. A grand piano is at one end, a sofa at the other. A table runs along an alcove, from which I am serving champagne to my friends, my parents and Lord and Lady Lloyd Webber. In return they have to listen to me play through the entirety of K447.

A speech seems in order. Things need saying, thanks need giving – to Dave, to Kevin, to Andrew Lloyd Webber who, being a former horn student, has consented not only to lend the venue but even to drop in despite a rival invitation to the birthday party of Lady Thatcher. Above all, an explanation must be laid before my suffering audience. So I tell them about my odyssey, about Dave and Kevin and K447. I have always hated speaking in public, and I note when halfway into my speech I reach out my left hand – the Lídl being in my right – to take a sip of water from a wineglass standing on the grand piano, that I have lost control of my own body. I have called it my boutique concert to make it sound intimate, unintimidating. But as the clock ticks down towards the moment I stop talking and start playing, there is no getting away from the fact that it is, in the final analysis, a concert.

My final practice the day before went badly.

'That was absolutely terrible,' said Kevin after the final B flat.

'It was, wasn't it?' There have been more euphonious motorway pile-ups.

'The good news is that it can't possibly be that bad again. I think it's gonna be a laugh.'

The irrepressible Kevin is seated at the other end of the piano. Can he see what I can see? I watch, horrified but intrigued, as my all but disembodied hand seeks out the glass. I have the motor skills of someone trying to operate a mechanical arm by remote. Can any of those arrayed in a standing semicircle around me see the hand actually quivering? How is this hand meant to operate three valves under these conditions? My hand fastens round the glass and I drink. This is a tough crowd. Some of my friends don't like classical music even when played by professionals. They look nonplussed by this scheme of mine.

'Take it away, Kevin.' The words do not sound as cool on my lips as they did in my head. I make a mental note never to utter them again so long as I breathe.

Kevin takes it away. With the semicircular audience not five yards away from me, I stare impassively at the music on the stand and try to imagine an empty room. Hit the D, I tell myself as I play the opening bars Mozart inserted as a favour to Leutgeb. Hit the D. I breathe like Darth Vader, hit the D and edge uncertainly into the crests and swoops of the Allegro. Within a couple of bars I can feel nuts coming loose from bolts. Notes go absent without leave, and in the oddest places. My breath sits high and shallow in my throat. My fingers and my brain aren't talking to each other. The wheels are coming off. A glorious set of eight rising phrases which I've polished and buffed with obsessive compulsion till I can see my reflection in them now splat out of the Lidl as if dunked in mud.

It's only when I get to the recapitulation at the top of the second page, Dave tells me later, that I start to settle. This doesn't bode well for the British Horn Society. I need a whole page to overcome my nerves. A whole page! The speech was meant to do that. That was its job. The one gratification is that the faster passages now trip more or less daintily off my tongue. A finger trill – the cop-out alternative to a lip trill – comes out just so. Suddenly I'm putting my foot down and accelerating through a cascade of triplets towards the cadenza. Kevin at the piano draws to a halt.

I am fresh from a session on my cadenza with Dave. He knows there's no fixing it now, but he can minimise the damage. 'If you can't hit the pedal F,' he advises, 'make a joke out of it. Say, "Oh sod it," and move on. You'll get them on your side.' He advises me not to even bother with the high B flat, three-and-a-half distant octaves above it.

I am on my own. This place, this split second at the start of the cadenza, doesn't get any less lonely the more I visit. I start to tell my musical jokes. Bits and pieces of the Rondo spliced and patched. Notes bent downwards by the hand in the bell. Gobbets of Strauss 1 and Mendelssohn's Nocturne. The hilarious Great C major transposition gag. There is a brief purr of pleasure from one section of the audience when I slip in and out of a phrase from the Andrew Lloyd Webber musical. But when it's time to run down through three octaves into the very basement of my range, the pedal F just refuses to show up. It's a breath of air, nothing more. I try again, to no avail. There's nothing for it.

'Oh sod it.' I switch to Dave's Plan B. It gets a laugh. Then I really think 'sod it' and try to crank it out one more time. It's sitting there this time, in a sulk, but it rears its head long enough to be welcomed by a bigger laugh. I ignore Dave's advice and decide to attempt my top B flat. It squeaks out with scarcely less reluctance, and then the Allegro is over. I take the momentous decision there on the spot that I will never play the first movement of Mozart's third horn concerto in public again.

'I hope you've all remembered to switch your mobile phones on.' It's my party and I'll talk between movements if I want to. Anything to drain away the tension. I empty spit into a champagne box I have placed at my feet to spare the grey tiles.

'Eurgh!' Madeleine Lloyd Webber is unfamiliar with the quirks of the horn's plumbing.

The Romanze beckons. My nerves have been vanquished. I look across at Kevin, take another deep Darth breath and hit the B flat smack dab in the middle. After losing the second note, the whole things works a treat. The soaring, the yearning, the sobbing – I throw them all in, crank them all up. This is the piece I played to these people nearly a year ago at my birthday party. What a difference nearly a year makes. All of a sudden I am playing the horn competently in public. By the time I bring the movement home I'm actually looking forward to the Rondo. So this is what it feels like to be confident with a horn in your hands. As I surge into the galloping rhythm of the final movement I have a sensation a bit like that moment in the movies where the crackpot inventor testing his prototype biplane, which is no more than a bucket with wings held together with string, after numerous attempts to get the contraption airborne only for it to smack its nose into the grass, can feel it rising, hovering, dipping, wavering, then rising again and shuddering upwards away from the earth. In other words, I'm flying. I am miraculously unshackled from the anxiety that sometimes keeps the feet of even real horn players lashed to the ground.

Appreciative applause is offered by guests who are, after all, a couple of sheets to the wind. Kevin and I sink into a bow. The audience holds its position until Dave breaks the semicircle and folds me in a bear hug.

'You see,' he says, 'you can do it!' I can do it with certain provisos. I need a whole speech to calm my nerves, plus four minutes of playing time before I actually settle. I need an audience of friends and family to be pumped full of booze. With all those preconditions met, it would appear that, yes, I can just about do it.

They are unrecognisable without their moptops, moustaches and Sgt Pepper regalia. For our meeting I have chosen a pub in the West End called the Green Man and French Horn. They introduce themselves as Richard Steggall (who wore the green suit of John), Matt Gunner (the pink of Ringo), Adam Walters (George, orange) and his brother Joe (Paul, blue). I buy them drinks and invite them to explain how they landed a berth playing the horn at the top of the biggest gig of all time.

'They were looking for people the same age as the Beatles in their suits,' says Matt, who got the call first and had to postpone his Cornish holiday. It was only once the four of them, all jobbing London freelances in their twenties, were signed that outfits were mentioned. They went along to be measured and fitted, much as the Beatles once did when the suits were originally created. 'To perform with Paul McCartney and U2,' Matt adds, 'I would probably have done it naked.'

At the fitting they discovered that U2 were keen on donning the uniforms themselves. But McCartney was too nervous to be dressing up as a Beatle. In keeping with the half-realised concept of the original album, McCartney earmarked the Sgt Pepper suits for the French horn section, and even decided who would be who. Matt, being the shortest, was Ringo. Richard was given round specs. 'By offloading the uniform onto us,' he says, 'that took the pressure off them.' McCartney wore jeans and a long-sleeved black T-shirt.

The sheet music written out by John Burden for the original quartet of horn players had long since disappeared. Only after the horn players had been booked did George Martin receive a panicked communiqué from the McCartney camp.

'I was in Montreal,' he tells me. 'I got a message saying, "Paul is desperate to have the horn parts. Have you got them?" I said, "No but I can probably sketch it out for you again." I wrote the parts for the horn again as I remembered them and emailed them to London, where they were printed out and got to the group just in time so they could actually rehearse it.'

The rehearsal was at a studio in Bermondsey. 'We turned up, these lads who had the look he wanted,' says Richard. 'He was really surprised the first time we did the run-through. "You can play!" And it was like, "Yeah. That's what we do. That's our job."' McCartney told them about the horn's introduction to the Beatles, about how Alan Civil was hired to play the scarily high solo on 'For No One' as 'a dep for a bloke who'd been recently deceased', says Adam. This was presumably Dennis Brain, who had in fact died nine years earlier. One can only conclude that in 1966 McCartney was somewhat out of touch with the horn world. 'If you can believe that!' says Richard.

They rehearsed with U2 the day before Live 8. Bono had just come from a meeting with the Prime Minister at 10 Downing Street. 'They laughed when they walked in,' says Matt. 'We were in costume.' The Edge had difficulty conquering the guitar break played by McCartney in the original recording. 'It was funny watching him struggle to play it,' says Joe. 'It took about half an hour to get this tiny rhythmic detail right.' 'When the Edge was practising his little bit,' says Adam, 'Paul McCartney came over to us and said, "Fantastic."'

At the sound check the next morning in Hyde Park, the focus moved on to their stage entry halfway through the song. Their cue to start marching on was 'So let me introduce to you ...' They had sixteen beats to get into position. 'It was walk walk walk walk walk two three breath play,' says Matt. They practised it three times. As the hour hand ticked around to two o'clock, they posed for a portrait, the four horn players and the Beatle, and once again the non-horn player in the middle held an instrument. Fittingly it was Joe, wearing the same blue-coloured suit that the Beatle wore on the cover of *Sgt Pepper's Lonely Hearts Club Band*, who handed over his instrument. Like John Lennon at the recording of 'A Day in the Life', Paul McCartney wasn't sure how to hold it.

For the performance itself, their path was initially blocked by the huge swarm of backstage celebrities eager to watch the opening act. 'The stage manager was effing and blinding,' says Adam. '"I don't care who you are, if you're not in the fucking act, fuck off!" It was all geared for us to be able to get on the stage.' When they got to their marks, they had to come to a halt, raise their horns to their lips, breathe and instantly blow. 'We could all play those notes any time in our lives,' says Matt, 'but when you have to play on 140 channels of live television of the biggest concert ever from memory ... It was only three minutes' worth of horn playing. You couldn't think about how many people were watching. You didn't think about how big a gig it was. I was ten for the last one and had only just started the horn then. To be up there twenty years on – quite incredible. Dynamics,' he adds, 'were not involved. It wasn't the studio version. It was the live version. We were giving it one.'

Between them they have racked up a lot of years' study under some distinguished professors of horn. But nothing had prepared them for this. 'It wasn't just the biggest gig we'll ever do,' says Joe. 'It was probably the biggest gig that Paul McCartney and U2 will ever do as well. Which is an unusual thought.' And yet somehow they contrived to conquer the terror which should, according to all the available evidence, have littered their performance with split notes. 'Most of the time when you get nervous,' says Richard, 'it's because you are relating it to something that happened back in the past. But we had nothing to relate to standing in front of 200,000 people playing with U2 and the Beatles. It was, this is like nothing we've done before, therefore we might as well just do it. It just goes to show there is something inside your body that's taught you how to play the horn. Your brain wasn't saying, "You've got to get this right." Your brain was saying *nothing*.'

The performance was immaculate. At the end, they looked up for the applause and realised they couldn't see the back of the crowd. Within three minutes one of them got a baffled text message, saying simply, 'Was that *you?*' Within half an hour, their performance was available for download all over the world. Offstage, McCartney gave them a hug.

'We made history together,' said the Beatle.

10
The Pass Door

Are you finishing? Thank heavens! – enough, enough!

Mozart

The pass door opens. The pass door of the concert hall of the Guildhall School of Music and Drama. A short walk. Ten paces perhaps, the Lídl in my right hand, to a solid wooden stand where the sheet music of Mozart's third horn concerto, K447, awaits. Ten small steps for mankind. A giant leap for an amateur horn player. The pass door swings shut, cutting off the possibility of retreat. I advance. Kevin Amos, who taught me for two years until I gave up at seventeen and is now my accompanist, takes his seat to my right at a massy grand piano. In front of me, just the other side of the music stand, is my audience.

I've been having bad dreams about the French horn. In one of the milder scenarios I am pressganged into an amateur orchestra. We are due to rehearse Mahler's Sixth Symphony. It's just about the biggest blow in the repertoire. I agree to participate so long as it's in the key of F, the horn key. I'm assured that it is. I turn up to an old school gym to find only two seats in the horn section, but the second horn's seat is occupied. I'm principal horn. I sit. The strings start to play and I stare gormlessly at a snowstorm of untransposed notes on the page before me. (When I wake up I check the key of Mahler 6. It's in A minor.)

I'm driving home to London from Somerset after playing the concerto to my daughters, nephews and nieces and stop off in a pretty village to visit a friend (whom in reality I've never met). My friend's grandfather has a collection of horns and Wagner tubas, one of which has been pulled straight so that it resembles an Alphorn with valves. I can extract only a few scratchy notes from it. I'm handed a child's tiny toy horn instead, and this time fail to produce a single note.

I am in the front room of Dave Lee's house. Dave isn't there, but four or five burglars are, all of them dressed in hooped T-shirts. Each has a sack which may as well be marked 'swag', into which they are loading copious knick-knacks and gewgaws from a low shelf running the length of a large L-shaped window. They have their backs to me and although I keep on saying, 'Hey. You can't take that! It's Dave's,' they ignore me. They don't even seem to hear. (What can this mean? Can it mean anything other than that in the horn world, as represented by Dave, I am even more of an intruder than a gang of cartoon burglars?)

Before my boutique concert I dream that I'm to perform the whole of Mozart 3 in a tall thin townhouse littered with clutter and detritus. The Lloyd Webbers are invited. They step warily through a minefield of junk to sit on a moth-eaten sofa. They are keen to get things rolling by 6.30 but not enough other guests have turned up. At 6.55 I decide to perform anyway, and go to the lidded cabinet where I keep the hi-fi to cue up the recording by Alan Civil which I will play along to. I raise the lid. The cabinet is overflowing with rubbish. I run up four floors to retrieve a Radovan Vlatković CD from my office, run downstairs again only to realise I've not actually brought the CD down. I run up four floors again. By the time I come to play I am too out of breath to perform.

The most graphic dream finds me on the edge of a large paved courtyard, the hub of some sort of country holiday complex. We must be somewhere in the very far north in midsummer, because it is warm and barely dark at two in the morning. People lounge around the courtyard, drinking. Children are still up and running around. There is no sign of a piano or pianist. Just me and a music stand. The terracotta paving is herringbone, I notice. As I take the Lídl out of its case it starts to come to pieces in my hands. The slides and valves all fall away from the main body of the instrument as soon as I touch them. Turning my back on the audience, I hurriedly attempt to fix it back together but to no avail. Not without relief I turn round again and announce that sadly there will be no concert.

The dreams are over. I look out into a large wide hall with high concrete walls and take my bearings. Hundreds of faces in long rows look back at me. A year ago many of these people were on the stage with me. I was one face in seventy, performing the Hallelujah Chorus in a massed horn ensemble conducted by Mike Thompson. But that was then, and this isn't. This is now. Somewhere out there are the other sixty-nine. As are Mike Thompson, Hugh Seenan and the great and the good of the British Horn Society. Somewhere out there are Dave, the New Person In My Life, my two girls and a dozen or so friends. Truly this is the stuff of nightmares. Not just mine. Anyone's, everyone's. The stage, the lights, the expectant audience, the lack of an escape route.

'I know you're wondering who the hell I am,' I say, 'and what on earth I'm doing on a bill sandwiched between the President of the International Horn Society and the horn section of the London Philharmonic Orchestra.' Beyond announcing me, Hugh Seenan has left it to me to introduce myself. 'Come to think of it,' I add, 'I'm slightly wondering myself.' I begin to tell them about giving up the horn. It was twenty-three years ago today.

The British Horn Society is twenty-five years old. To celebrate, it is holding its annual jamboree in rather more imposing surroundings than the sort of venue it normally musters in. The Guildhall with its flat wide auditorium and beetling concrete ramparts looks like a Soviet palace of culture. This being an important birthday, the bill also features an immodest gathering of talent. Most major British players have answered the summons. David Pyatt, who has advised me on positive visualisation and breath control, is leading a quartet of London Symphony Orchestra horns. Andrew Clark, the Orchestra of the Age of Enlightenment principal horn who inspected Dennis Brain's Alexander with me, is booked to play on Dennis Brain's Raoux. Hugh Seenan, who auditioned me, is playing Poulenc's Elegy, written in memory of the maestro after the car crash. Tony Randall, who played on *Sgt Pepper's Lonely Hearts Club Band*, is here to conduct his own composition. Sarah Willis, my chum from the Berlin Philharmonic, is flying in for a day. Over the course of the weekend the members of the British Horn Society are going to hear the great old instrument played to the very highest standard, and in every imaginable permutation: solo, solo with piano, solo with string quartet, duet, trio, quartet, octet and, for the grand finale, sixteen horns of the London Horn Sound are going to club together and give us their 'Bohemian Rhapsody': a fitting finale for an instrument whose first great soloists came from Bohemia. And at some point the entire society will cram onto the stage for the annual massed ensemble and play a version of Beethoven's *Egmont Overture*, conducted by Barry Tuckwell.

Barry Tuckwell, as I explain in my speech to those friends of mine who may by some oversight be unfamiliar with the name, is the godfather of the instrument, the gunslinger; the Pele and Pavarotti. In recognition of his services to the instrument the Queen has bestowed on him an Order of the British Empire medal and the British Horn Society has honoured him with its presidency. At the inaugural festival, he performed a duet with Alan Civil. A quarter of a century on, he has flown over from his native Australia. I am about to perform to the greatest horn player since the death of Dennis Brain.

To accommodate all this talent, the festival has extended backwards from its regular start time on Saturday morning into Friday evening. I sit in the audience at the opening concert listening to real horn players teasing beautiful sounds out of their instruments when the gigantic absurdity of my quest hits me squarely in the solar plexus for the very first time. In a year of preparation I have just about survived the series of hurdles I have placed in my own way: performing at my fortieth birthday, at horn camp in New

Hampshire, to my family in Somerset, in a Royal Academy masterclass and finally at my boutique concert. I have always been able to count on the deferral of improvement to a later date. But in twenty-four hours' time there will be no more preparation time left, no more deferral. The clock will have ticked down. A full year will have expired and I will be attempting, now or never and for one night only, to pass myself off as a horn player to a room full of hundreds of horn players, some of them the best in the country, one or two among the best in the world. I had always assumed I would be tucked away in the schedule on Sunday morning or Saturday afternoon. But the glossy festival programme, bulging with the CVs of famous horn players, says otherwise.

'We'll do all right by you,' Hugh Seenan has told me. 'We'll make sure you get a good slot.' The good slot is straight after the interval on the Saturday evening concert. It says so, here in incontrovertible print.

7.30 SATURDAY GALA STAR CONCERT

The first half consists entirely of guests from the European mainland. The principal horn of the Rotterdam Philharmonic is followed by the principal horn of the Gothenburg Symphony Orchestra duetting with Frøydis Ree Wekre, perhaps the most illustrious female horn player in the instrument's entire history. Before the interval it's the turn of Frank Lloyd who, according to the blurb, played at the inaugural festival along with Barry Tuckwell and Alan Civil, now has Hermann Baumann's old job as a professor of horn at the Folkwang-Hochschule in Essen, and is indeed the current president of the International Horn Society. Then it says this:

Interval 15 mins

Mozart	Jasper Rees plays Mozart
Bach	Fugue arr. Shaw for Horn Quartet
	London Philharmonic Orchestra Horn Quartet
	Richard Bissill, Gareth Mollison, Chris Parks,
	Martin Hobbs

Martin Hobbs! Martin Hobbs was the first horn player I confided in about performing a solo at the festival. He had just played the fourth horn solo in Beethoven's Ninth, to a rousing ovation. I distinctly remember his advice. 'My advice,' he said, sounding spooked, 'is don't do it. It's *really* scary playing at the British Horn Society festival.'

It's all too much. I turn to the New Person.

'I feel sick.'

'I'm not surprised.'

Before the festival gets under way I have a pint with Barry Tuckwell. We stand among the Friday-after-work suits in a heaving City pub. Barry is deep into his seventies now. His signature goatee has gone white. He is sniffling with a bug caught on the jumbo coming over, and walks in tidy little granny steps. Before he retired a decade ago, his playing was celebrated as much for its muscle as its dazzle.

'I quit before everyone found out I was going off,' he tells me. 'You've got to have a lot of strength to play the horn. I realised I was losing the strength. I thought, tell-tale sign, if you're not strong enough, quit.' He lived in Baltimore for a while, but has since returned to Australia. As for many a horn player, the marriages came and went. Scientific studies have not been made, but there must be a correlation between the high risks of horn playing and the high rate of marital casualty. I ask Barry if horn players are wedded, ultimately, to their instruments.

'They tend to get divorced from their wives,' he replies. Barry is dry as dust. 'In general the spouse tends to resent her husband's preoccupation with his career. And with the horn you are preoccupied.'

He grew up in Sydney and only alighted on the horn after trying piano, organ and violin. 'I was playing professionally in about six or seven months. When I was fifteen I got a job. I could read music. Learning the horn was all I had to do. One note at a time – it seemed easy. Later on you find it's more complicated. You need nerves of steel and if you have doubts about what you can do, you don't survive. A horn misses a note, the critics write it up in the newspaper. If a pianist misses a note they don't bother.'

In due course Barry came over to the UK. He reckons he met Dennis Brain a dozen times in the 1950s, the first at a concert in Chelsea Town Hall where Brain was playing Haydn's first horn concerto. 'I went and said hello. He was still playing the Raoux piston horn. He'd had this extra valve put on, showed me the instrument, what he'd done to it, *handed* it to me. I was *nothing*. I was nineteen or twenty. With respect I'd say he was a simple person. I don't mean he was stupid. He was very open, very pleasant, and nice to everybody. He'd sit around and drink tea with a sticky bun. No bullshit. Aubrey Brain was no less phenomenal than his son, but Dennis brought something extra. He had a sunny personality when he walked on to the stage. Everything lit up.'

Barry landed the job of principal horn with the LSO in 1955 after John Burden led a walk-out of principals in protest at the management. After thirteen golden years he left to go freelance. Almost all the work that came his way was as a soloist. His unfussy, unflappable temperament must have been a solid bedrock to build a career on. For a time only he and Hermann Baumann were making a living on the solo instrument in Europe, but Barry was the one to exploit its full commercial potential. Hermann recorded the Mozart concertos twice, one with valves, one without. Barry recorded them no fewer than four times. I ask him about K447. 'In a way I think it's my favourite. The slow movement has some beautiful things. You know he did it with affection – for the instrument, and for Leutgeb. They were certainly very personal works. The first time I played it was in Sydney on an ABC broadcast. I was eighteen or nineteen. I've got a record of it. It's not bad. A young brazen fellow playing the horn. And the last time was the last time I played in public. That was in Baltimore. A very good old colleague and friend went to the concert. He said, "I want to hear the last note that you play." And it didn't occur to me until I suppose a second before the end. I thought, I'm going to leave the last note out. So I didn't play the last note. And of course all the horn players spotted that.'

The opening concert is due to start. We amble back from the pub towards the Guildhall along darkening streets.

'What instrument do you play?' asks Barry as we walk. The usual question.

'Er, a Lídl,' I say apologetically.

'A Lídl, eh? Good horns, those.' I'm not sure I've heard correctly. I've been waiting all year for someone to say that. It's the first time anyone has said a pleasant thing about my instrument.

'Well, adds Barry, 'they were seventy years ago.'

A day later Barry is somewhere out there in the audience. 'At this moment,' I say, 'with Barry Tuckwell sitting somewhere out there, I can think of a million things I'd rather be doing.' I am flagrantly luring the members of the BHS on to my side. 'Like having my fingernails pulled out, or my eyelids sewn up, or being abducted by aliens.' Despite my aversion to public speaking, so far it's going quite well.

'I gave up the horn when I left school. I was never very good and I didn't practise enough. Twenty-two years later, as I approached my fortieth birthday, I suddenly felt an urgent need to take it up again. So I got this old Josef Lídl, made in a country that doesn't exist any more, out of its case in the attic and took it to last year's British Horn Society festival. I played in the massed horn blow and in both senses of the word had a blast. I set myself the target of playing a solo at the festival a year on.'

The announcement is greeted with a huge, spontaneous outbreak of applause and even cheering. A gust of warmth flows up towards me from the auditorium. Relief floods through my body like water through a burst dam. My God, I think, they do actually get it. I *knew* they would. To stand up alone as an amateur in front of this of all crowds, and after twenty-two years off? They know the instrument, these fellow travellers along the high lonely ridges, and grasp the epic scale of my folly.

On the other side of the pass door the usual flock of symptoms have been circling like vultures. They are my familiars. I can do a roll-call. Parched mouth? Here, sir. Heart pecking against ribcage? Tick. Nausea? Yup. Uncontrollable lateral leg judder? Check. But hold on. What the hell's this new sensation? Five minutes before we go on I turn to Kevin, who for the past hour has been doing his pragmatic best to keep me distracted.

'Kevin? Why am I feeling faint?' My focus is swimming. My head is giddy.

'Lack of oxygen to the brain,' Kevin explains. 'It'll pass. You'll be fine as soon as you get out there.' Kevin's chirpiness is bulletproof. He's right though. As I work the audience, the vultures lose the whiff of carrion. The nerves settle. The speech must be doing its job.

'There is a change to the advertised programme. Or rather the programme I advertised to Hugh Seenan.' I have told Hugh Seenan I am going to play the first movement, the Allegro. His original invitation made reference to 'one or two movements'. After my boutique concert, though, I've decided to play the second and third movements instead. They allow for more contrast, and together have more of a narrative. Plus I'm much less likely to come off the rails.

'I was going to play the first movement of Mozart's third horn concerto,' I tell my audience. 'But the first movement calls for a cadenza.' They laugh. 'And you don't want to hear my cadenza.' And laugh. 'And you really don't want to hear my lip trilling.' I'm starting to enjoy this speech a bit too much. It may be the oratorical equivalent of Jeremy Thal's three bananas. 'So instead I'm going to play the second and third movements of the same concerto.' I might end up *too* relaxed.

'I don't know how many of you know the work of Dave Lee.' I had meant to bring a copy of Dave's CD, *Under the Influence*, out onstage with me, but I've forgotten. 'You will not hear more powerful and daring and imaginative horn playing anywhere.' It's impossible for me to find an adequate way of paying tribute to Dave. His generosity has been unstinting. 'Dave has very kindly borne the full brunt of my obsession and given me lessons over the year.' Money has never been discussed. There's been nothing in it for him apart from a few drinks. In return, he has somehow found his reputation, through no fault of his own and in this very public way, hitched to mine. 'Anything musical you hear in the next few minutes,' I say, 'is down to him.' I take this opportunity to put at least some distance between him and my playing. 'Any errors are my own.' They start laughing again. 'And trust me there will be errors.' I'm in the grip of an addiction.

I have in fact been able to repay Dave in one small way.

'Oh we've got that, have we?' says a curator when I make a preliminary visit to the Music and Rare Books reading room to order it up. In 1986 a substantial part of the Stefan Zweig Collection, the private library of the Austrian Jewish playwright – and librettist of Strauss's *Die schweigsame Frau* – who committed suicide in Brazil in 1942, came into the possession of the British Library. The collection includes the handwritten thematic catalogue of his own works that Mozart began in 1784. It also contains a document that will be of as much interest to Dave as it is to me: the autograph manuscript of K447.

We meet in the piazza at the front of the new library in Euston Road and enter a gleaming atrium through sliding doors. Dave signs up for a short-term membership and we take the lift to the second floor. Pushing through one set of thick double doors, then another, we present our light green cards at a security desk. Above our mugshots run the words 'Researching the world's knowledge'. Someone was handsomely paid to come up with this trendy convolution. We enter a large low room where row upon row of leather-topped desks are occupied by people of every age and ethnicity. There is perhaps a relatively high preponderance of spectacles, unruly hair, general dishevelment and other semaphores of the academic calling. The room is dense with a consensual hush, although talking is permitted at the lending desk.

'I have asked to look at a manuscript?'

'Can I see your card?'

I collect a thin bound hardboard volume and carry it to a nearby desk. Dave pulls a second chair across from a neighbouring berth while I untie a ribbon and open the cover. Within the limits imposed by the surroundings, Dave and I are beside ourselves with excitement. We are in the presence of – we are actually touching – the very parchment once handled and scrawled on by Mozart. It says so at the top right-hand side of the first page: '*von Mozart und seiner Handschrift*'. His handwriting. The words are written by Georg Nikolaus von Nissen, the Danish diplomat who married the composer's widow Constanze in 1809 and did much, in the form of a respectful biography and the preservation of documents and mementoes, to guarantee his legacy. Apart from the headings, every last inkspot is Mozart's. K447 is the only one of Mozart's horn concertos for which a completed autograph manuscript exists. And here it is, open on the desk in front of us.

The central heading, in Mozart's hand, says '*Concerto per il Corno Solo*'. Instead of the word 'Allegro' Mozart has jotted a time-saving contraction, 'allo'. Down the left-hand margin, across the first six of twelve staves, the instruments are listed opposite the music to be played by them: '*Corno principale, 2 Violini, Viola, 2 Clarinetti in B, 2 Fagotti* [over a crossing out], *Bassi.*'

'This is the only one of the four concertos,' Dave explains, 'where he used clarinets and bassoons.' He whispers like a conspirator. 'In the other two completed concertos he used oboes and horns. It meant he got a much darker sound. Bassi,' he adds, 'would have been cellos.'

The folios are 22.5 cm wide and 17 cm deep. The Allegro takes up ten pages, the Romanze four and the Rondo eight. In the Allegro he fits only eight bars across the opening page, while in the Rondo he can squeeze in as many as sixteen. There is no clarity about the date of composition. A date on the top right-hand side of the first page, probably written by Nissen, says '1783', though the 3 looks oddly tampered with. The concerto is certainly not mentioned in his private catalogue of compositions begun a year later, but another theory is that the paper is written on the same parchment as that used for the score of *Don Giovanni*, which dates it to 1787. The relative narrowness of the concerto's range, compared with that of K417 and K495 and especially K407, the quintet for horn and strings written for Leutgeb in 1781, suggests that Mozart was newly aware of his horn player's declining physical powers. The *corno principale* was now deep into his fifties. There is another theory that the Allegro was written at a different time to the second and third movements, which would explain why at the start of the second movement Mozart has written across the top of the page:

Larghetto   *Romanze*   *di Wolfgango Amadeo Mozarto*

He has put his signature (with a florid scroll under the O of 'Mozarto') halfway through the concerto. There is also a difference in the way he writes the bar lines down the face of the page. In the Allegro the lines have gaps, where the ink didn't flow smoothly off the nib, as if Mozart was less bothered about precision. They are firmer in the Romanze and the Rondo, and the notation is recorded a little more precisely and distinctly.

'He would have written this out late at night,' says Dave, poring over the Allegro. 'He would have had a glass of wine on the table and done it in a hurry.' He can't have drunk too much of the wine because he is on his best behaviour. There are no jokes for Leutgeb's enjoyment as there are on other concertos, no differently coloured inks. Curiously there is an almost total absence of dynamics, apart from the occasional call for an orchestral crescendo. Aside from an indication where notes are either slurred or staccato, the horn is left to its own devices.

'That's because Leutgeb wouldn't have been playing from the orchestral score,' says Dave. 'He'd have had his own part.' Now and then Mozart does ask for a slur between notes, and he never fails to indicate where a trill is required. Above a G held over a whole bar he has written 't' with a squiggle waving out along the bar like a tadpole tail. A similar hieroglyph at the appropriate point is the only sign that Mozart is asking for a cadenza.

'Would he have composed this directly from his head, Dave? Or do you think this is a fair copy of a rough draft?'

'Definitely from his head,' says Dave.

We turn to the Romanze. Mozart's script is small but so clear I could almost take it onto the festival stage instead of my own edition of the concerto. With the thirty-two semiquavers, he knows he has to fit them into narrow bars, so he pays particular attention with his quill and they come up a treat. It's also instantly apparent that there are many fewer slurs, indicating a smooth untongued glide between notes, than in most published editions of the movement.

'He would have left it up to Leutgeb to decide all that,' says

Dave. We follow the score through the teasing series of false endings until the quizzical round-off of the last bar: B flat quaver, quaver rest, then two B flat quavers down an octave.

'Why does he conclude on such an inconclusive note?' I ask. I've often wondered. For the horn all three movements end on the same note, but the middle movement is in the subdominant key of A flat, so the horn B flat is not the tonic note and has a different role within the final chord. 'There would be much more resolution with an E flat than a B flat.'

'Because a horn E flat is not a natural note on the harmonic,' says Dave. 'Leutgeb didn't have valves. He could have played it as a stopped note with his hand muting the air flow out of the bell to bend the note down a tone from F. But it would have sounded muffled. It would have sounded unsatisfactory. I could swear Dennis Brain plays the E flat on his recording.' (Later I check on the Nomad. He does.)

There is no mention of the word 'Rondo' in the Rondo. Instead, under the *corno principale*'s opening note, Mozart has written 'Allegro' (not 'allo' again). The movement is in 6/8 and the hunting rhythm calls for a lot of quavers, so the composer is again careful to differentiate each note. The orchestrations are written out with a little less attention. We turn over the pages and get the horn's penultimate entry. There, above the upbeat, Mozart has inscribed a single word with a trim little flourish: 'Leitgeb'. It puzzles me. It seems an odd decision to doff a cap to his horn player for the first time on the final page of the concerto. Dave looks carefully at the manuscript. He starts to leaf slowly back through the movement in search of clues.

'He's mentioned Leutgeb there too, look.' Dave points at the horn's second entry, after the orchestra has replayed and elaborated on the opening statement. The letters are little more hunched, as they are on the second line, squeezed into the gap between the sixth and seventh stave. That must be why I missed it. It doesn't answer my question though.

'Why mention his horn player at the second entry of the third movement, and then again just before the concerto ends altogether? There's no reference to Leutgeb in the Allegro or the

Romanze.' Dave flicks back to the second mention of Leutgeb, then to the first.

'It's because he's entering alone. That fermata there' – he points to the sign for a musical stop – 'means the orchestra comes to a halt on a suspended chord. The horn then enters on the upbeat by itself before the orchestra comes back in. He's written "Leitgeb" in there because it's the horn that gets the piece going again.' I'd never have worked that out. I'm glad I've brought Dave along with me. We close the autograph manuscript of K447 inside its hardboard case and I tie up the ribbon.

'How do you feel about seeing that, Dave?'

'Wonderful,' he says. 'I enjoyed that. Really special.' Dave is not a gusher.

'Me too.' Nor am I. I hand the manuscript back at the lending desk and we make our way out through the rows of haircuts and glasses and serious faces bent over laptops. We may not have researched the world's knowledge, whatever that entails, but for an uplifting half-hour we have looked over the shoulder of genius and watched it at work by candlelight, late one night (or possibly two separate nights) in Vienna. Two centuries and two decades have shrunk to a vanishing point. We emerge – slightly changed – into the broil of Euston Road.

The day of the concert is grim. I get a haircut. The woman clipping me into shape is some kind of reiki master. Hairdressing is only one of her lines. Alternative therapies are her daily bread. She says she knows a lot of witches.

'It'll be cool,' she says cheerfully into the mirror when I tell her about the concert. She seems remarkably convinced of this. The L in 'cool' is more of a W, which for some reason makes me distrustful of her wisdom. The haircut is fine though. I do some Farkas warm-ups in the afternoon and, heeding Dave's advice, rest the lip. At six o'clock we climb into the car and drive across town to the Guildhall School of Music and Drama. The New Person tries to keep me chipper but I feel cold with dread. While they park in the underground vault of the Barbican Centre I peel off and enter the foyer alone. It is long and narrow and teeming. The first day of the festival is all but done. The horn manufacturers,

Paxman and Schmid and Hans Hoyer, have packed away their displays of gleaming horns. British Horn Society members mill around in a state of suspended animation, the concert still half an hour off.

I find Kevin in an underground bunker. It looks like a steeply raked lecture hall, but with a piano instead of a lectern. He is trotting through the accompaniment. We've agreed to wear suits but no ties. I've never seen him looking so dapper. Kevin has been denied access to the concert hall to get a feel for the piano, because an ensemble of thirty-two horn players are using it to rehearse the night's grand finale.

'How are you feeling?' he says.

'Not great.'

Kevin recommends that we try just a little bit of each movement and leave it at that. Time drags so slowly. I go upstairs to make sure my friends have got their tickets. The hall is emptier now as people file into the concert hall. Dave comes in from the street. I tell him about my dream, the one where the horn falls apart in my hands as I'm about to perform.

'Perfectly normal,' he says nonchalantly.

'Really?'

'Oh yeah. It's a bog-standard dream about performance anxiety. Everyone's had that dream.' I'm not sure whether to feel reassured. 'If you're not nervous,' he adds, 'you won't perform as well. You've done all the work. I know it sounds daft, but try to enjoy it.'

'Do you enjoy performing, Dave?'

'No!' He laughs. I'm reminded of a story Dave once told about James Buck Snr, who was one of the horn players who did the Sgt Pepper session. He was once booked to play Strauss's first horn concerto. 'He used to do quite a bit of work with Aubrey Brain,' says Dave, 'and asked him for some advice on quelling nerves at the start of Strauss 1. Aubrey Brain being terribly pompous and important, said, "What I do is I put confidence-boosting words to the opening fanfare." You have to imagine Jim asking this in a cockney accent,' says Dave. 'Jim says, "What exactly do you mean?" And Aubrey says, "Here am I, Aubrey Brain man of fame." He said, "You try that, James, I'm sure it'll work." "Thank you very much, Aubrey," says Jim. A fortnight later, he sees Aubrey and Aubrey says, "James, how did the Strauss go?" Jim says, "Terrible." "Did you do what I told you to do?" "Didn't work." "What did you sing?" "Here am I, Jimmy Buck scared as fuck."'

Without Dave I wouldn't have got this far. I just hope I don't embarrass him. He wishes me good luck and follows the stream down the corridor. I won't see him again until afterwards. In a minute or two the place is empty and through the thick walls I can hear the principal horn of the Rotterdam Phil get under way. I go back to find Kevin. He is talking to the New Person and the girls, who do their best to keep me buoyant. At a certain point the second item on the bill will have started. Attempts to steer the subject clear of the impending examination prove fruitless. There seems nothing for it but to wander around to the far side of the concert hall before the interval starts. The New Person and the girls say their goodbyes and good lucks and leave. Kevin and I walk through a succession of double doors until we find ourselves in the long thin corridor that runs the length of the concert hall on the opposite flank to the foyer. After a few yards, and a right turn through another double door, we come to the pass door. On tables and on the floor there are piles and heaps of horn cases. If I counted they'd no doubt come to thirty-two. Through the pass door comes the sound of the president of the International Horn Society performing death-defying stunts on his instrument. I've never in my life been more grateful for a fifteen-minute interval. To go on straight after that would be verging on vandalism.

The applause that greets the performance sounds loud enough even before the pass door opens and a short trim man with silver hair steps offstage. He is beaming. There are cheers and whistles. I have a sudden *déjà vu*. The last time I was in this position it was a competition. Frank Lloyd is summoned back to take another bow. The pass door opens again. He nods curtly and wanders away down the corridor. Kevin and I are alone with the sound of dying applause. A surge of hubbub rises to fill the silence as the members of the British Horn Society rise to stretch their legs, get a coffee, marvel over what they have heard. The bustling figure of

Mike Thompson appears. He is conducting the thirty-two horn players.

'How are you feeling?' he asks brightly.

'I've felt better.' The vultures are gathering.

'Don't be surprised if your mouth dries up,' he says, 'or if your heart feels like it's going to burst out of your chest, you feel dizzy, you can't breathe. Don't think you're having a heart attack. It's perfectly normal.'

'That's good to know, Mike.' I find myself wondering out loud what Barry Tuckwell did to kill time on this side of the pass door.

'Why don't you ask him? I'll go and get him.' Mike hurries off down the corridor in search of the greatest living horn player.

'Wow,' says Kevin.

'I had a drink with him yesterday,' I say. I start telling Kevin how in the final performance of his career Barry left out the last note of K447, only to see the man himself shuffling along the corridor towards me. He is carrying a white plastic shopping bag and wearing a tie emblazoned with horns. I introduce him to Kevin.

'A great honour,' says Kevin deferentially. When Kevin was studying the horn, Barry was in his pomp. I ask the president of the British Horn Society how he's feeling today.

'Pretty good.' His Australian accent is clipped. 'Looking forward to this.'

'I'm glad *you* are.'

'There's nothing you can do about it now.' He smiles, but more with his eyes. The smile tells me that I've only got myself to blame.

'Any final advice, notwithstanding?'

'Just do what you know you can do,' he says. 'Don't concentrate on the things you know you don't do terribly well. And just do your best.'

'I'll bear that in mind.'

A rumble of noise gathers behind the pass door. People are taking their seats. As the president of the British Horn Society turns and walks back down the corridor, the chairman pops up behind me. We've spoken, we've emailed, but this is the first time

I've seen Hugh Seenan since my 'lesson' with him months ago.

'We're all looking forward to this.' He slaps me lightly on the back. 'I'm sure it's going to be great.' We discuss the business of how he introduces me, how much he says about me. I tell him I've got a speech ready, waving a sheet of A4.

'Do you want us to put that out on the stand for you with your music?' I hand over both sheets of paper. It's the horn equivalent of having your rackets carried out for the Wimbledon final.

'OK to go in a couple of minutes?'

I look for a moment of peace a few yards down the corridor and take some slow deep breaths. Time is no longer dragging. I blow a couple of palsied notes.

'You ready?' It's Hugh's Glasgow rasp. I walk back towards Kevin and the pass door, through which Hugh now disappears. In the brief instance it is open I can see the reassembled audience talking among themselves. The noise muffles as the pass door closes and then dies altogether at the sound of Hugh's amplified voice.

'For the second half of our concert we are extremely privileged' – for a split second I think he's going to refer to me – 'to have the horn quartet of the London Philharmonic Orchestra play for us. They've been on tour in Korea for the last three or four days so they're probably very jet-lagged. Afterwards an ensemble of thirty-two horn players from eight music colleges are going to premiere a new composition. But first of all I'd like to introduce you to a very special chap called Jasper Rees, a professional journalist and amateur horn player. We first met last year at the Southampton horn festival and he's going to say a few words to you.'

My year of waiting is over. The pass door opens and, followed by my old horn teacher, I walk out of my private pipedream, away from a netherworld of shadows. Ten short paces perhaps, the Lidl in my right hand. Out to face the music. Out to *be* the music. People are clapping. I come to a halt and look up.

'I need to say a few words, partly to get my pulse rate down. But also I know you're wondering who the hell I am ...'

It's interesting to note the medicinal properties of laughter. The speech is a courtesy extended to an audience which has paid good money to attend this concert. It is also designed to reduce expectations to subterranean levels. I tell the potted version of my re-entanglement with the horn. Talking about it is a slam dunk. Talking about it is what I'm good at. The more they laugh, the more control I wrest back over myself, and extend over them. But they also laugh, I sense, because they are nervous too. They have no idea what to expect, and they didn't pay to see someone crash and burn.

In due course it's time to sign off. 'I'd like to thank Hugh Seenan and the British Horn Society,' I say, 'for their incredible generosity and indeed broadmindedness in allowing me to play. Finally, I'd like to thank you all for suffering the next few minutes. Thank you very much.' There is more heart-warming applause. I feel like the actress accepting her Oscar. They like me! But will they still like me in seven minutes? I raise the Lídl and play a sturdy B flat. The note spreads comfortably around the Soviet palace of culture. Nice acoustic! I've never played a horn in such a big room. Kevin sounds the same note on the piano and raises his eyebrows, indicating that I'm slightly flat. I push in the main tuning slide and blow again. Kevin nods discreetly. And now there is nothing for it but to play. I take a long slow breath and, peeling my eyes away from Kevin, send out the first note of the second movement of Mozart's third horn concerto, K447.

I hit it. I hit the B flat. Relief shoots through my body for the duration of a dotted crotchet as I snarl the slur up to the E flat quaver before sinking down onto the two Gs. I order myself to ignore that first glitch – it's nothing, it's nerves – and proceed as normal. But I'm not listening to myself. In the opening bars I contrive to split a freakish number of notes. I am a bull in a china shop. I don't just split them. I ram-raid, I blowtorch them. I'm playing as badly as eighty-year-old Harry in horn camp. It's an instant catastrophe. As Kevin's accompaniment now takes over for eight bars, I remember the New Person's advice about grimacing during performance. But behind my impassive face an internal critic is screaming abuse. How in God's name did you miss that G? It's the easiest note in the entire piece! Can't you even slur any more or something? You've played that right hundreds of times!

Emergency! We have a situation! We have a definite type of situation! Evacuate the building!

I feel myself freeze. The speech has gone far far too well. I've assumed that playing the horn will be as easy as speaking. I've warned them there will be mistakes, as if that somehow gets me off the hook. But five in the first eight bars? It's unconscionable. The high F entry is coming up, the one I failed to find in school, with the tumbling legato phrase to follow, and then the repeat. I suddenly can't play legato with a gun to my head. I take a solid early breath and split the F, hold it for a beat and a half then prepare to slide down into the tumbling phrase. There are ten notes to hit. It's falling-off-a-log easy. As I miss the first, I panic and feel my fingers flutter randomly over the three valves. They have lost radio contact with the mothership. I splatter every single note in the phrase, apart from the last. It sounds utterly appalling. Without exaggeration the worst two-bar passage I have perpetrated in my entire comeback. I sound like a wino.

There are two bars before I play the entire phrase again. I have to think quickly. This performance could not possibly have started worse. A year's methodical preparation has simply vaporised in front of the entire membership of the British Horn Society. On the evidence so far, I should not be here. I am breaking and entering in a burglar's stripey T-shirt. I will not be able to look Dave in the face. He will be tarred by association. Right now thousands of toes in hundreds of shoes are curling in horror. The entire audience will have to be ferried in ambulance fleets to A&E to have them surgically straightened. Hospitals won't be able to cope. And what can Barry Tuckwell possibly be thinking? He was looking forward to *this*? He flew from Australia for *this*? I imagine the commiserations afterwards. Caring smiles for the horn player who limped over the line. Despair creeps through my bloodstream like a fast-acting cancer. I am in shock. I am heading towards the waterfall. There are two bars to rescue this thing. There are sharp rocks at the bottom. Play it right! I become abusive. The Live 8 horns performed nervelessly to 250,000 people. Knock three noughts off that and you're still a jibbering husk! If you can't play this, don't even think of the damage you'll do to the semiquavers. Did they suffer performance anxiety outside the walls of Jericho? If you carry on cocking this up, you may as well skip the Rondo and let the LPO on early.

Just in time I remember Martin Hobbs's advice from nine months back. 'If you're nervous, play loud.' I lift the horn on two, breathe on three, place the mouthpiece on my lips on four and on one I am Roland summoning Charlemagne's reinforcements to the battlefield. My temples practically burst but, lo and behold, it works: I hit the high F smack in the centre. This time, instead of congratulating myself for being able to locate a cow's arse with a banjo, I focus on articulating the phrase. The notes glide smoothly out in the correct order. It's the first phrase I've played without making a mistake. It's a miracle. I can do legato after all. Thank you, Martin.

Now for the semiquavers. There's only a bar's rest to think about them, but in that bar I concentrate with renewed intensity on the music in front of me and the instrument in my hand. And bang, they fly out of the bell in perfect formation, all thirty-two of them, like a fleet of Red Arrows. I counted them out. Am I imagining things, or does the Soviet palace of culture breathe a sigh of relief? My audience knows this piece, it knows where the bodies are buried. Against all odds I have contrived to snake through the passage unharmed. The worst is surely over.

Now I get another eight bars' rest. I look across at Kevin, blow air through the horn to check for spit, anything rather than look out into the auditorium. I fiddle with my nose. Unlike Ewan McGregor, I stop short of wiping it on the back of my hand. The ardent E flat entry looms. I think very hard about not splitting it. Too hard, it turns out, because it splits like a coconut, neatly down the middle. The damage is somehow contained. The manly D is missed too, but doggedly I play on through. Whatever you do, I tell myself, don't get dragged back towards the rim of the waterfall. I'm not going to let it happen. According to the established pattern, the fear which had me clamped in its iron mitt is now loosening its grip. A phrase approaches, a particular favourite of mine which, the first time I played it for Hermann Baumann in New Hampshire, harvested a morale-boosting nod of approval.

Hermann likes his horn students to sing, so I try to sing the phrase and it emerges like a bloody bel canto aria. *Danke schön*, Hermann!

And on I step into the set of false endings, teasing little citations of the Romanze's opening melody. This is the phrase I proved incapable of playing at the start. Can I do any better now? It turns out that I can. At the final bar of each phrase Mozart ends with a rising series of three quavers, separated by a quaver's rest: B flat, D, E flat. The high E flats are a tad shaky on their pins, but otherwise I am more or less in command. I can see the final bar approaching. Relief is at hand. And here they are, the three amigos, the three B flats. I play the final low note, the one that Dennis Brain corrected to the tonic E flat, with an exaggerated firmness of purpose. Rather than the question mark written by Mozart, in my interpretation it's a resounding full stop.

I stop. Silence. And lower the Lídl. There are no coughs from the floor, and certainly no quips from the stage. I have already made merry enough with performance convention, the convention being that you don't perform a series of mistakes. I concentrate on emptying the horn. It's a labour-intensive pitstop. I pull out a slide with its twin apertures pointing upwards, turn it around and, with a flicking motion, deposit that slide's accumulation of saliva on the wooden concert hall floor. Herringbone, I notice. I replace the slide and move on to the next. There are five slides in all. Remove, flick, replace. It's nothing like as ostentatious as Dale Clevenger's routine. Remove, flick, replace. The audience patiently watches and listens to the familiar clink of brass on brass. I am much more efficient than I was as a ten-year-old curiously scoping the instrument for rogue liquids. It takes upwards of thirty seconds, each one of them a priceless respite. As I empty my horn I find my head emptying too. It's an involuntary process, an automated disk defragmentation. The clutter and the debris, the yadder-yadder-yak from the disputatious parliament inside my brain – they're gone, cut, deleted.

Only three minutes of this journey remain. I no longer feel any terror at all. The Rondo awaits, one of the most purely exhilarating tunes to emerge from the entire well of Mozart's imagination. In my head, despite an aversion to all things horsy, I clamber into an imaginary saddle, and prepare to gallop. I am going to enjoy this. I can feel it. I'm going to do what I know I can do. I look across at Kevin. He nods and lifts his hands from his lap to the keys. I take a long slow breath and crack the whip.

The wonderful thing about the Rondo is that it is virtually impossible to make a mistake in the first four bars. You can attack it with utter impunity, which I now do: F quaver up to six B flat quavers ... F quaver up to six C quavers. They trip off the tongue, they fly. The first hurdle, the resolution of the main melody, is a tricky little barrier, but on Dave's advice I've long since taken it to pieces and put it back together again. First fence easily cleared. Kevin takes the tune and leads it on a series of digressive twists and jinks while I ponder my next obstacle. 'Leitgeb,' Mozart inscribed carefully on the orchestral score here. Kevin pulls up and I kick off and charge on. So far there's not been a single split, I tell myself, a little prematurely. In the thrill of the chase I lose control of the reins and clip a note little too firmly. But it's quickly disappearing in the distance as I tear into a set of rousing hunting calls, first up to high F, then in an echo up to D. I'm just congratulating myself on how well I'm playing them when I botch the troubling round-off completely. It's the musical equivalent of clattering a gate rail. Whoops. Ignore it. It's gone. In a phrase or two the Rondo falls back into the main theme. I accelerate up towards it then on Dave's instruction diminuendo down into the six B flat quavers. They're my old friends now. The six C quavers. Good to be reunited with them. Another rest. I turn the page. There is only one page of Mozart's third horn concerto left. I have just enough time to empty water out of a small slide before the horn resumes with a witty up-tempo quotation from the Romanze. I rip through it. This really is going awfully well, I think as another hunting call looms. Could this be going any better? I'm starting to grow smug. Another note bites the dust. There are plenty of hurdles up ahead. Concentrate, I tell myself, as the Rondo reaches maximum volume with a crescendo up to the final resumption. I tiptoe up through a bar's worth of semitone increments into the main tune, only to miss the last note. That is positively the last split. It has to be. This movement may on balance be counted a success, but I can't afford any more. We're more than halfway down the page. Kevin leads me into a prancing phrase near the lower end of the movement's range which, when I first played it to Dave in what I thought was an appropriately dainty step, caused him to suffer convulsions of laughter and accuse me – once he'd recovered – of sounding like, and I quote, 'the fairies in the forest'. I now give it the most macho Dave Lee delivery I can muster. It segues into a final chest-pumping horn call before the tune interrupts itself to soar up to high F, then down again and then the most challenging section of the movement presents itself: an entire scale up to high G, but at warp speed. 'Just wiggle your finger on the first valve and slur it,' Sarah Willis told me. 'No one will know you're not playing the right notes.' That's what I do, and it sounds phenomenally competent. Thank you, Sarah! You're a pal! But the struggle's not over. The horn topples through the harmonics from a high F to a low B flat, vaults straight back up to the D and bumps down to a low F, all in the space of two bars. I've practised these two bars more than any others in the entire concerto and there's still no telling whether they'll come out the way Mozart intended. But by now nothing is going to block my path. Every single note troops out to order. I practically give myself a standing ovation. Kevin has four bars to himself and I know I'm home now. I can see it, the other side of the fermata where the accompaniment pulls up and there's another solo entry for 'Leitgeb'. Kevin has scarcely paused before I plough past him for the Rondo round-off. I play it with the flare, if not quite the flair, of Kendall Betts's acrobatic finale. And now all I have to do is count. One two there's no way I'm missing out the last note two two I look across at Kevin three two lift up the horn four two Darth breath five two high B flat straight to seven low B flats to a personalised and entirely unMozartian but profoundly terminal pedal B flat Da da da da da da Da-Da-DA!

I don't even have time to lower my instrument before a roar blasts in my direction from the floor of the concert hall of the Guildhall School of Music and Drama. It's the inchoate sound of peer approval. Undeserved, but overwhelming. I transfer the Lidl to my left hand and with my right gesture towards Kevin. I can't take this acclaim on my own. But Kevin is clapping too. I edge across towards him and put my arm around him. We're in this together.

'That was superb,' he says. It's my last flattering report from him.

'What about the start from hell?'

'Forget it!'

'I couldn't have done this without you.' I can feel him patting me on the shoulder.

He peels away and I am left to bow awkwardly to the audience. The room is a blur of raised hands and smiling faces. Don't milk this, I tell myself. You're not the president of the International Horn Society. You weren't *that* good. With the noise ringing in my ears I turn and walk towards the pass door. Ten short paces, the Lídl back in my right hand. The door opens. I go through. On the other side, hemmed into the cramped corridor, are the four horns of the London Philharmonic Orchestra.

'Jasper?' says one of them, a smallish man with short dark hair. 'Martin!'

It's Martin Hobbs, who tried to warn me off performing at the British Horn Society festival. He was right about how terrifying the experience would be. Afterwards people tell me they've not seen anyone ever looking so white. But I've never felt better about ignoring sound professional advice. Did I play well enough to get into music college? Er, no. Did I embarrass myself? After a dismal opening, I settled down and played the Romanze and Rondo of Mozart's third horn concerto, K447, to the best of my not exactly boundless ability. Did I do what I set out to do? Did I prove to myself that there's more to life than being young and not trying very hard? Did I enjoy myself more than I can possibly describe? Oh yes.

More than that, I stood up. I took a risk and lived, and breathed the sweet, rarefied air of utter, inner contentment. I've never experienced anything like it. From now on, when I go to the mirror in the small dark hours, I will be spared the accusing glare of an unfulfilled man. I have been released from my own private death row, and all thanks to the uncrowned king of musical instruments.

'I think you'd better go out again,' says Kevin. From beyond the pass door comes a thunder of stamping feet. Absurdly, the members of the British Horn Society are clamouring for another sight of me. Someone pulls open the pass door and I walk out alone to face an audience who turn out to be generous beyond the wildest of my positive visualisations. I come to a halt. I face the front. I bow. I mouth the words 'Thank you'. And just as I turn to walk back to the life that waits on the other side of the pass door, it occurs to me at the final second to raise my French horn – this old friend, this old foe from a country that no longer exists – into the air.

Bibliography

Anyone wishing to read up further on the horn, its history and its repertoire is encouraged to seek out the following:

Reginald Morley-Pegge: *The French Horn: Some Notes on the Evolution of the Instrument and of its Technique* (Ernest Benn, 1960; second edition 1973)

Robin Gregory: *The Horn* (Faber & Faber, 1960)

Stanley Sadie (ed.): *The New Grove Dictionary of Musical Instruments II* (Macmillan, 1984)

Anthony Baines: *Brass Instruments: Their History and Development* (Faber & Faber, 1976)

Barry Tuckwell: *Horn* (Macdonald, 1983)

Horace Fitzpatrick: *The Horn and Horn-Playing in the Austro-Bohemian Tradition 1680-1830* (OUP, 1970)

Karl Geiringer: *Instruments in the History of Western Music* (third edition, George Allen & Unwin, 1978)

C. Paul Herfurth and Vernon R. Miller: *A Tune a Day for French Horn (F and Bb) and Tenor Horn (Eb) Book 1* (Boston Music Co., Boston Mass)

J.E. Philip Farkas: *The Art of French Horn Playing* (Summy-Birchard Music, 1956)

I also found the horn in the following sources:

Stephen Battersby: 'Is space rolled up like a funnel?' *New Scientist* (17 April 2004)

Juvenal: *Satires*, Book I Satire 2 (1st century AD)

Polybius: *Histories*, Book 29 (from c. 160 BC)

Ovid: *Metamorphoses* (AD 8)

Seneca: *Oedipus* (c. AD 40-65)

Vegetius: *De Re Militari*, Book III (c. AD 350)

Beowulf (8th century)

Ptolemy: *Geographia* (c. AD 150)

CK Scott Moncrieff (translator): *The Song of Roland* (Chapman & Hall, 1919)

Glyn Burgess (translator): *The Song of Roland* (Penguin, 1990)

John Pope-Hennessy: *Fra Angelico* (Scala, 1981)

William Tyndale (translator): *The Book of Exodus* (1525)

King James Bible: *The Book of Joshua* (1611)

Reginald Morley-Pegge: 'The Orchestral French Horn: Its Origin and Evolution', *Hinrichsen's Musical Year Book*, volume VII, 1952

W.F.H. Blandford: 'Studies on the Horn: The French horn in England', *The Musical Times*, 1 August 1922, p.544-7

Otto Erich Deutsch: *Handel: A Documentary Biography* (Adam and Charles Black, 1955)

Newman Flower: *George Frideric Handel: His Personality and His Times* (Cassell & Co, 1923)

Charles Burney: *The Present State of Music in Germany, the Netherlands and United Provinces* (1773)

H. C. Robbins Landon: *Haydn: Chronicle and Works – Vol. II. Haydn at Eszterháza, 1766-1790* (Thames & Hudson, 1978)

Wolfgang Amadeus Mozart and family: *The Letters of Mozart and His Family* edited and translated by Emily Anderson (Macmillan, 1938)

Wolfgang Amadeus Mozart: *Mozart's Letters, Mozart's Life*, selected letters edited and translated by Robert Spaethling (Faber & Faber, 2000)

Otto Jahn: *Life of Mozart*, translated by Pauline D. Townsend (Novello, Ewer & Co, 1882)

Edward Holmes: *The Life of Mozart* (Chapman & Hall, London, 1845)

H.C. Robbins Landon: *Mozart: The Golden Years* (Thames & Hudson, 1989)

Robert W. Gutman: *Mozart: A Cultural Biography* (Harcourt Brace & Co, New York, 1999)

Daniel Heartz: 'Leutgeb and the 1762 horn concertos of Joseph and Johann Michael Haydn', *Mozart Jahrbuch*, 1987-8

Madame Campan: *Mémoires sur la vie privée de Marie Antoinette, suivis de souvenirs et anecdotes historiques sur les règnes de Louis XIV-XV* (Paris, 1823)

Antonia Fraser: *Marie Antoinette: The Journey* (Weidenfeld & Nicolson, London, 2001)

The New Grove Dictionary of Music, Vol. X (Macmillan, 1980)

Ferdinand Ries and Franz Gerhard Wegeler: *Biographische Notizen über Ludwig van Beethoven* (1838)

Alexander Thayer: *Life of Beethoven*, revised by Elliot Forbes (Princeton University Press, 1964)

Michael Kelly: *Reminiscences of the King's Theatre and Theatre Royal Drury Lane* (London, 1826)

Michael Kennedy: *Richard Strauss* (Dent, 1976)

Michael Kennedy: *Richard Strauss: Man, Musician, Enigma* (Cambridge, 1999)

Norman Del Mar: *Richard Strauss: A Critical Commentary on his Life and Works* (Barrie & Rockliff, 1962)

Willi Schuh (tr. Mary Whittall): *Richard Strauss: A Chronicle of the Early Years 1864-1898* (Cambridge University Press, 1982)

Anne Applebaum: *Gulag: A History* (Allen Lane, 2003)

Stephen J. Pettitt: *Dennis Brain: A Biography* (Faber & Faber, 1976)

Benjamin Britten: *Letters from a Life: The Selected Letters and Diaries of Benjamin Britten 1913-1976* edited by Donald Mitchell (Faber & Faber, 1991)

Humphrey Carpenter: *Benjamin Britten: A Biography* (Faber & Faber, 1992)

Michael H. Kater: *The Twisted Muse: Musicians and the Music in the Third Reich* (OUP, 1997)

James Morris: *Coronation Everest* (John Murray, 1958)

M. Dee Stewart (editor): *Philip Farkas: The Legacy of a Master* (The Instrumentalist Publishing Company, 1990)

Ian MacDonald: *Revolution in the Head: The Beatles' Records and the Sixties* (second revised edition, Pimlico, 2005)

The Beatles Anthology (Cassell & Co, 2000)

Barry Miles: *Paul McCartney: Many Years From Now* (Secker & Warburg, 1997)

Mark Lewisjohn: *The Complete Beatles Recording Sessions* (Hamlyn, 1998)

George Martin with Jeremy Handsby: *All You Need Is Ears* (St Martin's Press, New York, 1979)

John Harris: 'The Day The World Turned Day-Glo', *Mojo*, March 2007

Acknowledgements

This book could not have been written without an immense amount of practical help and advice. I must first pay tribute to Dave Lee. For the generosity with which he shared his knowledge, time, wit, fund of (sometimes quite tall) stories and above all his love of the French horn, it is impossible to convey the extent of my gratitude. I will, however, mention that for those inclined to hear just how brilliant a musician he really is, look no further than his remarkable CD, *Under the Influence* (Quartz).

In the global community of horn players I never met with anything but a friendly welcome, and hereby pay my respects to Barry Tuckwell, Vincent DeRosa, Peter Damm, Radovan Vlatković and James Thatcher; Stefan Dohr, Fergus McWilliam, Sarah Willis and the horn section of the Berlin Philharmonic Orchestra; David Pyatt, Timothy Jones, Angela Barnes, John Ryan and Jonathan Lipton of the London Symphony Orchestra; Dale Clevenger and the horn section of the Chicago Symphony Orchestra; Günter Högner and the horn section of the Vienna Philharmonic Orchestra; Phil Myers and the horn section of the New York Philharmonic Orchestra; Andrei Gloukhov and the horn section of the St Petersburg Philharmonic Orchestra; Andrew Clark and Martin Lawrence of the Orchestra of the Age of Enlightenment; Martin Hobbs, fourth horn of the London Philharmonic Orchestra; Martin Owen, principal horn of the Royal Philharmonic Orchestra, Nigel Black, principal horn of the Philharmonia Orchestra, Richard Berry, principal horn of the London Chamber Orchestra; Simon Rayner and Roger Montgomery of the Orchestra of the Royal Opera House; Shirley Hopkins; Tim Ball, Brendan Thomas, Tim Locke and Richard Ashton of the West End and beyond; Joseph Walters, Matt Gunner, Richard Steggall and Adam Walters of Paul McCartney's Live 8 horn quartet; John Burden, Tony Tunstall and Tony Randall, who among many other things played for the Beatles; Terry Johns, who played at Darth Vader's funeral; and Jérôme Oriou, who gave me a tutorial on the *trompe de chasse*.

I owe a huge debt to Michael Thompson, the Aubrey Brain professor of horn at the Royal Academy of Music, in which guise I found him unstintingly helpful on the many occasions I approached him. My thanks also go to those of his students who were asked to put up with my interloping.

Howard Pink, for thirty-four years until Hurricane Katrina the fourth horn of the Louisiana Philharmonic Orchestra, is now resident in Nashville, Tennessee, where his Musical Garden Hoses show is available for bookings. My thanks to him for sharing his story.

I had an idyllic week at the Kendall Betts Horn Camp in New Hampshire. My gratitude above all is due to Kendall Betts (the new owner of Lawson Brass Instruments) and his faculty, a veritable Mount Rushmore of eminent American pedagogues, including Jeffrey Agrell, Richard Chenoweth, Douglas Hill, Richard Mackey, Randy Gardner, Mike Hatfield, Abby Mayer and Lowell Greer. I would also like to thank some fellow campers: Richard Sachs, Sister Monica Elmer, Gretchen Zuk, Herb Foster, Susan McCullough, Jesse McCormick, Richard J. Martz, Alec Zimmer, Harry Harrison, Julia Pearring and KBHC's trilling latrines attendant, Jeremy Thal.

Of all the Titans of the instrument I encountered, Hermann Baumann was the only one apart from Dave who actually had to listen to me day after day. He was patient, generous and bracingly honest. I salute him.

I would also like to thank Chris Huning, Luke Woodhead and Steve Flower of Paxmans Musical Instruments for sharing their expertise, as well as Raimund Pankratz of Gebr. Alexander of Mainz.

In expressing my gratitude to the horn community, I leave till last the former chairman of the British Horn Society, Hugh Seenan, as well as Barbara MacLaren, Simon de Souza and the committee. Without their backing, this book would simply not exist. I would also like to thank the members of the British Horn Society and anyone else who was in the audience that evening. They know who they are, and I hope they also know how much their generosity of spirit meant to me then and means to me still.

I had immense help from outside the horn world too. Without Kevin Amos's calming bedside manner and impeccable musicianship, the trip would have been a great deal lonelier. I was also helped by three further pianists: Clair Friedman, Clement Ishmael and Ros Jones. My thanks to them all.

The Duc and Duchesse de Brissac invited me into the world of the *trompe de chasse* in the Loire Valley. Lord and Lady Lloyd Webber loaned out the conservatory of the Really Useful Group. Sir George Martin dug deep into his bulging library of Abbey Road memories. Frances Palmer, curator of the York Gate Collections at the Royal Academy of Music, allowed me to handle Dennis Brain's 1818 Raoux. Brigitte Sebald gave me a fascinating tour of Salzburg and retrieved articles on Joseph Leutgeb from the library of the Internationale Stiftung Mozarteum. Ewan McGregor admitted me to his dressing room and reminisced. Simon Callow shared his enthusiasm for Haydn, Caroline Ross Pirie her knowledge of Vivaldi, and Dallas Edmonds his total recall of Beachcomber. My profound thanks to them all. I would also like to express gratitude to Jan Eade of RUG, and to Liz Sharp (now Mrs Dave Lee) and Stringendo for playing along.

Paul Gent, former third horn in the City of Salford Youth Orchestra, let me write about my resumption of the instrument at the BHS festival for the *Daily Telegraph*. The article proved a handy calling card. My thanks to him and other commissioning editors who allowed me to air my enthusiasm along the way: Helen Hawkins of the *Sunday Times* Culture section, Simon Hills of *The Times Magazine* and above all Paul Kampen of *The Horn*. I would also like to thank Dillon Brydon and Christopher Cox for their photography, and Tom Beard and Andrew Palmer of KEO Films for filming my appearance at the BHS Festival.

I have relied on the expertise of several linguists. William Ward translated Mozart's exuberant Italian, Susie Dent translated Leutgeb's low German and James Morwood translated Punto's Latin epitaph. Engelbert Schmid interpreted for me when I quizzed Peter Damm, and Nina Apollonov was my interpreter when I met the horn section of the St Petersburg Philharmonic. My thanks to them all.

I am indebted to Pat Kavanagh, who did not flinch when I said I'd like to write about the French horn. I would also like to thank Sarah Ballard, Sabine Durrant and Claudia Daventry for their indispensable thoughts on style, tone and content. My thanks, penultimately, to Alan Samson, Lucinda McNeile and Tom Graves of Weidenfeld & Nicolson, and to Salvatore Rubbino for his wonderful illustrations.

My final thanks go to my parents, Simon and Jacquy, who put up with the spit and lack of polish the first time round and thirty years later entered into the spirit all over again, to my friends who listened to the performances, and to Richard Friedman, the distinguished violinist, with whom I had many conversations about orchestral life. Above all, I would like to pay homage to Sonia, Pascale and Florence. The three of them endured a year of monomania with more grace than I had any right to expect. Without their tolerance none of this could have gone ahead. I can only apologise to them that, whether they like it or not, they will be humming K447 for the rest of their lives.

Index